PC ARCHITECTURE FROM ASSEMBLY LANGUAGE TO C

PC ARCHITECTURE FROM ASSEMBLY LANGUAGE TO C

DAVID HERGERT
Miami University

NANCY THIBEAULT
Miami University

Prentice Hall

Upper Saddle River, New Jersey   Columbus, Ohio

Library of Congress Cataloging-in-Publication Data

Hergert, David.
    PC architecture from assembly language to C / David Hergert, Nancy
Thibeault.
        p.   cm.
    Includes index.
    ISBN 0-13-653775-8
    1. Microcomputers.   2. Microprocessors.   3. Computer architecture.
4. Assembler language (Computer program language)   5. C (Computer
program language)   I. Thibeault, Nancy.   II. Title.
QA76.5.H4447   1998
004.16--DC21   97-20688
                                                                              CIP

Cover art: © 1997 Photo Disc, Inc.
Editor: Charles E. Stewart, Jr.
Production Editor: Alexandrina Benedicto Wolf
Cover Design Coordinator: Karrie M. Converse
Cover Designer: Russ Maselli
Production Manager: Pamela D. Bennett
Marketing Manager: Debbie Yarnell
Editorial/Production Supervision: Custom Editorial Productions, Inc.

© 1998 by Prentice Hall, Inc.
Upper Saddle River, NJ 07458

Notice to the Reader: The publisher and the author do not warrant or guarantee any of the products and/or
equipment described herein nor has the publisher or the author made any independent analysis in connection
with any of the products, equipment, or information used herein. The reader is directed to the manufacturer for
any warranty or guarantee for any claim, loss, damages, costs, or expense arising out of or incurred by the
reader in connection with the use or operation of the products or equipment.

    The reader is expressly advised to adopt all safety precautions that might be indicated by the activities and
experiments described herein. The reader assumes all risks in connection with such instructions.

This book was set in Times Roman by Custom Editorial Productions, Inc. and was printed and bound by
R.R. Donnelley and Sons Company. The cover was printed by Phoenix Color Corp.

Printed in the United States of America

10 9 8 7 6 5 4 3

ISBN: 0-13-653775-8

Prentice-Hall International (UK) Limited, *London*
Prentice-Hall of Australia Pty. Limited, *Sydney*
Prentice-Hall of Canada, Inc., *Toronto*
Prentice-Hall Hispanoamericana, S. A., *Mexico*
Prentice-Hall of India Private Limited, *New Delhi*
Prentice-Hall of Japan, Inc., *Tokyo*
Pearson Education Asia Pte. Ltd., *Singapore*
Editora Prentice-Hall do Brasil, Ltda., *Rio de Janeiro*

PREFACE

Over the past decade, there have been many books on PC assembly language written for computer science and engineering technology programs. Some texts place a heavy emphasis on microprocessor hardware, and others have a stronger focus on assembly language and operating systems. This book, while placing a slightly stronger focus on assembly language, seeks to provide a practical balance between hardware and software. Timing diagrams, 80x86 bus configurations, PC bus configurations, and a set of interfacing experiments make up the hardware components of the text. A complete coverage of assembly and how it relates to the PC hardware, the BIOS, and C make up the software component of the book. Numerous examples are given to supplement topics in the text.

This book can be used as a text or as a reference manual. As a text, it presents the history of the microcomputer. It starts with a crude microprocessor unit (the Easy4), evolves to .COM files (with structure derived from the CPM operating system), .EXE files (which allow memory segmentation), and ends with C files. As a reference, the appendixes contain valuable information on BIOS and DOS interrupts (Appendixes A and B), PC memory and port maps (Appendixes C and D), a summary of 8088-based instructions (Appendix E), an ASCII table (Appendix F), installing the Easy4 software (Appendix G), and a set of interfacing experiments (Appendix H). The Easy4 software and the library file ASY.LIB are included with the text. ASY.LIB is on Disk 2 and can be copied to the MASM directory.

The PC operating system (whether it is DOS, Windows® 3.1, or Windows 95) has a common core of BIOS and DOS interrupts. These interrupts are explained with numerous examples, along with an introduction to 80x86 assembly language and the PC memory map. This book emphasizes programming as a means to teach PC architecture. The text is designed for instructors desiring to give their students a solid understanding of how the PC operating system works. Students who have had an introductory course in the C language and want to broaden their programming knowledge by learning how C relates to assembly will find this book useful. The prerequisite for this book is, at minimum, a course in the C language. Although this is not absolutely necessary, it would also be helpful if the student had or is taking a course in digital systems.

The text begins at an elementary level and advances to coverage of interrupt service routines, terminate and stay resident programs, and DOS memory configurations. A simple processor called the Easy4 is used to help introduce basic architecture without relying on advanced 80x86 topics like segmentation. At Miami University, a separate course is used to teach such hardware topics as bus architecture, address decoding, DMA, and other related concepts. The authors envision this book being used in two- or four-year computer or electrical engineering technology programs. It may also be useful in computer technology or computer science programs.

Learning assembly language on 80x86 processors can be a daunting task for students. Not only do they have to learn the CPU registers and assembly language mnemonics, but they must also understand the segmented architecture of the 80x86 and the structure of .EXE files on the PC. To this end, the book gradually introduces these topics. Chapters 1 through 10 include topics normally covered in a course on PC assembly language, and can be covered in a single semester. Chapters 11 through 14 introduce advanced topics, and can be included in a second course or as selected extensions to a first course.

Chapter 1 introduces students to bits and bytes, base conversions, and basic microprocessor architecture. Chapter 2 covers a pseudocomputer, the Easy4. It allows students to "see" the relationship between registers and memory by graphically displaying them on the screen. A simple stack is also introduced in this chapter, as well as instruction fetch, decode, and execute cycles.

Segments are introduced in Chapter 3 and are fully explained in Chapter 5. Since .COM files are easier to understand, they are introduced before .EXE files. This gives the student time to learn the 80x86 assembly language mnemonics before studying segmentation and the .EXE structure. This is a departure from most assembly language texts, which tend to introduce .EXE files when they are covering assembly instructions.

Chapter 6 introduces the ASY.LIB library provided on disk with the book. This library contains many common I/O routines for the keyboard, screen, and printer. The 80x86 stack is also introduced in this chapter. Chapter 7 provides some useful PC examples using the ASY.LIB library, including the clock timer, toggle keys, keyboard buffer, and writing directly to screen memory and printer ports. Chapter 8 covers basic string operations.

Chapter 9 gives some basic floating point operations, including transcendental functions. This chapter gives examples that engineering technology students may find useful. Chapter 10 covers interrupts and interrupt service routines. Examples are given using the screen and mouse.

Chapter 11 provides unique coverage of an assembly text. Using Microsoft C as an example, it disassembles basic C programs to show the equivalent 80x86 assembly language version of the .EXE file. This helps students understand how C is converted into assembly when compiled. There is also coverage of intermingling assembly and C code, including passing variables from C to assembly and back. Terminate and stay resident programs are also covered in this chapter, using combined C and assembly routines.

Chapter 12 covers the PC boot process and the memory map. Programs used to view the memory map are also covered. Chapter 13 covers advanced C memory and I/O routines, mainly oriented toward tips and techniques not covered in a standard introductory course in C. Chapter 14 covers mnemonics from the 80286, 80386, and 80486. Finally,

Appendix H contains a set of interfacing experiments including I/O ports, analog measurements that include maximum, minimum, DC, and RMS voltage readings, and frequency measurements. Also included is an experiment on creating an ISR for interrupt driven I/O.

Many hours of work have gone into the writing of this text. Thanks to all of the students at Miami University who have patiently tolerated the many revisions. We would also like to thank the following reviewers for their invaluable feedback: Mike Awwad, DeVry Institute; Boris Kovalchuk, Central Washington University; Michael A. Miller, DeVry Institute; and Gregory S. Romine, Indiana University-Purdue University at Indianapolis.

David Hergert
Nancy Thibeault

BRIEF CONTENTS

CONTENTS

3   COM FILES AND DEBUG   39

4   ADDITIONAL 80X86 INSTRUCTIONS   56

5   80X86 SEGMENTATION, .EXE FILES, AND MISCELLANEOUS INSTRUCTIONS   80

6   LINKING OBJECT FILES AND THE .ASY LIBRARY   100

7   ADVANCED MEMORY AND PORT I/O   112

8   STRING OPERATIONS   131

9   80X87 FLOATING POINT OPERATIONS   140

10   INTERRUPTS AND I/O   153

11   ASSEMBLY LANGUAGE AND C   169

12   BIOS, DOS, COMMAND.COM, AND THE PROGRAM SEGMENT PREFIX   191

13   ADVANCED C MEMORY AND I/O ROUTINES   204

CHAPTER 1

Microprocessor Architecture

THE STRUCTURE OF A COMPUTER

In twenty years' time, computers have shrunk from large mainframes that took up a whole room, to laptops that weigh less than six pounds. At the same time, microcomputers have advanced from a small box with no keyboard or monitor to multimedia machines capable of editing motion pictures. This book is about PC-based (or IBM®-compatible) microcomputer architecture. In a microcomputer, the electronic hardware that makes up the computer is contained in a variety of integrated circuits including the microprocessor, clock, memory, and port chips (Figure 1.1).

The **microprocessor** chip includes all of the circuitry needed to implement instructions coming from the operating system or programming language. In mainframe computers, the processor is contained in many separate circuits. In microcomputers, the processor has been squeezed onto one chip. Program instructions and data are stored in **memory** chips. Today's microcomputers have far more memory than a mainframe of thirty years ago had. Instructions are stored in one section of memory, and data in another. In order to interpret instructions stored in memory, a microprocessor must first fetch each instruction from memory before interpreting it.

Port chips control access to outside devices such as the keyboard, monitor, mouse, and printer. Think of a computer port chip as being similar to a shipping port. When a boat laden with goods comes from overseas, the boat must first stop at an assigned port before the goods can enter the country. The same is true for a computer port. When data comes from an outside source, it must be routed to a port in order for the microprocessor to have access to it. The microprocessor has instructions that allow it to send information to or receive information from a port.

All computers have a basic operational structure as shown in Figure 1.2. The **Operating System** and high-level *Programming Language* control the *Electronic Hardware* that comprises the physical layer (Layer 1) of the computer. The programming language could be BASIC, Pascal, C, FORTRAN, or any high-level language. When the computer is turned on, a core routine loads the operating system in first (this is called a system boot),

1

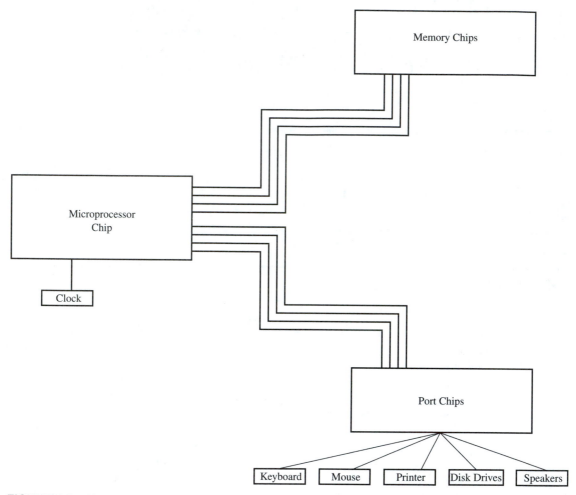

FIGURE 1.1   Microcomputer System

and the programming language is then loaded by the operating system. At higher layers, the computer is easier to use and program.

The **Application Program,** Layer 4, is a program that is frequently used, such as a spreadsheet, CAD program, or word processor. It is written in a programming language *(Layer 3)*. Most modern software is written in either the C or C++ language or a combination of Assembly and C. The operating system is also written in a combination of Assembly and C. The programming language communicates with the operating system *(Layer 2)* to control the electronic hardware *(Layer 1)*. Note the arrows connecting the four layers in Figure 1.2. All four are intertwined. This book slowly unravels the connection between them. You will study the underlying glue that holds them together. This "glue" is called machine language. Applications programs, programming languages, and the operating system must all be converted to a series of instructions that the microprocessor

FIGURE 1.2 Layers of a Computer System

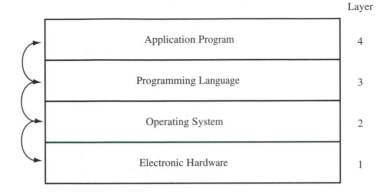

understands. These instructions make up the **instruction set,** or a list of the instructions the processor can interpret.

Machine language is the set of microprocessor instructions encoded as binary numbers. The binary numbers act as on-off devices to control the electronic hardware. Although the microprocessor uses machine language, no one actually programs in this language anymore. Instead, higher-level languages are used. At some point, these higher-level languages are converted to machine language. There are two methods to do this: through a compiler or through an interpreter. A **compiler** converts all of the code to machine language before the program is run. You first enter the code, then run a compiler to convert the file to machine language and combine (or link) it with any functions your program may use. An **interpreter** converts one line of code to machine language at a time while the program is running. Interpreters are much slower than compilers. This book uses the Microsoft® Assembler Compiler (MASM) to convert Assembly language to machine language. Actually, there is no benefit to programming in machine language, since Assembly language can be directly converted to machine language and is much easier to use.

Programming languages have a relationship to the machine language instructions they will eventually be converted to. If a language has a direct relationship to machine language, it is called a low-level language. If there is little relationship between the language and machine language, it is called a high-level language. Table 1.1 compares some of the more common languages.

TABLE 1.1 Programming Languages

Language	Level	Ease of Programming	Relative Speed	Power and Flexibility
BASIC	High	Easy	Slow	Poor
COBOL	High	Easy	Slow	Poor
Pascal	High	Fairly easy	Slow	Poor
FORTRAN	High	Moderate	Moderate	Moderate
C	Moderate	Fairly difficult	Fast	Good
Assembly	Low	Difficult	Very fast	Excellent

TABLE 1.2   Timing Test (Sieve of Eratosthenes)

Programming Language	Time to Run
BASIC	10 seconds
C	2.7 seconds
Assembly	0.18 second

Note that the lower-level languages are harder to program but provide more speed and power. In this case, power is defined as the languages' ability to make full use of the electronic hardware. To demonstrate the speed differences in languages, Table 1.2 shows the results of a timing test written in BASIC, C, and Assembly on an 80486 machine.

This example demonstrates the huge advantage obtained by programming in Assembly or C. In addition, only Assembly gives full access to the operating system and electronic hardware. As you will see in Chapters 10 and 11, such things as device drivers and terminate and stay resident (TSR) programs are best programmed in Assembly, or with a higher language with access to Assembly language (as is the case with C).

THE 80X86 FAMILY OF MICROPROCESSORS

The Intel® 8086 family of microprocessors is found in all PC compatibles. This includes the 8088, 8086, 80186, 80286, 80386SX, 80386DX, 80486SX, 80486DX, and Pentium® processors operating in the real mode. Since all of these processors are supersets of the 8086/8088, this book uses the term 80x86. All of the programs in this book will run on any of the processors in the 80x86 family.

Microcomputer Systems

All microcomputer systems have an **Address Bus,** a **Data Bus,** and a **Control Bus,** as shown in Figure 1.3. The 80x86 uses these three buses to connect with memory and ports. When communicating with the outside world, an address is first sent out from the processor to a device external to the processor (memory or port). Data is then transferred on the data bus. The data bus is bidirectional. If the data comes from the 80x86 to the device, a **write** operation occurs. If the transfer is from the device to the 80x86, a **READ** operation occurs. The control bus is also bidirectional. Among other tasks, it lets outer devices know if a read or write operation is occurring. Note that the address bus is unidirectional. The address is placed on the bus by the 80x86, not the external device.

All microprocessors are driven by a **clock.** The clock is usually a quartz crystal (like the one in your watch). Through wave-shaping hardware, the clock appears as a square wave to the microprocessor. The length of time to complete one cycle of the clock is called the period, or **clock cycle.** More than one clock cycle is needed to complete an instruction. The **instruction cycle** describes the time to complete an instruction. Normally this is three

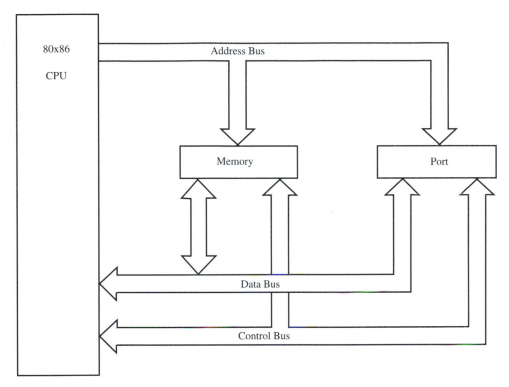

FIGURE 1.3   Microcomputer System Diagram

or more clock cycles. A generic instruction is retrieved from memory using a Read operation as shown in Table 1.3

Microprocessor Architecture

Microprocessors contain a ***Central Processing Unit*** **(CPU),** which is divided into two sections, the ***Control Unit*** and the ***Arithmetic Logic Unit*** **(ALU),** as shown in Figure 1.4. The control unit is responsible for interpreting instructions and operating the control bus.

TABLE 1.3   Read Operation from Memory to the Microprocessor

Clock Cycle	Operation
1	The address is latched (or stored) by the 80x86 onto the address bus. A Memory pin on the control bus tells memory to get ready to read an address.
2	The Read pin on the control bus goes low to tell memory a READ operation is occurring.
3	The instruction is placed by memory onto the data bus. The processor reads the instruction in.
4	The Read pin goes high to indicate that the data bus no longer contains the instruction.

FIGURE 1.4   80X86 Micro-processor

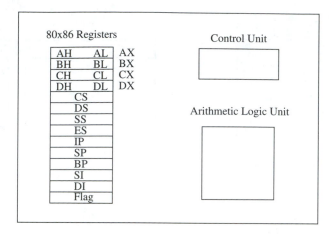

Groups of Bits

The microprocessor is composed of a series of digital circuits. These circuits operate due to a series of electrical voltages that are either present (On) or not present (Off). If a voltage is present, it is represented as a 1; if a voltage is not present, it is represented with a 0. The binary number system also has two states (1 and 0). Because of this, the binary number system can be implemented in a digital computer. Binary digits are often collected into groups with names as shown in Table 1.4.

Example 1.1

How many bits are in 5 paragraphs?

Solution   5 paragraphs * 8 words/paragraph * 2 bytes/word * 8 bits/byte = 640 bits.

Processor Size

The size of a microprocessor is defined by its data bus. There is an internal data bus (for such routines as routing between registers) and an external data bus (for routing between the processor and memory and ports). The size of the Intel processors are shown in Table 1.5.

TABLE 1.4   Groups of Bits

1 binary digit	- bit
4 bits	- nibble
2 nibbles	- byte
2 bytes	- word (This can vary on some systems.)
8 words	- paragraph
16 paragraphs	- page

TABLE 1.5 Comparison of Intel Microprocessors

Processor	Size of Internal Data Bus	Size of External Data Bus
4004	4	4
8008	8	8
8080	8	8
8085	8	8
8088	16	8
8086	16	16
80186	16	16
80286	16	16
80386SX	32	16
80386DX	32	32
80486SX	32	32
80486DX	32	32
Pentium	64	64

The 8008 through 8085 had similar instruction sets. The 8088/8086 had some funda-mental design changes requiring a new instruction set. The 8088 through Pentium have similar instruction sets. This book focuses on these instruction sets. It does not attempt to convert every instruction for every Intel processor; instead, it will focus on the most common instructions you need to know to be a good Assembly language programmer.

Contents of the Arithmetic Logic Unit

The **Arithmetic Logic Unit** (ALU) in the microprocessor performs arithmetic and Boolean operations. It consists of **registers, shift registers, counters, adders, flip-flops, and logic gates. Flip-flops** are storage cells used to maintain the state of a bit. They con-tain either a 1 or 0 (in many computers, this translates to 5 volts, or 0 volts, respectively). The present state is maintained until a new state is brought in. It is best to think of them as small storage cells. Flip-flops are combined into groups of eight, sixteen, or thirty-two to produce registers. Some memory chips (such as static RAM) are comprised of flip-flops. The registers in Figure 1.4 are 8 bit. Each has eight flip-flops.

    Shift registers rotate bits in a register to the left or right. Figure 1.5 shows the shift register rotating a register's bits to the left. Note that the shift register shown introduces a 0 into the right-most bit. Shift registers are covered in detail in Chapter 6. **Counters** incre-ment or decrement the bits in a register. The counter shown in Figure 1.5 adds a 1 to the right-most bit. Counters are covered in Chapter 4. **Adders** add two registers together and store the result in one of the two registers. In Figure 1.5, the adder is adding registers A and B and storing the result in register B. Adders and subtracters are covered in Chapter 4. Figure 1.5 also shows a **Boolean** AND operation performed on registers A and B. Boolean concepts are introduced in this chapter, and Boolean instructions are covered in Chapter 6.

Counting in Binary and Decimal

In order to understand how the digital computer performs arithmetic operations, it is im-portant to know how to count in binary. Counting in decimal may come quite naturally, but

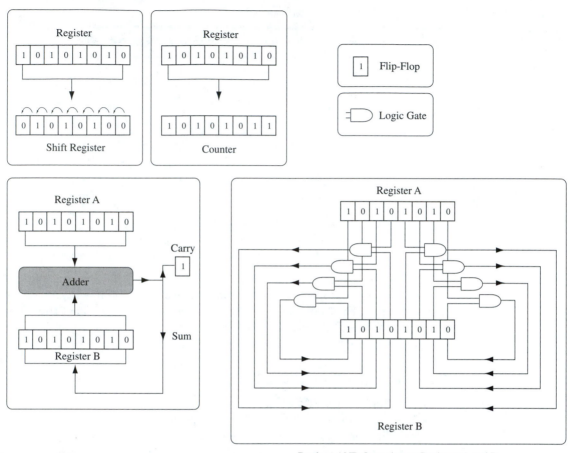

FIGURE 1.5   Arithmetic and Logic Unit

let's think about some of the rules when adding. Look closely at how the decimal system increments:

```
00
01
02
03
04
05
06
07
08
09
10
11
```

Note that when the count exceeds 9, the right column is reset to 0 and the left column is incremented. Addition works the same way. If the addition produces 10, the sum column is reset to 0 and the next column is incremented. This is demonstrated in the decimal addition shown below:

```
  332
+ 486
  ───
  818
```

Note that the right column increments the number 6 twice. Since the result is less than 10, no carry is needed and the answer is stored in the sum. Next the 8 in the middle column is incremented 3 times as shown below:

8 ← start
9 ← first increment
0 ← second increment (Second column is reset to 0. Carry generated.)
1 ← third increment

In other words, if the addition produces a sum greater than 9, the column is reset to 0 and the next column is incremented. Table 1.6 compares binary and decimal numbers.

Translating Binary to Decimal

Binary numbers carry certain weights for each column. The weight is 2 to the power of the column number. The first column has a weight of 2^0, the second a weight of 2^1, the third a weight of 2^2, etc. The number (1 or 0) is then multiplied by the weight to obtain a decimal representation for that column. All of the columns are added together to obtain the decimal equivalent.

Example 1.2

Convert 11011101 binary to decimal.

Solution   The binary weights are shown below:

```
2⁷  2⁶  2⁵  2⁴  2³  2²  2¹  2⁰
1   1   0   1   1   1   0   1
```

The conversion is shown below:

$$2^7*1+ \quad 2^6*1+ \quad 2^5*0+ \quad 2^4*1+ \quad 2^3*1+ \quad 2^2*1+ \quad 2^1*0+ \quad 2^0*1 = 221 \text{ decimal}$$

Translating Decimal to Binary

A decimal number can be converted to binary by using the successive division by 2 method. The decimal number is divided by 2. The integer part is saved, while the remainder is the next least significant bit of the binary number. The integer part is again divided by 2 and the process repeated. The procedure terminates when the integer part is 0.

TABLE 1.6   Binary and Decimal Number System

Binary	Decimal		Binary	Decimal
0000	0		1000	8
0001	1		1001	9
0010	2		1010	10
0011	3		1011	11
0100	4		1100	12
0101	5		1101	13
0110	6		1110	14
0111	7		1111	15

Example 1.3

Convert 221 decimal to binary.

Solution

Division	Integer	Remainder	
221/2	110	1 (.5 * 2)	(LSB)
110/2	55	0	↑
55/2	27	1	
27/2	13	1	
13/2	6	1	
6/2	3	0	
3/2	1	1	
1/2	0	1	(MSB)

MSB means most significant bit, or the bit farthest to the left. **LSB** means least significant bit, or the bit farthest to the right. The binary number equivalent is then read from bottom to top, or 11011101.

Hex Representations

Hex is the base 16 number system. It is comprised of 16 digits; 0 through 9 are used, as well as A through F. Table 1.7 compares the binary, decimal, and hex number systems. Hex is particularly useful when representing groups of 4 bits.

TABLE 1.7   Comparison of Number Systems

Binary	Decimal	Hex		Binary	Decimal	Hex
0000	0	0		1000	8	8
0001	1	1		1001	9	9
0010	2	2		1010	10	A
0011	3	3		1011	11	B
0100	4	4		1100	12	C
0101	5	5		1101	13	D
0110	6	6		1110	14	E
0111	7	7		1111	15	F

Example 1.4

Convert 1011011110100110 to hex.

Solution   Starting at the right, break the binary number into 4 bit nibbles and place the appropriate hex digit below each nibble.

```
1011  0111  1010  0110
B     7     A     6
```

The answer is B7A6 hex.

Example 1.5

Convert 5FE3 to binary.

Solution   Convert each hex digit to binary and string the numbers together.

```
5       F       E       3
0101    1111    1110    0011
```

The answer is 0101111111100011. As can be seen, it is much shorter to represent a number in hex than binary.

Representation of Instructions in Memory

Instructions are encoded in memory as 1s and 0s. An 8-bit memory address might have an instruction stored in it that looks like this:

```
10011010
```

This instruction could also be written in hex as:

```
9A
```

Since 9 = 1001 and A = 1010, it is easier to represent instructions and data in hex. 4 bits of binary can be directly translated to hex, and hex notation is shorter and easier to use than binary. While all of the examples in this chapter use hex for representing data and instructions, remember that the computer sees the same data and instructions as binary. Arithmetic operations occur between registers, or between a register and a number in memory. The result is always stored in the first register indicated in the operation. For example, the instruction

```
SUB Register1,Register2
```

will subtract Register1–Register2 and store the result in Register1.

Binary Addition

Look at the right-most binary column in Table 1.6. The highest number is 1, so if 1 is incremented, the right column is reset to 0 and the next column is incremented. Binary addition is performed following the same set of rules:

```
  1001
+ 0011
  ----
  1100
```

The right-most column shows $1 + 1$. This equals 10. So the sum is set to 0 and the carry to 1. The second column shows $1 + 0 +$ carry. This is the same as $1 + 1$, or sum = 0, carry = 1. The third column from the right shows $0 + 0 +$ carry, or sum = 1, carry = 0. The left-most column shows $1 + 0$, or sum = 1, carry = 0. Note the decimal equivalents of the binary numbers:

$$
\begin{array}{r}
9 \\
+\ 3 \\
\hline
12
\end{array}
$$

Example 1.6

Perform an ADD operation between a register and a number in memory. The register equals 10111011, and the number equals 11110000. The result is stored in the register.

Solution

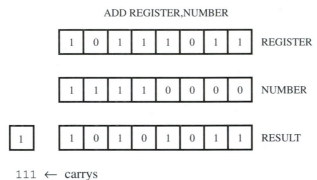

ADD REGISTER,NUMBER

```
 111  ← carrys
 10111011  (register)
+11110000  (number)
110101011  (result..stored in register)
```

Binary Subtraction

What about binary subtraction? First let's look at negative binary numbers. In binary, counting is similar to an odometer. Note that there is a fixed number of bits (in this case, 4). When the highest number is reached (1111), the counter is reset to 0 and counting starts again, as shown below:

```
1100
1101
1110
1111  ← Highest 4-bit binary number.
0000  ← Start over from 0000.
0001
0010
0011
```

What is a negative 1 in this system? If 000 is decremented, 1111 is the result. This is −1 in binary. Let's try another example. If 0000 is decremented three positions, 1101 is obtained. This is −3 in binary. Unfortunately, 1101 does not look like −3. The 2's complement method can help make the number look recognizable. This method inverts the bits of the negative number and adds 1. Thus

1011

becomes

```
0100
 + 1
0101
```

Since 0101 equals decimal 5, 1011 must equal −5. Actually, most microprocessors do not contain a unit in their ALU capable of performing subtraction. Instead, they add using 2's complement. This method performs an addition, while first changing the sign of one of the numbers. Look at the following example:

```
  1001   (9)
− 0101   (−5)
```

First, 2's complement the minuend:

```
0101
1010   (Inversion of 0101.)
  +1   (Add 1.)
1011
```

Now add 1011 to 1001.

```
  1001
+ 1011
  0100
```

Note that an extra carry is generated. While this carry is ignored as part of the sum, it is important. If a carry is generated, the answer is positive. If no carry is generated, the answer is negative. Look at the opposite case:

```
  0101   (5)
− 1001   (9)
```

This time complement 1001 (which is 0110) and add 1.

```
0110   (complement of 1001)
  + 1
0111
```

Now perform the addition:

```
  0101
+ 0111
  1100
```

Since no carry is generated, the answer is negative. To see a positive representation of the answer, 2's complement 1100, which is 0011. Next add 1.

$$
\begin{array}{r}
0011 \\
+\ 1 \\
\hline
0100
\end{array}
\quad \text{(decimal 4)}
$$

Thus 0101 (decimal 5) minus 1001 (decimal −9) equals 1100 (decimal −4).

Example 1.7

Perform a SUBTRACT operation between a register and a number in memory. The register equals 10111011, and the number equals 11110000.

Solution

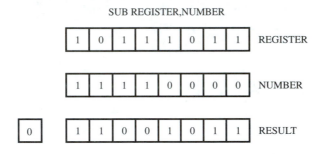

SUB REGISTER,NUMBER

$$
\begin{array}{r}
10111011 \\
-\ 11110000
\end{array}
$$

The 2's complement of 11110000 = 00010000.

$$
\begin{array}{r}
10111011 \\
+\ 00010000 \\
\hline
11001011
\end{array}
$$

Since a carry was not generated, the answer is negative. The 2's complement of 11001011 is 00110101 binary.

Boolean Operations

In addition to algebraic operations such as addition and subtraction, there are Boolean operations. Boolean operations produce an output based on certain combinations of binary inputs. The most common operations are **AND, OR, XOR,** and **NOT.**

Boolean AND Operation.   The AND operation produces an output equal to the minimum of two or more inputs. Often a comparison chart is shown in the form of a truth table, as shown in Table 1.8.

Note that the output is always equal to the smallest value of the two inputs. Since a 0 appears in every case except the last, the output is also 0 except if all inputs equal 1.

TABLE 1.8   Boolean AND Truth Table

Inputs xy	Output z (minimum of x,y)
00	0
01	0
10	0
11	1

Example 1.8

Perform an AND operation between a register and a number in memory. The register equals 10011011, and the number equals 11110000. The result is stored in the register.

Solution

AND REGISTER,NUMBER

| 1 | 0 | 0 | 1 | 1 | 0 | 1 | 1 | REGISTER

| 1 | 1 | 1 | 1 | 0 | 0 | 0 | 0 | NUMBER

| 1 | 0 | 0 | 1 | 0 | 0 | 0 | 0 | RESULT

10011011 AND'd with 11110000 equals 10010000. Note that each column has an AND operation performed on it.

Boolean OR Operation.   The OR operation produces an output equal to the greater of two or more inputs. If any of the inputs are 1, the output is 1, as shown in Table 1.9.

Example 1.9

Perform an OR operation between a register and a number in memory. The register equals 10011011, and the number equals 11110000. The result is stored in the register.

TABLE 1.9   Boolean OR Truth Table

Inputs xy	Output z (Maximum of x,y.)
00	0
01	1
10	1
11	1

Solution

OR REGISTER,NUMBER

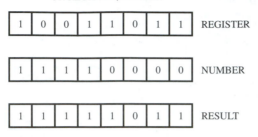

10011011 OR'd with 11110000 equals 11111011.

Boolean XOR Operation. A third type of Boolean operation produces a 0 output if all inputs are equal, else the output is 1. The eXclusive OR (XOR) output is shown in Table 1.10.

Example 1.10

Perform an XOR operation between a register and a number in memory. The register equals 10011011, and the number equals 11110000. The result is stored in the register.

Solution

XOR REGISTER,NUMBER

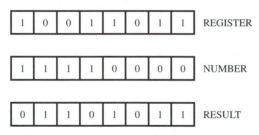

10011011 XOR'd with 11110000 equals 01101011. Note that any bit XOR'd with 1 is inverted. Any bit XOR'd with 0 remains the same.

Boolean NOT Operation. The final Boolean operation covered is the NOT, or complement operation. This function simply inverts an input as shown in Table 1.11.

TABLE 1.10 XOR Truth Table

Inputs xy	Output z	
00	0	←Inputs equal
01	1	
10	1	
11	0	←Inputs equal

TABLE 1.11 NOT Truth Table

Inputs x	Output y
0	1
1	0

CHAPTER 1 PROBLEMS

1. Explain the purpose of the address, data, and control bus in a microcomputer system.
2. How many bits are in 6 words?
3. How many paragraphs are in 10000h bytes? Express your answer in hex.
4. How many words are in 16 nibbles?
5. Convert the following binary numbers to decimal:
   a. 101b
   b. 11101b
   c. 1010101010b
6. Convert the following decimal numbers to binary:
   a. 6
   b. 121
   c. 16,646
   d. 32,766
7. Add the binary numbers shown below:
   a.   110
      + 011
   b.   101101
      +011010
8. Subtract the binary numbers shown below:
   a.   110
      − 011
   b.   101101
      − 011010
   c.   011101
      − 100010
9. What is the difference between an adder and a counter?
10. Suppose register A equals 10110111 and register B equals 01110111.
   a. Perform an AND operation on each corresponding bit of registers A and B.
   b. Perform an OR operation on each corresponding bit of registers A and B.
   c. Perform an XOR operation on each corresponding bit of registers A and B.
11. Invert the following set of bits:
   a. 10110001
   b. 01010101
   c. 11111111
12. Determine the 2's complement of problem 11.
13. Convert the binary numbers shown below to hex:
   a. 1011
   b. 00010001
   c. 111101010
14. Convert the hex numbers shown below to binary:
   a. F3
   b. 345
   c. FACE

CHAPTER 2

Easy4 Programming and Architecture

THE EASY4 MICROCOMPUTER

This book comes with software that runs in Microsoft® Windows® 3.1, Windows for Workgroups, or Windows 95 in 16-bit mode. This software simulates an early microcomputer called the Easy4. No computer with this name was actually built, but many early microcomputers (circa 1971–1975) were similar to the Easy4. The Easy4 processor is not able to do much, but is ideal as a prelude to the Intel series of microprocessors since the instructions are similar. Perhaps the greatest feature of the Easy4 is that it allows you to peer inside it, observing the internal registers and external memory. It contains one general-purpose register, an instruction pointer, a stack pointer, an adder, and a small amount of memory. Figure 2.1 shows the case of the Easy4.

The Easy4 uses a seven-segment light-emitting diode (LED) for a display and a **Hex Keypad** for a keyboard. Since the Easy4 is only capable of working with 1s and 0s, a seven segment display and hex keypad are all that is needed. Many microprocessor-driven machines in industry still use this type of input and output. The Easy4 also contains four buttons. The one on the lower left turns the computer on and off. The upper two buttons are used to **RUN** a machine language program and **STEP** through a program, one instruction at a time. The **RESET** button on the lower right resets internal registers to default values. The architecture of the Easy4 is shown in Figure 2.2.

The seven-segment LED in the case is connected to port A of the computer; the computer can output any hex number to the LED. The hex keypad is connected to port B. A keyboard buffer chip is used to store keystrokes. Without it, there would be no memory of what key was pressed when the computer reads port B. There are 16 nibbles of memory available in this computer, occupying memory addresses 0 through 15. Figure 2.2 shows a memory address on the right and the data contained in the address on the left. The CPU contains an instruction pointer, a register named A (for accumulator, because it stores the results of operations), a stack pointer, a carry flag, and a zero flag. Flags are binary numbers that indicate the result of an operation. For example, if an addition produced an overflow, the carry flag is set. The stack pointer is used to indicate a position in memory.

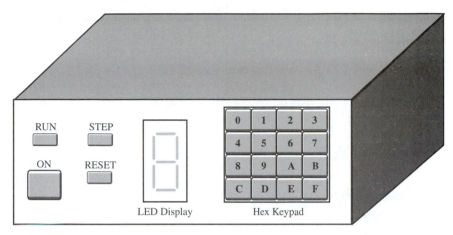

FIGURE 2.1   Easy4 Enclosure

The Easy4 operating system allows you to enter an Assembly language program and run it. On early microcomputers such as the Easy4, you would have had to enter a program in machine language from the hex keyboard. In this simulation program, instructions are entered from the list on the upper left of the screen.

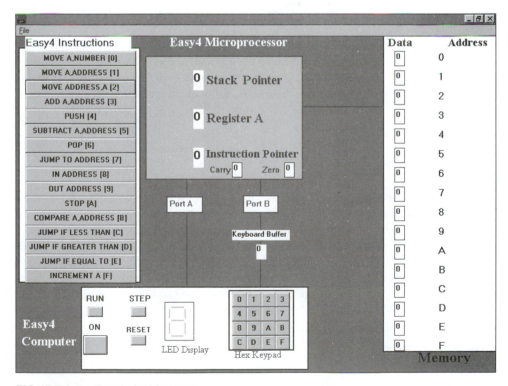

FIGURE 2.2   Easy4 Architecture

EASY4 INSTRUCTIONS

The instructions for the Easy4 are shown in Table 2.1. On the left is an English-like translation of the instruction, and on the right the representation of the instruction in memory. Remember, computers only work with 1s and 0s (binary). Hex representations of the opcode are used instead of binary.

Easy4 MOVE Instructions

The MOVE instructions operate on register A. They can move a number or contents of a memory address to register A or vice versa. The instruction

```
MOVE A,NUMBER
```

moves a hex number into register A. Whatever was in register A is erased to make room for the new number. The number is stated immediately after the instruction. Note the backwards notation used in the instruction, or a right-to-left movement (NUMBER is on the right, and A is on the left in the instruction statement).

Move A, Number

This instruction moves Number
into Register A

By loading the accumulator with a number, no other action is taken. The output LED does not show the contents of the accumulator, nor does the statement in any way read the hex keypad. You must program the computer with other instructions to do this. NUMBER is stored in memory in the address following the instruction.

The instructions

```
MOVE A,ADDRESS
```

and

```
MOVE ADDRESS,A
```

operate on the accumulator and memory. MOVE ADDRESS,A loads the value from register A into a memory address specified immediately after the instruction. For example, MOVE ADDRESS F,A loads the contents of A into memory address F. To understand how this instruction works, think of delivering a package to a house. You need to know the address to deliver the package to. The package is the data in the accumulator, and the street address is the same as the memory address in the computer.

Data can be transferred from a memory address to register A by using the instruction MOVE A,ADDRESS, as shown below.

Move A,Address F

Results

A

| Data | ←————— | Data |

Address F

TABLE 2.1   Easy4 Instruction Set

Easy4 Instruction	Hex Representation (Op-code)	Description
MOVE A,NUMBER	0	Moves a number into the A register. The number to be used follows the instruction.
MOVE A,ADDRESS	1	Moves the number contained in an address into A. The address follows the instruction.
MOVE ADDRESS,A	2	Moves the contents of A into an address. The address to be used follows the instruction.
ADD A,ADDRESS	3	Adds the contents of A and the contents of an address. The address to be used follows the instruction.
PUSH	4	Pushes the contents of A onto the stack.
SUBTRACT A,ADDRESS	5	Subtracts the contents of the contents of an address from A. The address to be used follows the instruction.
POP	6	Pops the contents of the stack into A.
JUMP TO ADDRESS	7	Transfers program execution to another address. The address to jump to is indicated after the instruction.
IN ADDRESS	8	Inputs data from a port into register A. The port address is indicated after the instruction.
OUT ADDRESS	9	Outputs data from register A to a port. The port address is indicated after the instruction.
STOP	A	Halts program execution.
COMPARE A,ADDRESS	B	Compares A to the contents of an address. Flag registers are set as a result of this operation.
JUMP IF LESS THAN	C	Jumps to an address if carry flag = 1.
JUMP IF GREATER THAN	D	Jumps to an address if carry flag = 0.
JUMP IF EQUAL TO	E	Jumps to an address if zero flag = 1.
INCREMENT A	F	Increment A (adds 1 to it).

Easy4 Algebraic Instructions

The Easy4 contains two instructions for adding and subtracting, **ADD A,ADDRESS** and **SUBTRACT A,ADDRESS.** In the first case, data contained in an address is added to the accumulator. Whatever was in the accumulator is replaced by the sum A + ADDRESS. In the latter case, data contained in an address is subtracted from A. Whatever was in the accumulator is replaced by A – Data in ADDRESS. The ADD and SUBTRACT instructions also set the carry flag, as shown below:

Case	Result
Two numbers are added together, with the sum being greater than F.	Carry flag = 1. Zero flag = 0. True sum = A + 10 hex.
Two numbers are added together, with the sum being F + 1.	Carry flag = 1. Zero flag = 1. A = 0. True sum = 10 hex.
Two numbers are subtracted, with the result being less than 0.	Carry flag = 1. Zero flag = 0. True difference = 2's complement of A.
Two numbers are subtracted, with the result being 0.	Carry flag = 0. Zero flag = 1. True Difference = 0.

If the first case, two numbers are added together and the result is greater than F. Since the largest number the accumulator can hold is F, some sort of error must occur. After F, the microprocessor starts counting from 0 again (see the binary odometer in Chapter 1). Since the result will not be correct, the carry flag is set to show that a carry has occurred. Fortunately, you can still calculate the correct answer by realizing that A equals the sum − F. As an example, suppose 9h + 8h are added. The result is shown below:

9	Number
A	Number + 1
B	Number + 2
C	Number + 3
D	Number + 4
E	Number + 5
F	Number + 6
0	Number + 7, carry flag is set when sum is greater than F.
1	Number + 8, results in accumulator.

The true sum is the contents of the accumulator + 10 hex, or 11 hex. You can think of the carry flag being 10 hex added to the accumulator. As a check, 9 + 8 = 17 decimal, or 11 hex.

Now add 9h + 7h. This sum is 16 decimal, or 10 hex. In this case A = 0, and both the carry and zero flags = 1. Whenever an algebraic operation resulting in 0 is stored in the accumulator, the zero flag = 1. Once again, think of the carry flag as 10 hex and add it to A. The result is 10 hex + 0 = 10 hex, which is the right answer.

Let's look at the case of subtraction. If the result of a subtraction is less than 0, an error has occurred since A cannot be negative. The Easy4 once again sets the carry flag. Look at the case of 2 − 4; this equals −2, but register A = E hex, as shown below:

2	Number
1	Number − 1
0	Number − 2
F	Number − 3
E	Number − 4

The true difference can be found by taking the 2's complement of E. Since E equals 1110: 1110 inverted = 0001.

$$\begin{array}{r} 0001 \\ + 0001 \\ \hline 0010 = 2 \end{array}$$

The true difference is −2. If a difference = 0, the zero flag is set to 1, since A = 0.

Easy4 Conditional and Jump Instructions

The Easy4 contains instructions for looping and branching. A loop cycles through a section of code a set number of times, as with the **for** loop in C. A branch instruction goes to another section of code, as with the **JUMP TO ADDRESS** instruction. This instruction loads the instruction pointer with the address following the instruction statement. For instance, if the instruction JUMP TO ADDRESS A is executed, the next instruction will be seen at address A. This instruction is similar to the GOTO instruction in the BASIC language.

The Easy4 can also simulate the IF statement in higher-level languages such as C or BASIC. Instead of IF, use **COMPARE A,ADDRESS.** This instruction compares the accumulator to data in a specified address. The result of the compare sets the carry and zero flags. If A is less than the number in the address, the carry flag = 1. If A is greater than the number, the carry flag = 0. If A equals the number, the zero flag = 1. A summary of how COMPARE sets the flags is shown below:

A>NUMBER   carry = 0, zero = 0
A<NUMBER   carry = 1, zero = 0
A=NUMBER   carry = 0, zero = 1

Conditional JUMP instructions are used after COMPARE. These instructions transfer program control to another address based on the state of the carry or zero flag.

The **JUMP IF LESS THAN** instruction checks to see if A is less than NUMBER in the COMPARE A,NUMBER instruction. What it really checks is the state of the carry flag. If carry = 1, a jump will occur after the statement. If carry = 0, the next instruction after JUMP IF LESS THAN is executed.

JUMP IF GREATER THAN transfers control if carry = 0. If carry = 0, program control is transferred to the address included in the instruction. Otherwise, the instruction after JUMP is executed.

JUMP IF EQUAL TO looks at the zero flag. If zero = 1, the address included in the instruction is loaded into the instruction pointer. Otherwise, the next instruction is loaded into the instruction pointer.

Easy4 Stack Instructions

The stack is an area of memory that contains present or previous values of Easy4 register A. Imagine a set of dishes suspended from a ceiling, as shown in Figures 2.3 and 2.4. When a plate is added to the set, it is pushed up onto the bottom. When a plate is taken off, it is pulled from the bottom of the set. This is comparable to a memory stack in a computer. The uppermost plate represents the top of stack memory. When you push or pop, you are placing data on the bottom of the stack, or taking data off the bottom of the stack.

Every time a **PUSH** operation is executed, the stack pointer is decremented one position, and the value of the A register is placed in memory at the address pointed to by the stack pointer. The stack pointer starts at 0. The PUSH instruction begins by first decrementing the stack pointer one position, making it point to address F (remember the binary odometer). If PUSH is executed again, the stack pointer is decremented again and points to E. The data in A is placed in memory at the address pointed to by address E. The **POP** instruction takes the data pointed to by the stack pointer and places it in A, then increments the stack pointer. If the stack pointer were pointing to address E, it would now point to address F.

Easy4 Miscellaneous Instructions

The **STOP** instruction stops the program from running. At this point, you can revise the program, add data, run or step the program again, or perform any other operation.

FIGURE 2.3   PUSH
Instruction

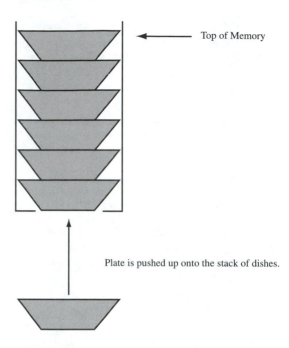

INCREMENT A adds 1 to the A register. It can be used instead of ADD A,AD-DRESS because it takes up less memory.

The **IN** and **OUT** instructions transfer data between the ports and register A. In the Easy4, port B is connected to the hex keypad, and port A is connected to the LED. When-

FIGURE 2.4   POP
Instruction

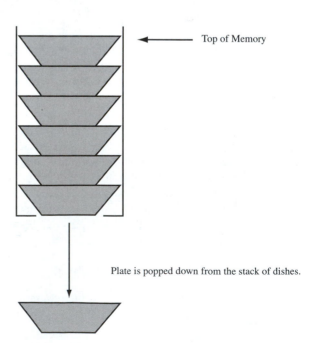

ever IN B is executed, the contents of the keyboard buffer are loaded into the accumulator. Likewise, OUT A sends the data contained in register A to the LED.

HOW MACHINE LANGUAGE IS STORED IN MEMORY

The representation of instructions as 1s and 0s is called machine language. Each machine language instruction occupies one or more memory addresses. A memory address can be thought of as a storage container for an instruction or datum.

Each instruction has a number representing it, and it is this number that is stored in memory. The binary (or hex) number representing the instruction is called the op-code. Easy4 op-codes can have one or no operands. The operands always come after the op-code, as shown below:

```
op-code, operand
```

The **op-code** defines an operation to be performed (hence the name), and **operand** describes the tools to be used in the operation.

An Assembly language instruction is an English-like translation of machine language code. The memory address can be thought of as a line number in a higher-level language, except instructions often take up multiple addresses. In a higher-level language, each instruction is assigned only one line number, but here MOVE A,F uses addresses 0 and 1. This may seem confusing at first. The op-code or hex representation of the MOVE A instruction uses address 0, and the operand F is stored in address 1.

Notice that addresses 1 and 2 both contain F but represent different things. The first F at address 1 is the operand of the instruction and represents the number used by MOVE A,F. It is the number to be moved into register A when the program is run, as described earlier. It uses the address after the instruction to find the number to use. The second F represents the op-code for INCREMENT A. This instruction simply increments (or adds 1 to) register A. This is a one-address instruction. The JUMP TO instruction transfers program control to another address. The address to jump to is found after the instruction, in this case address C. After the JUMP TO instruction, the next instruction executed is the one located at address 12.

TABLE 2.2 Machine Language Versus Assembly Language for the Easy4 Microprocessor

Instructions Stored in Binary (Machine Language)		
Memory Address	HEX Representation of Instruction	Assembly Language Instruction
0	0	MOVE A,F
1	F	
2	F	INCREMENT A
3	7	JUMP TO C
4	C	
5	A	STOP

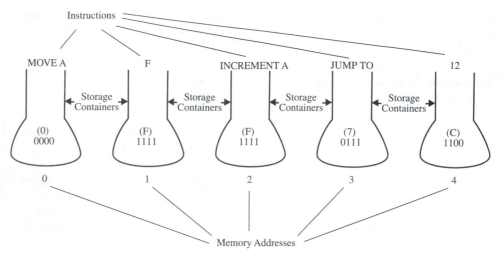

FIGURE 2.5   Easy4 Storage of Instructions in Memory

Think of each address as a storage container. Figure 2.5 represents how the first three instructions are stored.

Which is easier to remember, 0 and 9 or MOVE A,9? Assembly language makes more sense from a programmer's standpoint. The statements are English-like and fairly easy to remember. It is important to see here that there is a physical relation between the 1s and 0s in memory and an instruction.

Programming the Easy4

Before trying to load the software, see Appendix G for instructions on running the install utility supplied with the disk. As noted in the appendix, you will need a PC compatible running at least Windows 3.1, with an SVGA monitor that has at least 800x600, 256-color resolution. After installing Easy4, click on the Easy4 icon to load the program. You should see a figure similar to Figure 2.1 on the screen. The Easy4 is initially in the OFF state. To turn it on, press the ON button with the mouse. You will now see a figure similar to Figure 2.2 on the screen.

The examples shown below use the **RUN** button. You should also try running them with the **STEP** button. This button steps through the programs one instruction at a time, allowing you to view register A, the instruction pointer, the input/output (I/O), and memory. When using the STEP button, you must reset the instruction pointer to 0 if you want to start from the beginning of the program. You can do this by pressing the RESET button, or clicking on the instruction pointer address and setting it to 0.

Let's start by entering a simple program. To enter the program shown below, first set the instruction pointer to 0. To do this, click on address 0 in the memory box. The instruction pointer should now show 0. Next select the instructions from the Easy4 instructions box. Instructions with operands will require a second entry. A dialog box (called the input box in the examples) will appear to enter the operand.

Example 2.1

Write an Easy4 program to load the accumulator with the number 5. Run the program to see if this occurs.

Solution The program is shown below:

```
MOVE A,NUMBER    Enter 5 in the input box.
STOP
```

After entering these instructions, the memory map should look like this:

Instruction	Address
0	0
5	1
A	2

Press the address 0 in the memory box to reset the instruction pointer to 0. Press the RUN button on the front panel of Easy4 to run the program. Register A should now contain the number 5.

Example 2.2

Write a program to load the number B into memory address 9.

Solution The accumulator must first be loaded with the number B, then B is transferred to address 9. The following instructions accomplish this:

```
MOVE A,NUMBER     Enter B in the input box.
MOVE ADDRESS,A    Enter 9 in the input box.
STOP
```

Press the address 0 in the memory box to reset the instruction pointer to 0. Press RUN to start the program. You should now see B in register A, and B in address 9 in the memory box.

Example 2.3

Write a program to solve the operation

$9 + 5 - 2$

After solving, disassemble the program and send it to a printer.

Solution The program is shown below. First load A with 2. Next store the contents of the accumulator in address F. You want to use the highest possible address to separate data from the program (otherwise they will overwrite each other, sometimes causing disastrous consequences!). Next, the program loads 5 into the accumulator and subtracts the contents of address F from it. So far, you have subtracted $5 - 2$. The program then stores the difference in address F. Now load the number 9 into the accumulator. Then add the accumulator to address F, which gives the answer of C in the accumulator. (9 + 3 = 12, or C hex).

Enter and run the program. Don't forget to reset the instruction pointer prior to pressing the RUN button.

`MOVE A,NUMBER`	Enter 2 in the input box.
`MOVE ADDRESS,A`	Enter F in the input box.
`MOVE A,NUMBER`	Enter 5 in the input box.
`SUBTRACT A,ADDRESS`	Enter F in the input box.
`MOVE ADDRESS,A`	Enter F in the input box.
`MOVE A,NUMBER`	Enter 9 in the input box.
`ADD A,ADDRESS`	Enter F in the input box.
`STOP`	Stops the program.

Next disassemble the program. This is done by selecting **File** from the top of the window and **Disassemble File.** A purple window will now appear with the memory addresses, instructions, and op-codes listed. Press the PRINT button to print the disassembled program. Press CLOSE to exit the Disassemble File window.

Example 2.4

Write a program to add 9 + C. Interpret the results.

Solution   A simple program to add 9 + C is shown below.

`MOVE A,NUMBER`	Enter 9 in the input box.
`MOVE ADDRESS,A`	Enter F in the input box.
`MOVE A,NUMBER`	Enter C in the input box.
`ADD A,ADDRESS`	Enter F in the input box.
`STOP`	Stops the program.

The result is 5, with the carry flag set to 1. Look at the table below:

9	**Number**
A	Number + 1
B	Number + 2
C	Number + 3
D	Number + 4
E	Number + 5
F	Number + 6
0	Number + 7
1	Number + 8
2	Number + 9
3	Number + A
4	Number + B
5	Number + C

Due to the odometer effect (or rolling over of numbers), this table shows that 9 is number, and number + C = 5. Since you crossed 0, the carry flag is set to 1.

Example 2.5

Write a program to input a number from the keyboard. If the number equals 6, display it to the LED and stop the program. Otherwise, stop the program.

Solution   The program is shown below. Before entering the program, insert a 6 in the data box in memory address A.

Address	Instruction	
0,1	IN A,ADDRESS	Enter B in input box.
2,3	COMPARE A,ADDRESS	Enter A in input box.
4,5	JUMP IF EQUAL TO,ADDRESS	Enter 7 in input box.
6	STOP	
7,8	OUT A,ADDRESS	Enter A in input box.
9	STOP	Stops the program.
A	6	

This program compares the number read in from the keypad to a number at address A. If two are equal, the number is printed to the LED by the instruction OUT A,ADDRESS.

Example 2.6

Write a program that outputs to the LED the greater of two numbers stored at memory addresses E and F.

Solution   To begin, store a number at addresses E and F. Click on the data box at address E in the memory box and change it to 7. Now click on the data at address F and change it to B. Enter the program shown below:

MOVE A,ADDRESS	Enter F in input box.
COMPARE A,ADDRESS	Enter E in input box.
JUMP IF GREATER THAN	Enter 8 in input box.
MOVE A,ADDRESS	Enter E in input box.
OUT ADDRESS	Enter A in input box.
STOP	Stops the program.

This program first reads the data at address F into the accumulator. This number is then compared with the data at address E. If F is greater than E, the accumulator is sent to the LED. Otherwise, address E is loaded into the accumulator and sent to the LED.

Example 2.7

Explain the condition of the stack after each instruction shown below is executed:

```
MOVE A,7
PUSH
MOVE A,2
```

```
PUSH
POP
POP
```

Solution   Before the program starts, the stack pointer equals 0. Address F contains the value of the accumulator, or 7. The stack pointer is equal to F. After the next PUSH, address E contains 2 and the stack pointer equals E. After the first POP, the stack pointer is incremented to F and register A is loaded with the contents of address E. After the final POP, the stack pointer is incremented to 0 and register A is loaded with the contents of address F.

The Easy4 Bus

The Easy4 has three buses: a data bus, an address bus, and a control bus. The address and data bus each contain four lines and are labeled A0,A1,A2,A3, and D0,D1,D2,D3, respectively. The control bus has three address lines called P/$\overline{M}$, Read, and Write. You can see the buses by selecting **Show Easy4 Bus** from the File menu. The Easy4 bus appears in Figure 2.6.

A READ or WRITE operation is viewed with respect to the microprocessor. A READ operation means that data is to be sent from a port or memory to the processor (or read into the computer). A WRITE operation means that data is to be sent from the

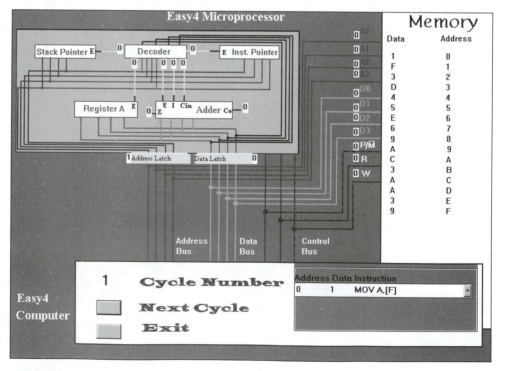

FIGURE 2.6   Easy4 Bus

processor to memory or a port. The P/$\overline{\text{M}}$ pin determines if memory or a port is to be accessed. If high, the port specified by the address on the address bus is to be connected to the data bus. If low, the data bus is connected to memory. The IN and OUT commands both set P/$\overline{\text{M}}$ high. If P/$\overline{\text{M}}$ is low, memory is to be accessed. This occurs when an instruction specifies a memory operation (such as MOVE A,ADDRESS).

The Easy4 CPU

The Easy4 has an internal CPU that runs the machine language programs. It consists of register A, the adder, the instruction pointer, the stack pointer, and, perhaps most importantly, the machine language decoder. These devices are connected to the address and data bus through two output latches.

The Easy4 Decoder

Have you wondered how the Easy4 CPU translates an op-code of 1 into a procedure that loads data from a memory address into register A? The decoder takes the op-code from memory and determines what needs to be done to implement the related instruction. Figure 2.6 shows a series of binary 0s surrounding the decoder. These are decoder outputs that are either set high or low to control the various devices. The outputs are connected to enable pins (marked **E** in Figure 2.6). A diagram describing an enable on a three-state buffer is shown in Figure 2.7. This buffer does not perform any digital logic, it simply sends the input to the output when enabled.

A 0 at the enable physically disconnects the output from the buffer. This is called the high-impedance state (marked **H** in Figure 2.7). The output is neither high nor low, but simply floats in space, much like a wire that is not connected to anything. When a 1 is placed on the enable, the device is activated. In the example in Figure 2.7, when the enable is high the input is transferred to the output. The enables allow data to be transferred to a specific device, without interference from other devices. This avoids a state called bus contention, in which two or more devices send out conflicting outputs on the bus at the same time, as shown in Figure 2.8.

FIGURE 2.7   Diagram of
Three-State Buffer

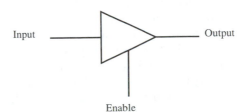

Input	Enable	Output
1	0	H
0	0	H
1	1	1
0	1	0

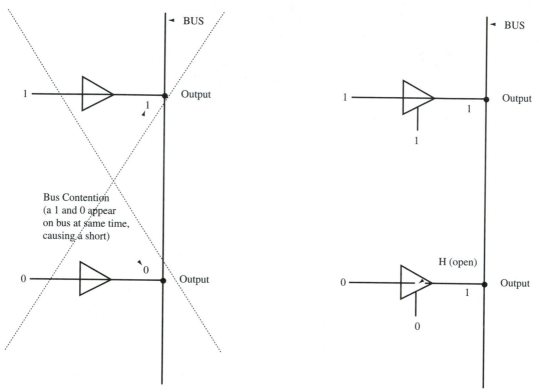

FIGURE 2.8   Diagram of Bus Contention

This figure shows a wire connecting the input to the output. On the left there are no enables, so a short is produced on the bus. On the right, a 0 enable causes a break in the connection. In this case, a 1 appears at the lower right output, even though a 0 is at the input. The 1 comes from the upper-right output. In this case there is no conflict. A single buffer is enabled only when all the other outputs on the bus are not enabled.

What the decoder places on the register A, adder, and instruction pointer enables is, for the most part, determined by the input to the decoder. The decoder input is the op-code from memory. Note that the input lines are connected to the data bus through the data output latch. New instructions are always sent in over the data bus. Although each instruction is executed differently by the decoder, the process of fetching the instruction from memory to the decoder is always the same. In order to synchronize the instruction loading and decoding process, all operations occur during predefined time intervals, called clock cycles.

Clock Cycles

All operations of the Easy4 are run by a system clock. The clock is actually a crystal, much like the one in your watch. The clock looks like a square wave, as shown in Figure 2.9. The wave alternates between logic 1 and logic 0 at a fixed rate called its frequency.

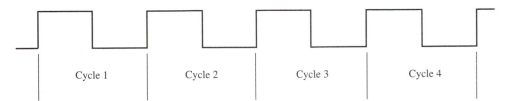

FIGURE 2.9   The Easy4 Clock

A clock cycle begins on the rising edge of the square wave, and ends at the start of the next rising edge. During each clock cycle, specific operations occur. Groups of clock cycles are combined into machine cycles: the first two machine cycles for all instructions are reserved for fetching instructions from memory, the remaining clock cycles are reserved for decoding and executing an instruction.

Fetching an Instruction from Memory

Machine language instructions are stored in memory addresses. The CPU decoder decides when to read in the instruction. To do this, the decoder performs the following steps:

During machine cycle 1, the decoder places the contents of the instruction pointer on the address bus. Immediately upon receipt of the address, memory determines the address is requested.

During machine cycle 2, the Read pin goes high and the $\overline{P/M}$ pin goes low. This means that data is to be transferred from memory to the CPU. Reading and writing are with reference to the CPU. A READ operation means data is being sent into the decoder. $\overline{P/M}$ going low means the data is coming from memory. Memory then places the instruction on the data bus. The decoder reads it and begins processing.

Interpreting an Instruction

How an instruction is interpreted depends on what the instruction must do. For example, an ADD or SUB operation will use the adder, while a MOVE operation will not. Let's look at a few of the instructions on the Easy4 Architecture screen.

Example 2.8

Explain each cycle of the MOVE A,[F] operation.

Solution   Select **Show Easy4 Bus** from the File menu. The default instruction to be analyzed is MOVE A,[F]. This instruction is a shorthand way of saying MOVE A,ADDRESS F. The square brackets around F indicate that F represents an address rather than a number. To view each machine cycle, press the Next Cycle key with the mouse.

Cycle 1—This cycle shows the decoder placing 0000 on the address bus (A0 through A3). This is because MOVE A,[F] is stored at address 0. Note that the **address output latch** is enabled. This allows the decoder to route the contents of the instruction pointer to memory, to indicate which instruction to place on the data bus.

Cycle 2—Cycle 2 shows the P/$\overline{\text{M}}$ pin low and the Read pin high. Memory now places the instruction located at address 0 onto the data bus. Since MOVE A,[F] has an op-code of 1, the data bus equals 0001. Note that the **data output latch** is set to 1 so that the data is sent to the decoder. The instruction pointer is then incremented to point to the next address.

Cycle 3—During cycle 3, the address latch is enabled, placing 0001 on the address bus.

Cycle 4—The Read pin goes high and the data at address 1 is loaded onto the data bus. The data at address 1 equals F. The decoder now knows the address needed to perform the complete instruction. The instruction pointer is incremented to point to the next address.

Cycle 5—During this cycle, the decoder analyzes the instruction. Since the operation requires more information to be obtained from the operand address, F is transferred from the data bus to the address bus, and the address output latch is set to 1. The decoder takes care of loading F onto the address bus without the help of the instruction pointer. Since the instruction pointer is not enabled, it does not contain the new address. It is important that it keep the next memory instruction position (address 2) intact. Note that the enables of register A and the data output latch are equal to 0. This means that register A is not yet connected to the data bus.

Cycle 6—During machine cycle 5, memory found the correct data for address F. Now the read pin goes low (P/$\overline{\text{M}}$ also remains low) so the proper data can be loaded onto the data bus. Note from the memory map on the upper left that address F contains the number 9. The data bus contains 1001, which is the binary representation for 9. The decoder sets the enables for register A and the data output latch high so that register A now contains the number 9. At this point, the desired outcome of the instruction has been achieved.

Example 2.9

Explain each cycle of the ADD A,[D] instruction.

Solution   Select **Show Easy4 Bus** in the File menu. Next select ADD A,[D] from the menu on the lower left corner of the screen. The first four cycles of this instruction are devoted to the instruction and operand fetch routines and remain essentially the same as Example 2.8. Cycles 1 and 2 load the instruction at address 0010 (2) into the decoder. Cycles 3 and 4 load the data in the next address (address 3). The data is equal to D. Cycle 5 transfers the data to the address bus. Note that the address output latch is high. During Cycle 6, register A is sent to the adder as the first number to be added (note the enables on the adder and register A). Although it is not shown here, an analysis of the program shows the number 9 resides in register A at this time (note that the first instruction loaded 9 from memory address F into register A).

During Cycle 7, the decoder loads the data from address D into the adder as the second number to be added. Note that the data bus is equal to 1010, or A. The number A is stored in address D. Also during this cycle, the decoder instructs the adder to add the two numbers (the 9 from register A and the A from address D). Since $9 + A = 13$, a carryout (Co) is generated on the adder (this is actually the carry flag). The 3 produced by the sum is sent to register A.

Easy4 Timing Diagrams

Timing diagrams show when specific operations occur and thus provide a deeper understanding of the workings of a computer system. A timing diagram for the Easy4 MOVE A,[address] instruction is shown in Figure 2.10.

The timing diagram describes the operation of the MOVE A,[address]. The timing of the instruction is controlled by a clock. Each machine cycle takes four clock cycles to complete. A change of state on the address, data, or control bus occurs during a positive transition of the clock pulse. During the first machine cycle, the address latch goes high during the first clock pulse. While the address latch is high, the address is loaded from the instruction pointer to the address bus. During machine Cycle 2, the data latch goes high and memory places the instruction onto the data bus. Also during machine Cycle 2 the Read pin goes high. This tells the processor to load the instruction into the decoder for processing. When the decoder interprets the MOVE instruction, it then uses machine Cycle 3 to set the address latch high again and load the next address onto the address bus. Machine Cycle 4 sees the Read pin set high to read in the address where the contents are to be moved to register A. Machine Cycle 5 sees the address latch placed high again, and finally the Read pin goes high during machine Cycle 6 so that the contents of the address can be read into register A.

The OUT instruction has a similar timing diagram (Figure 2.11).

The OUT timing diagram is split into five machine cycles. Cycles 1 and 2 are reserved for fetching the instruction and are the same as the MOVE instruction shown above. Cycle 3 places the next address after the op-code on the address bus. Cycle 4 reads in the data at this address. During Cycle 5, the address that was read in Cycle 4 is latched on the address bus. After this, the contents of register A are latched on the data bus. The Write pin goes low, sending the data to the specified address.

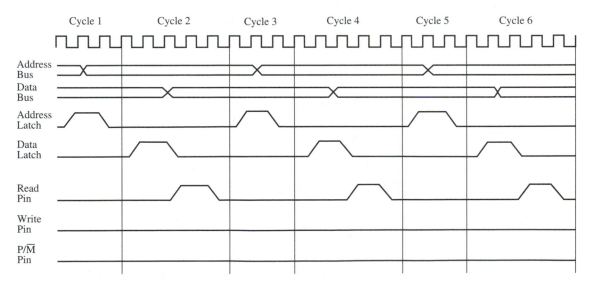

FIGURE 2.10 Timing Diagram for the MOVE A,[address] Instruction

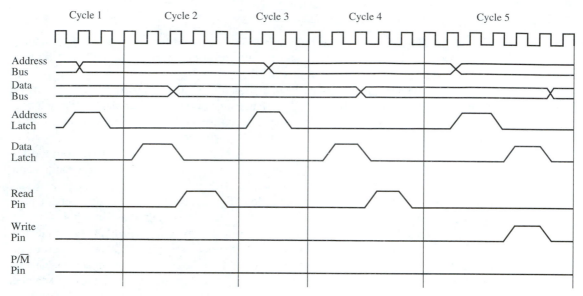

FIGURE 2.11　Timing Diagram for the OUT Instruction

Easy4 Versus 80x86 Processors

The Easy4 is a model of one of the simplest computers possible. On the other hand, all 80x86 processors are quite complex. They are similar in the sense that both take numerous clock cycles to complete an instruction. Any processor that takes more than one clock cycle to complete an instruction is called a CISC (complex instruction set computer). A processor that uses one clock cycle or less to complete an instruction is called a RISC (reduced instruction set computer). The RISC processors avoid complicated instructions; they require many instructions to complete the equivalent of a CISC instruction. This places more burden on the Assembly programmer, but, in general, allows for faster, more efficient programs.

There is some similarity in the 80x86 and Easy4 instruction fetch and decoding process, but there are also many differences. When an instruction is fetched in the 80x86, it is loaded into an internal queue for temporary storage. The CPU then grabs one instruction at a time from the queue. The advantage to this method is that future instructions to be processed can be loaded onto the queue, during the same clock cycle that the CPU grabs and decodes an instruction. This essentially combines the instruction fetch and decoding process into the same clock cycle.

Compiling Assembly Language Programs

The Easy4 assembler has no need to compile a program. The machine language code is entered into the next available memory address when an instruction button is pressed. Modern assemblers must compile Assembly language programs prior to running them. Compiling is the process of converting the Assembly language instructions to machine language. The result is a separate machine language program. On a PC, all machine language programs that are operational (i.e., can be run from DOS), end with a .COM or an .EXE extension. Assembly language programs end with an .ASM extension. In the next chapter, an assembler called DEBUG is covered. It is capable of allowing you to enter, run, and compile .COM files. In future chapters, you will work with the MASM, a full-featured assembler capable of compiling .EXE files. When you use MASM, Assembly language will begin to appear more like a higher-level language. You will be far removed from the days of small microcomputers like the Easy4. Still, the principles learned in this chapter will be helpful in future chapters.

CHAPTER 2 PROBLEMS

For all Easy4 programs, disassemble each program and send it to a printer.

1. Write an Easy4 program to print the letter C to the LED.
2. Write an Easy4 program to display the contents of memory address D to the LED.
3. Write an Easy4 program that subtracts the numbers stored in addresses E and F from address D.
4. Write an Easy4 program that reads in two numbers from the hex keypad and sends the sum to the LED. *Hint:* You will need to use STEP instead of RUN to do this.
5. State which instructions shown below set either the carry flag or zero flag to 1. Enter the program into Easy4 and use the STEP button to view the program one line at a time. Assume address $D = 5$, $E = A$, and $F = 6$ (you can set these values in the memory data boxes).

```
MOVE A,6
ADD A,E
SUBTRACT A,D
INCREMENT A
ADD A,F
STOP
```

6. Decipher the Easy4 machine language program shown below. Verify by entering the program in the memory data boxes and disassembling it.

```
0
2
3
A
F
B
F
E
D
A
```

7. Describe the differences between using the RUN button and the STEP button. What purpose does the STEP program have when developing a program? How are the registers affected when using RUN or STEP?

8. Write an Easy4 program that sends the lesser of two numbers stored at address F and the keyboard buffer to the LED.

9. Write an Easy4 program to push the numbers 1, 2, 3, and 4 onto the stack. Restore the stack pointer to its original value prior to issuing a STOP instruction. Use compare and increment instructions in the program.

10. Write an Easy4 program that pushes the contents of register A onto address F, loads a new value into register A from the keyboard, adds the new value to the contents of address F, outputs the sum to the LED, and restores A to its original value.

11. Describe each clock cycle of the OUT A instruction. You can find it on the Easy4 Architecture menu.

12. Describe each clock cycle of the PUSH A and POP A instructions. You can find them on the Easy4 Architecture menu.

13. The Easy4 is incapable of subtraction, only addition. Subtraction is accomplished through the 2's complement method described in Chapter 1. Describe each clock cycle of the SUBTRACT A,[E] instruction. You can find it on the Easy4 Architecture menu.

14. Although it does not exist on the Easy4 Architecture menu, describe what you think each clock cycle of the INCREMENT A instruction might contain.

CHAPTER 3

COM Files and DEBUG

NEW INSTRUCTIONS IN THIS CHAPTER

Mnemonic:	**MOV**
	MOV *destination,source*
Description:	Transfers a byte or word from source to destination. The source can be a register, an immediate number, or an address. The destination can be a register or an address.
Examples:	MOV AL,13 (Copies 13 to AL.)
	MOV AX,BX (Copies BX to AX. BX is not changed.)
	MOV DL,CL (Copies CL to DL. CL is not changed.)
	MOV BL,[BX] (Copies the contents of the address pointed to by BX to BL.)
Flags Affected:	Carry, Overflow, Parity, Sign, Zero

Mnemonic:	**INT**
	INT *0-255*
Description:	Transfers program to a procedure specified by the interrupt number. The interrupt returns processing to the address after the INT instruction.
Examples:	INT 21h (Executes interrupt 21 hex. Used as DOS interrupt.)
	INT 20h (Executes interrupt 20 hex. Used as .COM exit interrupt.)
	INT 16h (Executes interrupt 16 hex. Used as keyboard interrupt.)
	INT 10h (Executes interrupt 10 hex. Used as screen interrupt.)
Flags Affected:	Interrupt

Mnemonic:	**JMP**
	JMP *address*

Description:	Transfers program to address.
Examples:	JMP 1234 (Jumps to offset address 1234.)
	JMP 12:34 (Jumps to segment 12, offset 34.)
Flags Affected:	None

Mnemonic:	**LOOP**
	LOOP *address*
Description:	Decrements **CX;** transfers program to address if CX > 0; transfers program to next instruction if CX = 0.
Examples:	LOOP 1234 (Loops to offset address 1234.)
Flags Affected:	None

Mnemonic:	**INC**
	INC *register*
Description:	Increments a register by 1.
Examples:	MOV CL,42
	INC CL (CL now equals 43.)
Flags Affected:	Overflow, Parity, Sign, Zero

Mnemonic:	**DEC**
	DEC *register*
Description:	Decrements a register by 1.
Examples:	MOV CL,42
	DEC CL (CL now equals 41.)
Flags Affected:	Overflow, Parity, Sign, Zero

THE 80X86 INTERNAL REGISTERS

Compared with the 4-bit registers in the Easy4 microprocessor, the 80x86 processor's registers are larger and there are many more of them. There are a minimum of 14 internal 16-bit registers in the 80x86 family that are accessible. The actual number of registers available depends on the processor. Some of the registers can be identified as two 8-bit registers, or one 16-bit register, as shown in Figure 3.1.

AX, BX, CX, and **DX** are word (16-bit) registers. **AL, AH, BL, BH, CL, CH, DL,** and **DH** are byte (8-bit) registers. Note that AL (L means low) and AH (H means high) combine to produce AX; AL and AH can be thought of as two rooms in a house called AX. The same is true for the BX, CX, and DX registers. The remaining ten registers are all 16 bit, and will be explained in later chapters.

Figure 3.1 80X86 Registers

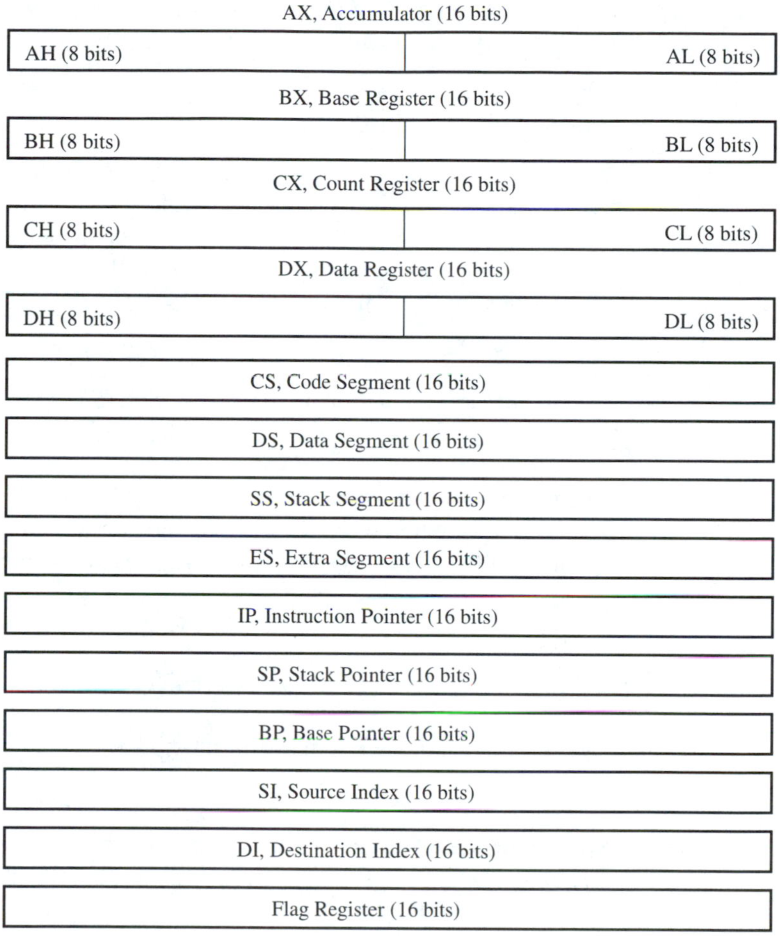

AX, Accumulator (16 bits)

AH (8 bits)	AL (8 bits)

BX, Base Register (16 bits)

BH (8 bits)	BL (8 bits)

CX, Count Register (16 bits)

CH (8 bits)	CL (8 bits)

DX, Data Register (16 bits)

DH (8 bits)	DL (8 bits)

CS, Code Segment (16 bits)

DS, Data Segment (16 bits)

SS, Stack Segment (16 bits)

ES, Extra Segment (16 bits)

IP, Instruction Pointer (16 bits)

SP, Stack Pointer (16 bits)

BP, Base Pointer (16 bits)

SI, Source Index (16 bits)

DI, Destination Index (16 bits)

Flag Register (16 bits)

Mnemonics and Operands

Mnemonics are the core part of an Assembly language instruction; MOV and ADD are examples of mnemonics. They state the purpose of the instruction. What comes after the mnemonic is called the operand. The operand states which registers or memory addresses the instruction operates on. For example, in the instruction

```
MOV AX,BX
```

MOV is the mnemonic, and AX,BX is the operand.

DEBUG and COM Files

This chapter introduces 80x86 Assembly language through .COM files. These files are the easiest type of Assembly program to create on PCs. A common way to create .COM files is through a utility program supplied with DOS entitled DEBUG, which allows you to write, modify, trace, load, and save 80x86 Assembly programs.

A First 8086 Assembly Language Program

You will find the DEBUG program included with DOS to be much more powerful than the Easy4 assembler. Also there are many more instructions in the 80x86 series of microprocessors than the Easy4. Let's try a simple example in DEBUG.

First go to the directory containing DEBUG. This is usually in the same directory containing your DOS files (either C:\DOS or C:\BIN). Next enter

```
DEBUG
```

You should now see a dash on the screen. Enter

```
-A100
```

This tells your program to begin at address 100 hex. All .COM files begin at address 100 hex. A funny looking set of numbers should appear on the left side. These are a hex representation of the address where your program begins. Enter

```
MOV DL,24
MOV AH,2
INT 21
INT 20
```

Press an extra carriage return to return to the dash. Now enter

```
G
```

You should see a $ printed to the screen. Congratulations! You have written and run your first 80x86 Assembly language program! You can see that the 80x86 has some different instructions than the Easy4 that help it print to the screen. How does it work? What do those funny numbers mean?

First of all, the program loads the DL register with 24 hex. All numbers in DEBUG are hex by default. Look at the ASCII (American Standard Code for Information Interchange) table in Appendix F. The number 24 hex corresponds to the $. Since the computer only works with numbers, characters are encoded as a number. The most common form of code is ASCII.

Secondly, the program executes the following instructions:

```
MOV AH,2
INT 21
```

MOV is similar to the MOVE instruction in Easy4. MOV AH,2 places 2 in the AH register. Putting a character on the screen or interpreting input from the keyboard is a fairly sophisticated accomplishment in Assembly language. The PC keyboard and monitor are far more sophisticated than the Easy4 keypad and LED display. Fortunately, a number of routines are available as interrupts on PCs. Software interrupts are functions included as part of the operating system. Interrupts are like subroutine calls. Control is transferred to the code corresponding to the interrupt number, executes, then returns to the calling program when done. Interrupts are identified by a number following INT and the contents of certain registers. The most common interrupt is:

```
INT 21
```

This interrupt (sometimes called the DOS interrupt) searches the value in the AH register to determine what action to perform. In this case, AH = 2. This tells the PC to run a section of code to print a character to screen memory. What could have been a complicated process has been made quite simple through the use of interrupts.

Viewing Registers

While in DEBUG, the contents of the 80x86 registers can be viewed at any time. Press

```
R
```

and ENTER to see the registers. The AX, BX, CX, DX, CS, DS, SS, SP, BP, and SI as well as the flag register are displayed. All of these registers are 16 bits. You will learn more about the unfamiliar registers later. You can view just one register by entering

```
R register
```

For example, **RAX** displays the contents of the AX register.

Printing More Characters to the Screen

Let's revise the program to print more characters. Enter

```
A100
```

and the following program:

```
MOV AH,2
MOV DL,30
INT 21
MOV DL,31
INT 21
MOV DL,32
INT 21
INT 20
```

What do you think appears on the screen when you run this program? Enter

```
G
```

to find out. By using AH = 2 and INT 21, you can print any character from the ASCII character set to the screen. In this example, three characters were printed in succession on the screen. AH and DL are registers inside the 80x86 used for storing information to be used by the interrupt. Now enter

```
U100
```

This command lists (or unassembles) the program onto the screen, starting at address 100.

Example 3.1

Write an 80x86 Assembly program to print "Pentium" on the screen.

Solution   From the ASCII table in Appendix F, the following representations are obtained:

```
Text:                P    e    n    t    i    u    m
ASCII code (hex):   50   65   6E   74   69   75   6D
```

The program could be written as:

```
MOV AH,2
MOV DL,50
INT 21
MOV DL,65
INT 21
MOV DL,6E
INT 21
MOV DL,74
INT 21
MOV DL,69
INT 21
MOV DL,75
INT 21
MOV DL,6D
INT 21
INT 20
```

Memory Addresses

What about those numbers that appear on the left of the screen as you enter a program? Note that the numbers to the left of the colon stay constant and the ones to the right increase as the program is entered. The numbers to the left represent the current segment (or block) of memory. Each segment can range from 0000 hex to FFFF hex. The numbers to the right represent the offset, which is the address of the instruction. The Easy4 microcomputer only had one block of memory, so only one set of numbers existed for all addresses. The 80x86 processors have many blocks. Each block is called a segment. Segments are explained in Chapter 7. All .COM files start at offset address 100h. You can use the U command to unassemble code anywhere in memory. For example, suppose you wanted to unassemble code at segment 12, offset 3456. Enter

```
U 12:3456
```

The code beginning at this address will now be shown on the screen.

An Easier Way to Print Messages

What if you wanted to print a long message to the screen? It can be rather clumsy to print one character at a time using AH = 2, INT 21. Instead, AH = 9, INT 21 works quite well. Try the following program:

```
100:MOV AH,9
102:MOV DX,109
105:INT 21
107:INT 20
109:DB '80x86 Assembly Language is Fun.$'
```

Enter **G** to run the program. You should see the message

```
80x86 Assembly Language is Fun.
```

printed on the screen.

The AH = 9, INT 21 routine looks at the DX register to determine the address of the beginning of a string (a string is a collection of characters). The routine continues to print characters to the screen until it encounters a $. At this point the printing is terminated. The $ is not printed. The DB directive at the end of the program specifies a series of data bytes (instead of instructions).

Example 3.2

Use AH=9, INT 21 to print

```
Assembly
Language
```

to the screen.

Solution   Although this example may appear simple at first, it does present a problem because a carriage return and line feed is required since "Assembly" and "Language" are on separate lines. You can solve this by placing the ASCII code for a carriage return and line feed into the text. According to Appendix F, the ASCII code for a carriage return is D, and the ASCII code for a line feed is A. You cannot place an A and a D inside the message quotes, because the two letters will be printed instead of the ASCII counterparts. You need to place them outside the quotes as shown below:

```
100:MOV AH,9
102:MOV DX,109
105:INT 21
107:INT 20
109:DB 'Assembly',A,D,'Language.$'
```

The DB directive interprets anything in quotes as text, and anything outside quotes as the ASCII equivalent. In the above example, the A and D represent the ASCII codes for carriage return and line feed. How can you be sure the data bytes were entered correctly? Try entering

```
U100
```

Note that the program is displayed, but not the data bytes! Instead, DEBUG attempts to interpret the data bytes beginning at address 109 as mnemonics.

Indirect Addressing with the MOV Instruction

You have learned how to use the MOV instruction to place numbers in registers and move the contents of one register into another. Another type of operation performed with MOV

46   CHAPTER 3   COM FILES AND DEBUG

is accessing bytes in memory by using a register to point to a memory location. The instruction to do this looks like:

```
MOV register, [BX]
```

and

```
MOV [BX], register
```

For these operations, the BX register is first loaded with an offset address. The data contained at that offset address in the data segment are then sent to a register. For example:

```
MOV BX,1100
MOV AH,[BX]
```

would place the contents of data segment:offset address 1100 (or address DS:1100) into the AH register. *Note:* BX is the only register that can be used for indirect addressing.

Example 3.3

Write a routine to place the number 9 hex into offset address 200 hex.

Solution   First load address 200h into BX. You could then try and force the number 9 into the address by:

```
MOV BX,200
MOV [BX], 9
```

This will not work because you are required to use a register (not an integer) as part of the transfer. The program below will perform the transfer:

```
MOV BX,200
MOV AL, 09
MOV [BX], AL
INT 20
```

Displaying Data Contained in Memory.   Since the U command does not display data, what command does? Try entering

```
D100
```

You should now see something similar to the data shown in Table 3.1 on the screen. Note that each line displays 16 bytes of memory.

The D command displays data beginning at the address indicated. The data is divided into three groups: addresses, hex data, and ASCII representations, as shown in Table 3.2.

In Table 3.2, the address of the hex data begins at 1B4A:0100 and continues sequentially across the row for 16 memory locations (16 bytes); 09 is at address 0101, and BA is at address 0102.

Example 3.4

What data are contained in address 1B4A:013A in Table 3.1?

Solution   Address 013A is in row 0130. Count over 10 (or hex A) digits to obtain 21. The hex number 21 is contained in address 1B4A:013A.

TABLE 3.1 Data Obtained from D Command in DEBUG

1B4A:0100	B4	09	BA	09	01	CD	21	CD	20	38	30	38	38	20	41	73	...!.. 80x86 As
1B4A:0110	73	65	6D	62	6C	79	20	4C	61	6E	67	75	61	67	65	20	sembly Language
1B4A:0120	69	73	20	46	75	6E	2E	24	DA	8B	C7	16	C2	B6	01	16	is Fun.$........
1B4A:0130	44	60	20	EA	40	7D	22	DE	42	89	21	DE	42	D9	21	DE	D`.@".B.!.B.!.
1B4A:0140	42	D9	21	DE	42	D9	21	DE	42	D9	21	DE	42	D9	21	DE	B.!.B.!.B.!.B.!.
1B4A:0150	42	D9	21	DE	42	D9	21	23	41	D9	21	23	41	D9	21	23	B.!.B.!#A.!#A.!#
1B4A:0160	41	D9	21	23	41	D9	21	23	41	D9	21	23	41	D9	21	23	A.!#A.!#A.!#A.!#
1B4A:0170	41	D9	21	23	41	D9	21	E2	43	D9	21	E2	43	D9	21	E2	A.!#A.!.C.!.C.!.

TABLE 3.2 D Command Data Representations

Address	Hex Data																ASCII
	0	1	2	3	4	5	6	7	8	9	A	B	C	D	E	F	
1B4A:0100	B4	09	BA	09	01	CD	21	CD	–20	38	30	38	38	20	41	73	......!. 80x86 As

The INC and DEC Instructions. The increment (INC) and decrement (DEC) instructions have the same effect as adding or subtracting 1 from a register. To implement these instructions, simply place the instruction before the register. Enter **INC BX** to increment BX, or **DEC BX** to decrement BX. INC is similar to the ++ (increment) operator in C, and DEC is similar to the -- (decrement) operator in C. *Note:* If BX equals 0000 hex and is decremented, FFFF hex is obtained. (See Chapter 2 for more information on the binary odometer.)

The LOOP Instruction. **LOOP** is a powerful 80x86 instruction that is similar to a DO-WHILE loop in a higher-level language. It works in the following manner:
The LOOP instruction is always followed by an address, for example, LOOP 100.

- CX must first be initialized with the desired number of iterations.
- When the LOOP instruction is encountered, the CX register is first decremented.
- If the CX register now equals 0, control is passed to the next instruction following LOOP.
- If the CX register is not equal to 0, control is passed to the address indicated by LOOP.

As an example, enter the program below:

```
100 MOV    AH,02
102 MOV    CX,20
105 MOV    BX,111
108 MOV    DL,[BX]
10A INC    BX
10B INT    21
10D LOOP   0108
10F INT    20
111 DB '80x86 Assembly Language is Fun.',A,D
```

Once again the message

```
80x86 Assembly Language is Fun
```

is printed to the screen. This time, the CX register is first loaded with 20 hex (or 32 decimal). This happens to be the number of characters in the message, including the A and D at the end. [BX] is used to point to each character in the message. *Note:* BX must be incremented to point to the next character. The combination of AH = 2 and INT 21 prints a character to the screen. When LOOP decrements CX to 0, control is transferred to the next instruction, which is INT 20. The LOOP instruction is similar to the DO-WHILE loop in C.

Saving the Program to Disk.   The DEBUG program can be saved to disk by following the procedure outlined below:

1. Set the BX register to 0.
2. Set the CX register to the number of bytes contained in the program.
3. Use the N command to name the program.
4. Use the W command to write the program to disk.

The BX and CX registers can be set to any value by using the R command. Try the following:

```
RBX
```

The contents of the BX register are displayed and the system waits for you to enter a new value. If you want to keep the present value, press the ENTER key. In this case enter

```
0
```

BX now equals 0. CX must now be set to the number of bytes in the program. The program itself ends at 111 hex, so you could set CX to 11, or 111 – 100, which is the ending address – the beginning address. The problem with this is that the data would not be saved. In order to save the data, you must use

```
D100
```

to see at what address the data ends. Note that the data ends at address 132h. You can then set CX to 132 – 100 + 1 = 33h to save the program plus the data. Why was 1 added? Because you had to include address 100h *and* address 132h.
    Enter

```
RCX
33
```

Now enter

```
NA:MESSAGE.COM
```
(assuming the program is saved on drive A)

to use the N (name) command, indicate the drive (i.e., a:), and identify MESSAGE.COM as the name of the program. Now enter

```
W
```

to save the program to disk; W is the WRITE command used for saving files.

Loading a File into Debug.   There are two ways to load a file into DEBUG. One way is to simply type DEBUG and the filename (with extension) at the DOS prompt, as shown below.

```
DEBUG FILE.COM
```

where FILE is whatever filename your program happens to be. DEBUG can also load .EXE files this way, but is incapable of saving .EXE files. Another way to load a program in DEBUG is with the L command. You must first specify the filename with the N command.

```
NFILE.COM
L
```

The program FILE.COM is now loaded into memory starting at offset 100h. You can use the U command to display the program, and the D command to display data.

Sending Messages to the Printer

INT 21 has a function to access the printer. This is AH = 5. Try the program below. *Note:* This example may not work on laser printers, some ink-jet printers, or network printers. It is intended for use on locally connected dot-matrix printers.

```
        MOV AH,5
        MOV CX,002D
        MOV BX,111
108     MOV DL,[BX]
        INC BX
        INT 21
        LOOP 0108
        INT 20
111     DB 'The quick brown fox jumps over the lazy dog.',0d,0a
```

After entering the program and returning to the dash, turn the printer on. Position the paper, and enter

```
G
```

The message **'The quick brown fox jumps over the lazy dog.'** should now be sent to the printer. Note that one character at a time was sent using the LOOP instruction. There is no function in INT 21 to send a stream of data to the printer, only one character at a time. In this program, CX specifies the number of characters sent to the printer.

Inserting a Breakpoint in DEBUG.   DEBUG contains a useful function that allows breakpoints to be inserted in a program. Instead of entering:

```
G
```

to run a program, enter

```
G Breakpoint Address
```

The breakpoint address is the location where you want the program to stop. When this command is used, the register values are automatically printed out so the state of the CPU is visible when the break occurred. If you want to continue from the break address, enter

```
G
```

or

```
G Breakpoint Address
```

TABLE 3.3   Bit Assignments for Flag Register

Bit	Purpose	ON Code	OFF Code
11	Overflow flag	OV	NV
10	Direction flag	DN	UP
9	Interrupt flag	EI	DI
7	Sign flag	NG	PL
6	Zero flag	ZR	NZ
4	Auxiliary carry flag	AC	NA
2	Parity flag	PE	PO
0	Carry flag	CY	NC

A new breakpoint address must be greater than the last one specified. When using the breakpoint command, it is important to reset the instruction pointer if you want to restart the program from address 100h. To do this, enter

```
RIP
100
```

RIP stands for register instruction pointer (the instruction pointer is actually a register in the CPU). If this is not done, the program will continue from the previous breakpoint address.

The Flag Register.   The flag register is a special register inside the 80x86 CPU whose bits are status indicators. Some of the important bit assignments in the flag register are shown in Table 3.3.

The **ON** code represents the code given by DEBUG when the bit is set to 1. Likewise, **OFF** is the code assigned by DEBUG when the bit is 0. The main use of flags is to record the state of an operation, so another instruction can act accordingly. The R command in DEBUG displays the flag states shown above. This book focuses on the **sign flag, zero flag, parity flag (even or odd), carry flag,** and **interrupt flag (enable or disable).**

Unconditional Jumps.   Many programming languages contain a GOTO instruction, of which the BASIC language is the most popular. While the GOTO instruction is discouraged in higher-level languages, there are times when it must be used in machine language. This is because machine language does not contain the more complex instructions such as FOR-NEXT or DO-WHILE loops. You have seen that the closest machine language instruction that compares with this type of instruction is LOOP. Some assemblers do provide limited FOR-NEXT capability, which is translated into GOTO statements when the program is compiled into machine language.

The GOTO instruction is implemented in the 80x86 through the JMP instruction. This instruction has many variations and is more complex than it first appears. The JMP instruction can take three different forms:

1. A short jump (+127 to −128 bytes from instruction).
2. An intersegment jump (jump to anywhere in segment).
3. An intrasegment jump (jump to anywhere in memory).

Short Jump.   This instruction uses a relative displacement from the current instruction pointer position to calculate the jump. Look at the DEBUG code below:

```
100    B80500      MOV AX,5
103    B80200      MOV BX,2
106    EB02        JMP 10A
108    88D1        MOV CL,DL
10A    8BC3        MOV AX,BX
```

While the code itself may seem like nonsense, let's study how the short JMP instruction determined its displacement. When you specify a JMP instruction, include the address to jump to. The statement **JMP 10A** instructs the computer to insert 10A into the instruction pointer, so that the next instruction begins at this address. Now notice the machine language translation, EB02. Note that address 10A does not appear here. EB is the op-code for a short JMP, and 02 is the displacement. The displacement is referenced from the instruction after the JMP (or the current instruction pointer position), as shown in Figure 3.2.

Note that address 10A is two displacements from address 108 (the position of the instruction pointer before JMP 10A is executed). This is the '2' in EB02.

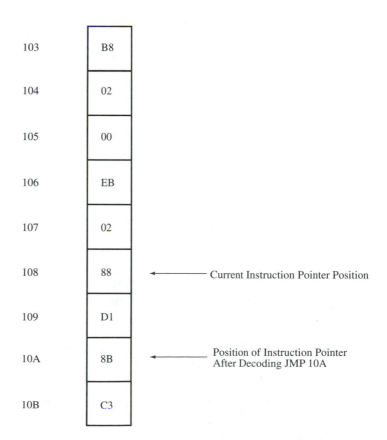

FIGURE 3.2   Relative Displacement of Short Forward JMP Instruction

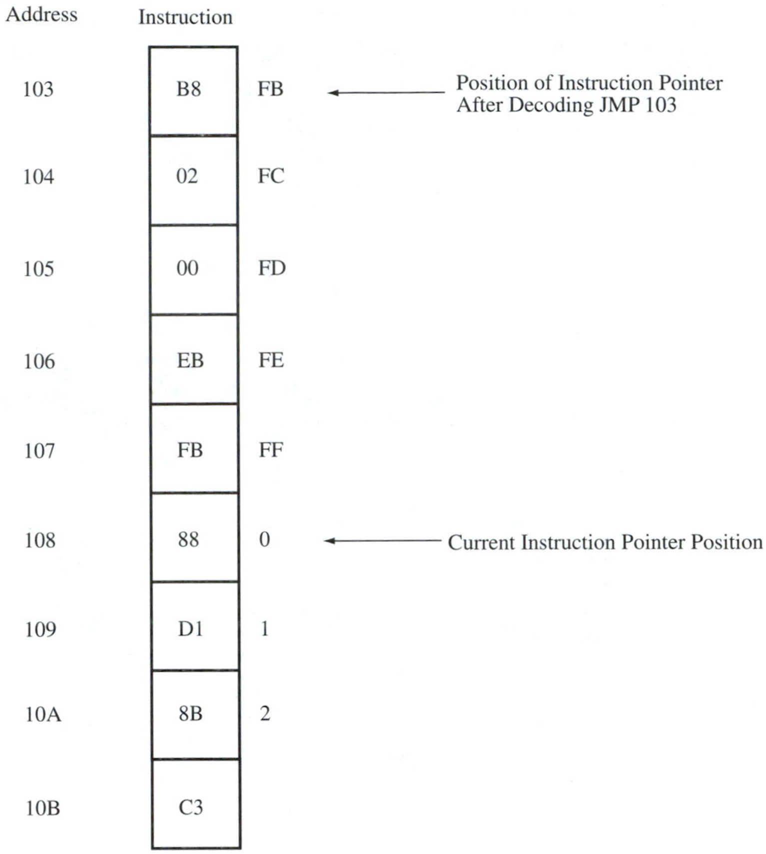

FIGURE 3.3 Relative Displacement of Short Backward JMP Instruction

Address	Instruction		
103	B8	FB	← Position of Instruction Pointer After Decoding JMP 103
104	02	FC	
105	00	FD	
106	EB	FE	
107	FB	FF	
108	88	0	← Current Instruction Pointer Position
109	D1	1	
10A	8B	2	
10B	C3		

Let's look at another example:

```
100    B80500    MOV AX,5
103    B80200    MOV BX,2
106    EBFB      JMP 103
108    88D1      MOV CL,DL
10A    8BC3      MOV AX,BX
```

A memory map for this program is shown in Figure 3.3.

Displacements from the instruction pointer are indicated to the right of the op-codes. Note that one displacement greater than FF is 0. This is similar to a binary odometer. The displacement is limited to 2 nibbles, so the next displacement after FF is 00, or 0. Limiting the displacement to 2 nibbles also affects the size of the displacement. For a short JMP, you can only move a displacement of 7Fh (127 decimal) forward, or 80h (128 decimal) back from the current instruction.

Example 3.5

Determine how the instruction JMP 103 is translated in the above program.

Solution Figure 3.3 shows the JMP displacement starting at address 108 and counting back to address 103, as seen below:

```
Address        108   107   106   105   104   103
Displacement   0     FF    FE    FD    FC    FB
```

Example 3.6

Write a program to fill the screen with the '$' character.

Solution From the ASCII table, you can see that the $ character is equal to 24h. You can use the JMP instruction in an infinite loop to keep filling the screen with the $ character. Enter the DEBUG program shown below:

```
100 MOV AH,2
102 MOV DL,24
104 INT 21
106 JMP 104
```

Now enter

```
G
```

to run the program. The screen will continue to fill with the $ character. The JMP instruction continually jumps to INT 21 to print another character. Since AH is not altered, it keeps the ASCII value of the $ character. This program has an infinite loop. Fortunately, INT 21 recognizes the CTRL-BREAK sequence. Enter

```
CTRL-BREAK
```

to break the program. You will need to reset the instruction pointer to address 100 to run the program again. Enter

```
RIP
100
```

to reset IP.

Intersegment Jumps. The second type of JMP command is the intersegment (or word) displacement. This is a 2-byte displacement that is only used if the jump exceeds +127 or −128 bytes. The instruction is entered in the same manner as the short jump.

Intrasegment Jumps. The third type of JMP allows jumps to far addresses. This refers to an address in another segment. The intrasegment jump requires that the segment be attached to the address. While you will not use this jump very often, it is implemented as shown below:

```
JMP 1234:5678
```

In this case, 1234 is the segment and 5678 is the offset.

Indirect Jump.   Another type of JMP command uses an indirect jump. It uses the contents of an address as a pointer to an address to jump to. For example, look at the DEBUG program below:

```
0100 B402       MOV AH,02
0102 B202       MOV DL,02
0104 CD21       INT 21
0106 FF260A01   JMP [10A]
010A 0401       ADD AL,01
```

The JMP [10A] instruction tells the processor to view the bytes contained in 10A as an address, in low–high order. Thus the address would be 04–low, 01–high, or 0104h. This type of jump is called indirect addressing, since the address you want to jump to is located in another address. The advantage of this instruction is that the contents of 10A can be changed to specify a new address, while the JMP [10A] instruction remains the same.

Jumps Using the PTR Operator.   Finally, another method of jumping is with the **near** or **far** operator. A near jump is shown below:

```
jmp near ptr NearLabel
```

This instruction allows a jump to anywhere in the segment.
    A far jump looks like:

```
jmp far ptr FarLabel
```

This allows a jump to be made in a far segment. The **ptr** operator refers to a pointer (or address) in memory. NearLabel and FarLabel are labels used to refer to near and far addresses, respectively.

CHAPTER 3 PROBLEMS

1. Write a program to print

   PC

   to the screen in DEBUG. Use function AH = 2, INT 21h.
2. State which part of the instruction is the op-code and which is the operand in the examples below:
   a. MOV DX,[1234]
   b. LOOP 102
   c. INC AX
   d. JMP 115
3. Write a program to print your name and address to the screen on separate lines using function AH = 9, INT 21h.
4. Write a program using the LOOP instruction to print the uppercase alphabet to the screen.
5. What is the purpose of the BX and CX registers when saving a program to disk in DEBUG?

6. Repeat problem 3, except send the output to the printer instead of the screen. Use function AH = 5, INT 21h.

7. Explain what the ON and OFF codes in the flag register mean (e.g., OV, NV, DN, UP).

8. Write the hex op-codes for the following code fragments:
   a. 110 JMP 115
   b. 109 JMP 102

9. What will the instruction pointer contain after the following code is executed?

```
106 FF260B01    JMP [10A]
10A F901
```

10. What type of jump is JMP [110]?

11. What does the **far ptr** operator do?

12. Write an instruction to jump to offset 0, segment FFFF.

13. Write a C program that simulates the DEBUG program shown below:

```
MOV DL,49
INC DL
MOV AH,2
INT 21
INT 20
```

14. What does the C program shown below do? Write a similar Assembly language program in DEBUG. A 0x in front of a number in C indicates it is a hex number.

```
#include <stdio.h>

void main()
{
int c=0x39;

do{
putc(c,stdout);
}
while(c-->0x30);
{
```

CHAPTER 4

Additional 80x86 Instructions

NEW INSTRUCTIONS IN THIS CHAPTER

Mnemonic:	**IN**
	IN AX, *port*
Description:	Transfers a byte or word from an external port to AX. If the port value is greater than FF hex, then it must first be placed in register DX.
Examples:	IN AL,13 (Sends the contents of 8-bit port 13 hex to AL.)
	IN AX,B3 (Sends the contents of 16-bit port B3 to AX.)
	MOV DX,FB00
	IN AL,DX (Sends the contents of 8-bit port FB00 to AL.)
Flags Affected:	None

Mnemonic:	**OUT**
	OUT *port,AX*
Description:	Transfers a byte or word from AL or AX to an external port. If the port value is greater than FF hex, then it must first be placed in register DX.
Examples:	OUT 13,AL (Sends the contents of AL to 8-bit port 13 hex.)
	OUT B3,AX (Sends the contents of AX to 16-bit port B3.)
	MOV DX,FB00
	OUT DX,AL (Sends the contents of AL to 8-bit port FB00.)
Flags Affected:	None

Mnemonic:	**XCHG**
	XCHG *register,register*
Description:	Exchanges the contents of two 8- or 16-bit registers.

Examples:	XCHG AL,DH XCHG AX,BX
Flags Affected:	None

Mnemonic:	**CMP** CMP *destination,source*
Description:	Compares a register or an immediate byte or word with a register by performing a SUB operation. The flag register is set based on the result. The result is discarded.
Examples:	CMP AL,13 (Zero flag set if AL = 13.) CMP AX,BX (Zero flag set if AX = BX.)
Flags Affected:	Carry, Overflow, Parity, Sign, Zero

Mnemonic:	**TEST** TEST *destination,source*
Description:	Tests a register or an immediate byte or word with a register by performing an AND operation. The flag register is set based on the result. The result is discarded.
Examples:	TEST AL,13 (Zero flag set if AL = 13.) TEST AX,BX (Zero flag set if AX = BX.)
Flags Affected:	Carry, Overflow, Parity, Sign, Zero

Mnemonic:	**JG** JG *address*
Description:	Jumps to an address if a CMP instruction produced a destination greater than a source.
Example:	CMP AX,13 JG 1234 (Jumps to address 1234 if AX > 13.)
Flags Affected:	None

Mnemonic:	**JE** JE *address*
Description:	Jumps to an address if a CMP instruction produced a destination equal to a source.
Example:	CMP AX,13 JE 1234 (Jumps to address 1234 if AX = 13.)
Flags Affected:	None

Mnemonic:	**JNE** JNE *address*

Description:	Jumps to an address if a CMP instruction produced a destination not equal to a source.
Example:	CMP AX,13 JNE 1234
Description:	Jumps to address 1234 if AX ≠ to 13.
Flags Affected:	None

Mnemonic:	**JL** JL *address*
Description:	Jumps to an address if a CMP instruction produced a destination less than a source.
Example:	CMP AX,13 JL 1234 (Jumps to address 1234 if AX < 13.)
Flags Affected:	None

Mnemonic:	**JGE** JGE *address*
Description:	Jumps to an address if a CMP instruction produced a destination greater than or equal to a source.
Example:	CMP AX,13 JGE 1234 (Jumps to address 1234 if AX ≥ 13.)
Flags Affected:	None

Mnemonic:	**JLE** JLE *address*
Description:	Jumps to an address if a CMP instruction produced a destination less than or equal to a source.
Example:	CMP AX,13 JLE 1234 (Jumps to address 1234 if AX ≤ 13.)
Flags Affected:	None

Mnemonic:	**ROR** ROR *register*,1 ROR *register*,CL
Description:	Rotates the register right by 1 bit. The LSB wraps over to the MSB. If more than 1 bit needs to be rotated, set the number of bits to rotate in the CL register first.
Example:	MOV AL,83h (83h = 1000 0011 binary.) ROR AX,1 (Rotates AX right by 1 bit. AX now contains 1100 0001 binary.)

MOV AL,83h
MOV CL,2
ROR AL,CL   (Rotates AX right by 2 bits. AX now contains 1110
                 0000 binary.)

Flags Affected: Carry, Overflow

Mnemonic: **ROL**
                          ROL register,1
                          ROL register,CL

Description: Rotates the register left by 1 bit. The MSB wraps over to the LSB. If
                          more than 1 bit needs to be rotated, set the number of bits to rotate in
                          the CL register first.

Example: MOV AL,83h   (83h = 1000 0011 binary.)
                          ROL AX,1   (Rotates AX left by 1 bit. AX now contains 0000
                                          0111 binary.)

                          MOV AL,83h
                          MOV CL,2
                          ROL AL,CL   (Rotates AX left by 2 bits. AX now contains 0000
                                          1110 binary.)

Flags Affected: Carry, Overflow

Mnemonic: **SHR**
                          SHR *register*,1
                          SHR *register*,CL

Description: Rotates the register right by 1 bit. The LSB is lost; it does not wrap
                          over to the MSB. If more than 1 bit needs to be rotated, set the
                          number of bits to rotate in the CL register first.

Example: MOV AL,83h   (83h = 1000 0011 binary.)
                          SHR AX,1   (Rotates AX right by 1 bit. AX now contains 0100
                                          0001 binary.)

                          MOV AL,83h
                          MOV CL,2
                          SHR AL,CL   (Rotates AX right by 2 bits. AX now contains 0010
                                          0000 binary.)

Flags Affected: Carry, Overflow, Parity, Sign, Zero

Mnemonic: **SHL**
                          SHL *register*,1
                          SHL *register*,CL

Description: Rotates the register left by 1 bit. The MSB is lost. It does not wrap
                          over to the LSB. If more than 1 bit needs to be rotated, set the number
                          of bits to rotate in the CL register first.

Example:	MOV AL,83h	(83h = 1000 0011 binary)
	SHL AX,1	(Rotates AX left by 1 bit. AX now contains 0000 0110 binary.)
	MOV AL,83h	
	MOV CL,2	
	SHL AL,CL	(Rotates AX left by 2 bits. AX now contains 0000 1100 binary.)

Flags Affected: Carry, Overflow, Parity, Sign, Zero

Mnemonic: **AND**
AND *destination,source*

Description: Performs a Boolean AND operation. The result is stored in the destination register.

Example: AND AX,13   (AND AX with 13. Result is in AX.)

Flags Affected: Carry, Overflow, Parity, Sign, Zero

Mnemonic: **OR**
OR *destination,source*

Description: Performs a Boolean OR operation. The result is stored in the destination register.

Example: OR AX,13   (OR AX with 13. Result is in AX.)

Flags Affected: Carry, Overflow, Parity, Sign, Zero

Mnemonic: **XOR**
XOR *destination,source*

Description: Performs a Boolean Exclusive OR operation. The result is stored in the destination register.

Example: XOR AX,13   (Exclusive OR AX with 13. Result is in AX.)

Flags Affected: Carry, Overflow, Parity, Sign, Zero

Mnemonic: **NOT**
NOT *register*

Description: Performs a Boolean NOT (or complement) operation. The result is stored in the register.

Example: NOT AX   (Complements AX.)

Flags Affected: Carry, Overflow, Parity, Sign, Zero

Mnemonic: **ADD**
ADD *destination,source*

Description: Adds a source to a destination. The result is stored in the destination register.

Example: ADD AX,13   (Adds 13 to AX. Result is in AX.)
ADD AL,DL   (Adds DL to AL. Result is in AL.)

Flags Affected: Carry, Overflow, Parity, Sign, Zero

Mnemonic: **SUB**
SUB *destination,source*

Description: Subtracts a source from a destination. The result is stored in the destination register.

Example: SUB AX,13   (Subtracts 13 from AX. Result is in AX.)
SUB AL,DL   (Subtracts DL from AL. Result is in AL.)

Flags Affected: Carry, Overflow, Parity, Sign, Zero

Mnemonic: **MUL**
(Byte version) MUL *8 bit source*

Description: Multiplies AL by a source value. The source can be a register or an address. The result is stored in AX.

(Word version) MUL *16 bit source*

Description: Multiplies AX by a source value. The source can be a register or an address. The high 16-bit result is stored in DX, the lower 16-bit result is stored in AX.

Example: MUL DL   (Multiplies AX by DL. Result is in AX.)
MUL BX   (Multiplies AX by BX. High result is in DX, low result is in AX.)

Flags Affected: Carry, Overflow, Parity, Sign, Zero

Mnemonic: **DIV**
(Byte version) DIV *8 bit source*

Description: Divides AX by an 8-bit source value. The source can be a register or an address. The result is stored in AX. The quotient is in AL, and the remainder is in AH.
(Word version) DIV *16 bit source*

Description: Divides AX by a source value. The source can be a register or an address. The quotient is in AX, and the remainder is in DX.

Example: DIV DL   (Divides AX by DL. Remainder is in AH, quotient is in AL.)
DIV BX   (Divides DX:AX by BX. Remainder is in DX, quotient is in AX.)

Flags Affected: Carry, Overflow, Parity, Sign, Zero

MORE ON INDIRECT ADDRESSING

Chapter 3 introduced indirect addressing with the MOV [BX] instruction. The next program loads the number 9 into address 200h.

```
MOV BX,200
MOV AL,9
MOV [BX],AL
INT 20
```

In order to see the number in memory, load DEBUG, type in the program, and enter

```
G
```

to run the program.
Now enter

```
D200
```

The memory dump shows that the contents of address 200h is 9.

Example 4.1

Place the number 1234h in address 200h and 201h.

Solution   One indirect MOV instruction can be used to accomplish this task. Enter the program below:

```
MOV BX,200
MOV AX,1234
MOV [BX],AX
INT 20
```

Now enter:

```
D200
```

What happened? The memory dump shows 200h equal to 34h and 201h equal to 12h.

Big and Little Endian Representations

In Example 4.1, the MOV instruction placed the most significant byte (MSB) in 201h and the LSB in 200h as shown in Table 4.1.

TABLE 4.1   PC Data
Representation in Memory

Value	Address
12	201h
34	200h

TABLE 4.2   Big Endian Data Representation in Memory

Value	Address
12	200h
34	201h

This type of memory organization is called little endian. It is common to all Intel microprocessors, dating back to the 8008 (manufactured in 1972). Some other computers use a type of memory representation called big endian, which stores numbers in reverse order, as shown in Table 4.2.

Many CPUs use the big endian data representation, including Digital Equipment Corporation (DEC®) and Motorola®.

Input and Output Ports

As indicated in Chapter 1, Intel microprocessors frequently communicate with the outside world through ports. Two instructions help do this, the IN and OUT instructions. These instructions are similar to the Easy4 IN and OUT instructions in Chapter 2. The IN instruction routes data from a specified port to the AL (8-bit data path) or AX (16-bit data path). If the port address is greater than 255, use the DX register to specify the address. Some examples are shown below:

```
IN AL,54              ;Route data in port 54 to the AL register.
IN AX,54              ;Route data in port 54 to the AX register.
MOV DX,FB00
IN AL,DX              ;Route data in port FB00 to the AL register.
```

The OUT instruction is similar, except it sends data from AL or AX to a port. Once again, if the port address is greater than 255, you must specify the port's address in DX. Some examples are shown below:

```
OUT 54,AL             ;Route data in the AL register to port 54.
OUT 54,AX             ;Route data in the AX register to port 54.
MOV DX,FB00
OUT DX,AL             ;Route data in the AL register to port FB00.
```

The Printer Port

One of the more common ports on a PC is the parallel printer port. Since this port is available on all PCs, it is used here as an example. The following examples were written for a dot-matrix printer connected to the parallel port. Laser printers and some ink-jet printers will not work for the following descriptions. The parallel printer port is comprised of three sequential addresses. The base address of the printer port changes with the make of the PC. Many PCs have more than one printer port, labeled LPT1, LPT2, and LPT3. Unfortunately, this does not tell where the printer's base port address is. Look at the series of addresses beginning at segment 40h, offset 8h to see what port addresses LPT1, LPT2, and LPT3 are assigned to, as shown in Table 4.3.

TABLE 4.3   Location of Base Printer Port Address in Memory

Segment 40h	Offset D,C	Offset B,A	Offset 9,8
	LPT3	LPT2	LPT1

The addresses shown in Table 4.3 can be displayed in DEBUG to determine the printer port locations. While in DEBUG, enter

```
D40:8
```

This will dump memory beginning at segment 40h, offset 8h. A sample copy of the memory display is shown below:

```
-d40:8
0040:0000                      78 03 00 00 00 00 C0 9F          x.......
0040:0010   27 C4 00 78 02 22 00 00-00 00 22 00 22 00 38 09    '..x."...."."".8.
0040:0020   0D 1C 64 20 6F 18 73 1F-0D 1C 64 20 65 12 62 30    ..d o.s...d e.b0
0040:0030   75 16 67 22 0D 1C 64 20-34 05 30 0B 3A 27 00 00    u.g"..d 4.0.:'..
0040:0040   52 00 C3 00 0E 00 00 A0-20 03 50 00 00 10 00 00    R....... .P.....
0040:0050   00 18 00 00 00 00 00 00-00 00 00 00 00 00 00 00    ................
0040:0060   0E 0D 00 D4 03 29 30 C2-11 45 76 FF 4B 6F 14 00    .....)0..Ev.Ko..
0040:0070   00 00 00 12 00 01 00 00-14 14 14 28 01 01 01 01    ...........(....
0040:0080   1E 00 3E 00 18 10 00 60                            ..>....`
```

Note that address 8 contains 78 and address 9 contains 3. For the PC shown, LPT1 is at address 378h. LPT2 and LPT3 show addresses of 0, so they are not implemented on this PC. The printer port is connected to a 25-pin female connector on the back of the PC. The pinout and addresses bit assignments are shown in Table 4.4.

Example 4.2

Write an assembly program to test if the printer is working and ready to print.

Solution   *Note:* This solution will only work on a dot-matrix printer. In this solution, the ACKNOWLEDGE pin will equal 1 if the printer is on and no errors are present. This pin equals 0 if the printer is off, or an error is present. The ACKNOWLEDGE position is Bit 5 port 2. If the printer base address is 378h, port2 on LPT1 is 379h. Turn off the printer and enter the DEBUG program below (assuming your printer base address is 378h):

```
100     MOV DX,379
103     IN AL,DX
104     INT 20
```

Now enter **RIP 100** to reset the instruction pointer, and enter **G104** to run the program. This will break the program at INT 20 and display the registers. Note that bit 5 of the AL register is 0. Now turn on the printer and enter

```
RIP
100
G107
```

again. The lower 6 bits of the AL register should now equal 20, or binary 100000. If bit 5, port 379h equals 1 the printer is on; if it equals 0, the printer is off.

The XCHG Instruction

This instruction exchanges the contents of two registers. You can exchange two 8-bit registers, or two 16-bit registers, but not an 8- and a 16-bit register. This instruction is commonly used when the result of an operation appears in one register and a quick way is needed to place the value in another register. For example, assume AL = 7Ah and DL = 60h. The instruction

```
XCHG AL,DL
```

TABLE 4.4 Bit Assignments of Printer Ports

Port 1	Printer Assignment	DB-25 Pin Number
Bit 0 =	Data 0	2
Bit 1 =	Data 1	3
Bit 2 =	Data 2	4
Bit 3 =	Data 3	5
Bit 4 =	Data 4	6
Bit 5 =	Data 5	7
Bit 6 =	Data 6	8
Bit 7 =	Data 7	9

Port 2	Printer Assignment	DB-25 Pin Number
Bit 0	Time out	
Bits 1 and 2	Unused	
Bit 3	Error	15
Bit 4	Online	13
Bit 5	Out of paper	12
Bit 6	Acknowledge	10
Bit 7	Busy	11

Port 3	Printer Assignment	DB-25 Pin Number
Bit 0	Strobe data to printer	1
Bit 1	Auto line feed	14
Bit 2	Initialize printer	16
Bit 3	Printer output	17
Bit 4	IRQ7 (Printer acknowledge)	
Bits 5–7	unused	

now places 7Ah in AL and 60h in DL, as shown below:

XCHG AL,DL

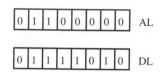

Conditional Operations

Conditional operators (such as JUMP IF LESS THAN) on the Easy4 processor were covered in Chapter 2. Conditional operations usually consist of two parts, a comparison and some action taken based on the results of the comparison. For example, the C statements:

```
if(a<d)
Less(a);
```

first use an if statement that compares **a** to **d.** If **a** is less than **d,** the function Less() is called and **a** is passed to the function. You can write similar statements in 80x86 assembly language. The **CMP** (Compare) instruction is used instead of if (as in the Easy4), and either the **JG** (Jump if Greater Than), **JE** (Jump if Equal), **JNE** (Jump if Not Equal), **JL** (Jump if Less Than), **JGE** (Jump if Greater Than or Equal), or **JLE** (Jump if Less Than or Equal) instructions are used for conditional jumps. Since the CMP instruction sets the flag register, the conditional jump instruction should appear immediately after. The CMP modifies the flag register in the same manner as the SUB instruction, but the results are not stored. For example, suppose you wanted to compare the AX register to the DX register. If AX is less than DX, then jump to address 160h. The following code fragment implements this process:

```
CMP AX,DX
JL 160
```

CMP AX,DX subtracts the value in DX from the AX without affecting the register contents. The flags are set or reset based on the result of the subtraction. The flags are then used by the conditional jump.

Example 4.3

Use the LOOP instruction to decrement the CX register from 20h to 0. When the CX register equals 5, store the CX register in the BX register.

Solution

```
100 MOV CX,20
103 CMP CX,5
106 JNE 10A
108 MOV BX,CX
10A LOOP 103
10C INT 20
```

If CX is not equal to 5, the instruction MOV BX,CX is passed over. Otherwise, the CX register is loaded into BX. When running the program, enter

```
G10C
```

to set a breakpoint at interrupt 20h. This will force the contents of the BX register to be displayed.

The TEST Instruction

The **TEST** instruction is also used for comparison. This instruction performs an AND operation on the two operators and sets the zero flag as a result. In other words, if the AND produced a 0, then ZF = 1. If not, then ZF = 0. For conditional operations, TEST can be used with JE, JZ, JNE, and JNZ.

ROTATE and SHIFT Instructions

It is often useful to shift bits in a register to the left or right. There are two instructions that allow you to do this, ROTATE and SHIFT. The two rotate instructions (**ROL** and **ROR**) rotate a register to the left or right, wrapping the last bit around to the first. For example, when the following instructions are executed:

```
MOV DL,1
ROL DL,1
```

the number 2 (or binary 10) is stored in DL. This occurs because the 1 is shifted to the left by one bit.

The leading bit is also moved into the carry as shown below:

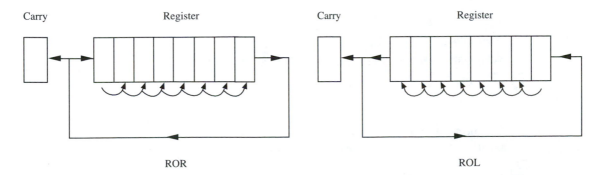

ROR   ROL

Example 4.4

What is stored in the AL register after the following instructions are executed?

```
MOV AL,81
ROL AL,1
```

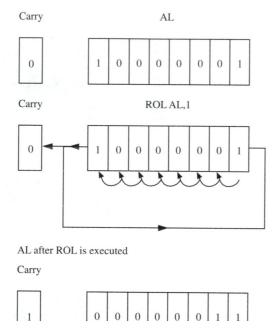

Carry   AL

Carry   ROL AL,1

AL after ROL is executed

Carry

Solution   The binary equivalent of 81 is 10000001. When the most significant 1 is shifted to the left by one position, it will wrap around to the carry and the first position. Therefore, the answer is 3, or 00000011, with the carry set to 1.

The ROTATE RIGHT instruction (ROR) is similar, except it shifts the bits in a register to the right. The LSB is shifted to the carry and the MSB.

Example 4.5

What number will appear in the AL register after the following instructions are run?

```
MOV AL,81
ROR AL,1
```

Solution   The binary equivalent of 8 is 10000001. By shifting these bits to the right one position, the result is 11000000, or C0. Notice that only 1 bit is shifted at a time. If more

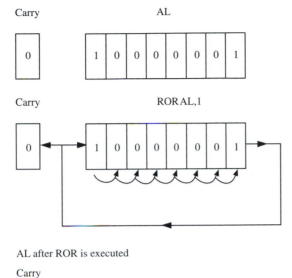

Carry   AL

| 0 |

| 1 | 0 | 0 | 0 | 0 | 0 | 0 | 1 |

Carry   ROR AL,1

| 0 |

| 1 | 0 | 0 | 0 | 0 | 0 | 0 | 1 |

AL after ROR is executed

Carry

| 1 |

| 1 | 1 | 0 | 0 | 0 | 0 | 0 | 0 |

than 1 bit is to be shifted, first load the count in the CL register and then execute the instruction:

```
ROL register,CL
```

or

```
ROR register,CL
```

Example 4.6

What number appears in the CH register after the following instructions are executed:

```
MOV CH,81
MOV CL,2
ROR CH,CL
```

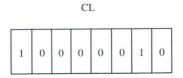

Carry   CH   CL

| 0 |

| 1 | 0 | 0 | 0 | 0 | 0 | 0 | 1 |

| 1 | 0 | 0 | 0 | 0 | 0 | 1 | 0 |

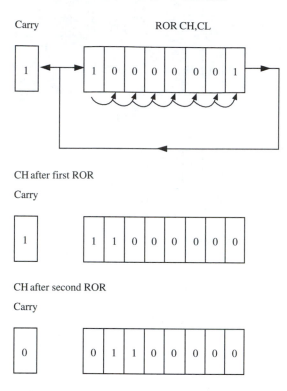

Solution   Start with an 8-bit register (CH) that is equal to 10000001. Shifting the bits two positions to the right produces 01100000 (remember the bits wrap from least significant to the most significant positions). Also note that the CH register does not rotate into the CL register. This will only happen if the CX register is specified instead of CH. A similar set of instructions shift bits to the left or right, but does not wrap. These commands include SHL (shift left) and SHR (shift right). A 0 is placed in the position left vacant by the shift, as shown below:

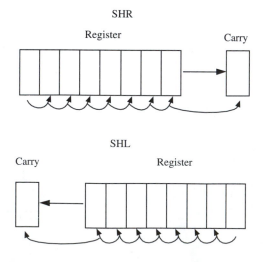

Note that neither SHL nor SHR wrapped one end to the other. Instead, a 0 is shifted into the LSB in the case of SHL, and a 0 is shifted into the MSB in the case of SHR. The SHL and SHR registers have the capability of multiplying and dividing registers by powers of 2. Suppose BL = 2 (binary 00000010) and the instruction

```
SHL BL,1
```

is executed. The result is binary 00000100, or decimal 4 in BL. The SHL instruction effectively multiplied BL by 2.

Example 4.7

Set the AL register to decimal 23 and use the SHL command to multiply the AL register by 256.

Solution　The binary equivalent of decimal 23 is 10111, or 17 hex. Shifting left eight times will multiply the register by 256 ($2^8 = 256$). Try entering the program below in DEBUG.

```
100 MOV AX,17
103 MOV CL,8
105 SHL AX,CL
107 INT 20
```

After entering the program, run it with a trap by entering:

```
G107
```

The registers show that AX now equals 1700 hex. You have shifted hex 17 to the left by 2 nibbles, or 8 bits.

BOOLEAN INSTRUCTIONS

Boolean operations include the AND, OR, XOR, and NOT. When working with 80x86 registers, Boolean operations are always performed on groups of 8 or 16 bits. Boolean operations on 8-bit registers were covered in Chapter 1. An example ANDing registers AL and DL is shown below:

Boolean AND Operation

```
AL = 10110110      AL
DL = 01110101      DL
     00110100      AL AND DL
```

Notice that each bit in AL is AND'd with a corresponding bit in DL. If the AND instruction is

```
AND AL,DL
```

the result is stored in AL.

Example 4.8

What is the OR and XOR output if AL = B6h and DL = 35h?

Solution   AL = 10110110 in binary. DL = 00110101 binary. The OR operation produces:

```
        10110110
OR      00110101
        10110111, or B7h.
```

The XOR operation produces:

```
        10110110
XOR     00110101
        10000011, or 83h
```

Example 4.9

What happens if you XOR a register with FF hex?

Solution   This is a special case of XOR. If you XOR a register with FF, you invert the register! Look at the case of AL = B6h:

```
        10110110 = AL
XOR     11111111 = FF
        01001001 = 49h, which represents the inversion of AL.
```

The NOT instruction performs the same task as XOR *register*,FF. This instruction inverts each bit in a register. Suppose you wanted to invert AX. The instruction to do this is:

```
NOT AX
```

Masking Bits in a Register

It is often useful to set certain bits in a register to 0. This is called masking the bits. You can do this by ANDing the instruction with a number containing 0 in the bits to be masked.

Example 4.10

Mask bits 4 and 0 in the DH register. Assume the DH register equals 96h.

Solution   Bits 4 and 0 need to be masked, so place a 0 in these slots, and a 1 everywhere else.

```
        76543210 ← Bit position
        00010010 = DH
AND     11101110 = Mask number, or EEh.
        10000010 = Result. Note that bits 4 and 0 are now equal to 0.
```

Example 4.11

Write an 80x86 instruction that masks the most significant nibble in register AH.

Solution   Mask the upper 4 bits with the instruction:

```
AND AH,0F
```

Bits can also be set to 1 (sometimes called enabling them). This is done using the OR instruction. To do this, insert a 1 in a bit position and OR with the desired register.

Example 4.12

What instruction enables bits 4 and 0 in DH without affecting the other bits in the register?

Solution   Since you want to enable bits 4 and 0, OR DH with 00010001, or 11h,

```
OR DH, 11h
```

A Routine to Print Hex Numbers to the Screen

There have been many examples in which a trap and a register dump were used to view the contents of a register. Unfortunately, no interrupt exists to print the contents of a register to the screen. In the program below, the DL register contains the number to be printed to the screen in hex. Since DL has two hex digits, you will need to display each digit separately. The number is temporarily saved in DH, and 1 nibble is isolated at a time to be printed. Once the nibble is isolated, you have to add 30h to convert the number to an ASCII character. The ASCII table for 0 through 9 is shown in Figure 4.1.

Note that after the number 9, there are seven intermediate codes (hex 3A through 40) before the letter A appears. You will have to jump over these characters when printing hex numbers to the screen. This can be done by adding 7 whenever the nibble to be printed is greater than 9. Also note that 0 is represented by 30 hex; 30h must be added to the nibble in the register because you are trying to print the ASCII representation of the number to the screen.

A DEBUG program that prints the DL register to the screen is shown in Figure 4.2. For this example, DL was set to FE. You can change DL to whatever you like and see it printed to the screen when the program is run. Comment statements explaining the program are shown to the right of the mnemonics. You cannot enter comment statements in DEBUG.

Algebraic Instructions

There are four algebraic instructions:

ADD—Used to add two registers, or a register and a number.
SUB—Used to subtract two registers, or a register and a number.

FIGURE 4.1   ASCII Code
For 0 through F

Hex Representation	ASCII Code
30	0
31	1
32	2
33	3
34	4
35	5
36	6
37	7
38	8
39	9
3A	:
3B	;
3C	<
3D	=
3E	>
3F	?
40	@
41	A
42	B
43	C
44	D
45	E
46	F

FIGURE 4.2   DEBUG Program to Print Hex Number in DL to Screen

```
MOV DL,A9     ;Load DL with A9 (sample).
MOV DH,DL     ;Save DL into DH.
MOV CL,04     ;Shift DL 4 bits to the right.
SHR DL,CL
ADD DL,30     ;Add 30 for ASCII adjust (30h = character 0).
CMP DL,39     ;Nibble greater than 9?
JLE 113       ;If so, add 7 (see Figure 4.2).
ADD DL,7
MOV AH,02     ;Print character to screen
INT 21
MOV DL,DH     ;Move other nibble into DL.
AND DL,0F     ;AND lower nibble.
ADD DL,30     ;ASCII adjust.
CMP DL,39     ;Add 7 if greater than 9.
JLE 127
ADD DL,7
MOV AH,02     ;Print second nibble to screen.
INT 21
INT 20        ;Terminate process.
```

MUL—Used to multiply two registers, or a register and a number.
DIV—Used to divide two registers, or a register and a number.

There are also two associated instructions:

INC—Used to increment a register (or add one to it).
DEC—Used to decrement a register (or subtract one from it).

The ADD, SUB, and INC instructions are similar to instructions in the Easy4 micro-computer. You can add immediate numbers or registers. You can also use indirect addressing.

Example 4.13

Write the instruction to add AL and DH and store the result in DH.

Solution

```
ADD DH,AL
```

Example 4.14

Write the instruction to add AX and DH and store the result in DH.

Solution   This cannot be done. You cannot add 16 bits to an 8-bit register.

Example 4.15

Write the instruction to subtract AL from DH and store the result in DH.

Solution

```
SUB DH,AL
```

MULTIPLYING AND DIVIDING NUMBERS

At one time, multiplying and dividing numbers was a difficult task for assembly language programmers to implement in microprocessors. This was because there were no implicit instructions to perform these tasks. Multiplication was usually performed through an algorithm called successive addition, and division through successive subtraction. On the 80x86, either the MUL and DIV instructions or the SHL and SHR instructions are used.

Multiplying and Dividing Using SHR and SHL

If you are multiplying or dividing by a power of 2, the SHR or SHL instructions can be used. For example, suppose you wanted to multiply 3 * 8. Since

$$8 = 2^3$$

a binary 3 can be shifted to the left three times.

Example 4.16

Write a DEBUG program to multiply AX times 8 using the SHL instruction. Assume AX = 3.

Solution

```
AX = 00000011
```

When SHL AX is executed three times:

```
AX = 00011000
```

which is equal to decimal 24. A DEBUG program fragment could be written as shown below:

```
MOV AX,3
MOV CL,3
SHL AX,CL
```

You can also divide by powers of 2 using SHR.

Example 4.17

Write a DEBUG program to divide AX by 16 using the SHR instruction. Assume AX = 32.

Solution

```
AX = 00100000
```

and

$$2^5 = 32$$

If you SHR AX five times you obtain:

```
000000010 = 2
```

The DEBUG program to do this is shown below:

```
MOV AX,32
MOV CL,5
SHR AX,CL
```

MUL and DIV Instructions

The MUL instruction can be used with an 8-bit or 16-bit register. If you use an 8 bit register, AL is the destination register and the result is stored in AX. If you use a 16-bit register, AX is the destination register and DX (high) and AX (low) contain the result. For example, multiply 5h * 30h using DEBUG as shown below:

```
MOV AX,5
MOV DL,30
MUL DL
```

AX will now contain F0h.

Example 4.18

Use DEBUG to multiply 16h*1132h.

Solution Since 1132h is too large for an 8-bit register, you must use a 16-bit operation. A DEBUG program to do this is shown below:

```
MOV BX,16
MOV AX,1132
MUL BX
```

The multiplication produces 16h*1132h = 17A4Ch. Register DX contains 1h, and register AX contains 7A4Ch.

Division is performed in a similar manner by using the DIV instruction. When you divide integers, a quotient and a remainder are produced. You can either divide a 16-bit register by an 8-bit register, or a 32-bit register by a 16-bit register. The 32-bit register is produced by combining DX and AX.

8-Bit Register DIV Instruction For this instruction, begin by putting a number in AX and another in an 8-bit register. Then use the instruction:

```
DIV 8 bit register
```

to perform the division. The remainder is in AH, and the quotient is in AL.

Example 4.19

Divide 345h by 13h by using DEBUG.

Solution This operation requires an 8-bit register. The larger number will be in AX, while the smaller number will be in an 8-bit register. In this case, you will use BL as the 8-bit register. The DEBUG program is shown below:

```
MOV AX,345
MOV BL,13
DIV BL
```

To run the program enter:

```
G 107
```

AL (the quotient register) now contains 2Ch and AH (the remainder register) equals 1.

16-Bit Register DIV Instruction For this instruction, begin by putting a 32-bit number in DX and AX. For example, if the number is 761234, DX = 76, and AX = 1234. A 16-bit register is then selected to contain the other number. Now use the instruction

```
DIV 16 bit register
```

to perform the division. The remainder is in DX, and the quotient is in AX.

Example 4.20

Divide 76FD34h by 56Ah using DEBUG.

Solution   Set DX equal to 76h and AX equal to FD34h. Now set a 16-bit register equal to 56Ah. In this case, use the BX register. The DEBUG program that performs the multiplication is shown below:

```
MOV DX,76
MOV AX,FD34
MOV BX,56A
DIV BX
```

To run the program enter:

```
G10B
```

The results show AX = 15FA for the quotient, and DX = 01B0 for the remainder.

The MUL and DIV instructions are easier to implement than successive addition and subtraction. However, the MUL and DIV instructions take many clock cycles to complete. Because of this, successive addition or subtraction is usually faster. The SHL or SHR method for multiplying and dividing powers of 2 is always faster and preferred over the other two methods.

CHAPTER 4 PROBLEMS

1. Write a program to load memory address 190h with 2Dh.
2. Write a routine to load memory addresses 130h with ABh and 131h with CDh.
3. What is wrong with the folowing code? What do you think it is trying to do? Correct the instruction with working 80x86 code.

   ```
   IN CL,100
   ```

4. Determine the base address of LPT1 on your PC.
5. Write a program that tests the least significant bit of the AH register. If this bit is high, print H to the screen. If low, print L to the screen. Try this program with various values in AH.
6. Write a program that cycles through the entire ASCII code in register AL. If AL = 'A' or 'B', then print the letters to the screen. Use the CMP instruction.
7. What is stored in the AL register after the following instructions are executed?

   ```
   MOV AL,24
   ROL AL,1
   ```

8. What is stored in the AX register after the following instructions are executed?

   ```
   MOV AX,64
   ROR AX,1
   ```

9. What number is in the CH register after the following instructions are executed?

```
MOV CH,11
MOV CL,3
ROR CH,CL
```

10. Repeat problem 9 if the last statement is

```
SHR CH,CL
```

11. What is AL equal to after the following instructions are executed?

```
MOV AL,43
MOV DH,69
AND AL,DH
```

12. What is AL equal to after the following instructions are executed?

```
MOV AL,43
MOV DH,69
OR AL,DH
```

13. What is AL equal to after the following instructions are executed?

```
MOV AL,00
MOV DH,FF
XOR AL,DH
```

14. What is AL equal to after the following instructions are executed?

```
MOV AL,43
MOV DH,69
XOR AL,DH
```

15. Write the code necessary to mask bit 13 of AX.
16. Write the code necessary to set bits 0, 3, and 5 to 1 in register BL.
17. Write the code necessary to invert bits 3, 4 and 5 in register DH.
18. Write the instruction to subtract CL – AH.
19. Write a program to add the following hex numbers. Store the result in AX.

```
43, 0C, 3E8
```

20. Write a program to multiply 15h * 10h using one of the shift instructions.
21. Repeat problem 20 using the MUL instruction.
22. Write a program to divide E6h by 4h using one of the shift instructions.
23. Divide 120000h by 742h using the DIV instruction.

CHAPTER 5

80x86 Segmentation, .EXE Files, and Miscellaneous Instructions

NEW INSTRUCTIONS IN THIS CHAPTER

Mnemonic:	**CBW**
	CBW
Description:	Converts byte to word. Extends the signed value of AL to AH.
Example:	CBW
Flags Affected:	Carry, Overflow, Parity, Sign, Zero

Mnemonic:	**CWD**
	CWD
Description:	Converts word to double word. Extends the signed value of AX to DX.
Example:	CWD
Flags Affected:	Carry, Overflow, Parity, Sign, Zero

Mnemonic:	**CALL**
	CALL *address*
Description:	Transfers control to address. Upon issue of RET, return to instruction after CALL. An intersegment call pushes IP onto stack. An intrasegment call pushes CS and then IP onto stack.
Example:	100: CALL 1234 (Transfers control to address 1234.)
	103: -------
	1234: RET (Transfers control to address 103.)
Flags Affected:	None

Mnemonic:	**RET**
	RET

Description:	Upon issue of RET, transfers control to instruction after CALL. An intersegment return pops IP from the stack. An intrasegment return pops IP then CS from the stack.
Example:	100: CALL 1234 (Transfers control to address 1234.) 103: ------- 1234: RET (Transfers control to address 103.)
Flags Affected:	None

Mnemonic:	**PUSH** PUSH *16 bit register*
Description:	Pushes contents of 16-bit register onto stack in little endian manner. Stack pointer is decremented 2 bytes.
Example:	PUSH BX (BX is pushed onto stack.)
Flags Affected:	None

Mnemonic:	**POP** POP *16 bit register*
Description:	Pops contents of 16-bit register from stack. Stack pointer is incremented 2 bytes.
Example:	POP BX (BX is popped from stack.)
Flags Affected:	None

Mnemonic:	**PUSHF** PUSHF
Description:	Pushes contents of flag register onto stack in little endian manner. Stack pointer is decremented 2 bytes.
Example:	PUSHF (Flag register is pushed onto stack.)
Flags Affected:	None

Mnemonic:	**POPF** POPF
Description:	Pops contents of flag register from stack. Stack pointer is incremented two bytes.
Example:	POPF (Flag register is popped from stack.)
Flags Affected:	None

Mnemonic:	**STC** STC
Description:	Sets carry flag to 1.

Example: STC   (Carry flag = 1.)

Flags Affected: Carry

Mnemonic: **STD**

                     STD

Description: Sets direction flag to 1.

Example: STD   (Direction flag = 1.)

Flags Affected: Direction

Mnemonic: **STI**

                     STI

Description: Sets interrupt flag to 1.

Example: STI   (Interrupt flag = 1.)

Flags Affected: Interrupt

Mnemonic: **CLC**

                     CLC

Description: Clears carry flag to 0.

Example: CLC   (Carry flag = 0.)

Flags Affected: Carry

Mnemonic: **CLD**

                     CLD

Description: Clears direction flag to 0.

Example: CLD   (Direction flag = 0.)

Flags Affected: Direction

Mnemonic: **CLI**

                     CLI

Description: Clears interrupt flag to 0.

Example: CLI   (Interrupt flag = 0.)

Flags Affected: Interrupt

Mnemonic: **LDS**

                     LDS *16 bit register,source*

Description: Transfers a word from source into any 16-bit register. Transfers a
                     word into DS from source+2.

Example:	LDS AX,LABEL (Sends the contents of LABEL into AX and LABEL+2 into DS.)
Flags Affected:	None

Mnemonic:	**LES**
	LES *16 bit register,source*
Description:	Transfers a word from source into any 16-bit register. Transfers a word into ES from source+2.
Example:	LES AX,LABEL (Sends the contents of LABEL into AX and LABEL+2 into ES.)
Flags Affected:	None

THE CALL AND RET INSTRUCTIONS

The CALL instruction loads the instruction pointer (and the code segment register, if needed) with the address of a subroutine. It is similar to the INT instruction, with a few minor differences. If a routine is to be repeated even a few times, it is probably best to place it in a subroutine. The RET instruction returns the program to the instruction after the CALL. Figure 5.1 shows the flow of a program using CALL and RET.

The CALL instruction in Figure 5.1 calls an imaginary subroutine named SUB; SUB refers to an address. The subroutine adds the contents of AH and DL. Upon issue of the RET statement, control is transferred to the instruction after CALL, or MOV AX,10. A DEBUG example with CALL and RET that prints a carriage return and line feed to the screen is given below.

```
100 B402      MOV   AH,02
102 B248      MOV   DL,48     ;Print H to screen.
104 CD21      INT   21
106 E80900    CALL  0112      ;Call CR-LF subroutine.
109 B249      MOV   DL,49     ;Print I to screen.
10B CD21      INT   21
10D E80200    CALL  0112      ;Call CR-LF subroutine.
110 CD20      INT   20
112 B402      MOV   AH,02     ;CR-LF subroutine.
114 B20A      MOV   DL,0A     ;Print LF to screen.
116 CD21      INT   21
118 B20D      MOV   DL,0D     ;Print CR to screen.
11A CD21      INT   21
11C C         RET
```

This example begins by printing the symbol for ASCII code 48h to the screen. This is the letter H. Next, address 112 in the current segment is called. The subroutine prints a line feed (MOV DL,A INT 21) and carriage return (MOV DL,D INT 21). The RET statement

FIGURE 5.1 Call and
Return

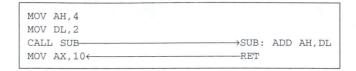

```
MOV AH,4
MOV DL,2
CALL SUB─────────────────────────→SUB: ADD AH,DL
MOV AX,10←─────────────────────────RET
```

returns control to address 109. The procedure is repeated for the symbol for ASCII code
49h, or the letter I. The above example prints

```
H
I
```

to the screen. Care must be taken when calling subroutines, because registers might be altered.
In the above example, the DL register is still equal to 0Dh on returning from the subroutine.

THE PUSH AND POP INSTRUCTIONS

The **PUSH** and **POP** instructions are similar to the Easy4 PUSH and POP in Chapter 2, but
are more complex. Both sets of instructions make use of the stack. Every microprocessor,
whether it is an 80x86, a 68000, or an Easy4, contains a **stack,** which is a reserved area of
memory (usually the highest part) used for the temporary storage of data. Stacks are an
easy way to store and retrieve data to and from a register. On 80x86 machines, the stack
can be in a variety of locations. In .COM files, everything is in one segment, so the stack
sits at the top of the segment. Similarly, the Easy4 stack is at the top of memory. The stack
in an .EXE file can either be combined with the data segment, or placed in its own segment, depending on how the file is compiled. The stack pointer (SP) points to the address
of the current position of the stack, as shown in Figure 5.2. Note that once data is pushed
onto the stack, it is not erased from memory after a pop.

When a register is pushed, the value in the register is copied onto the stack. The
stack pointer points to the value of the last pushed register. When CX is pushed, the stack
pointer points to the low-order byte (in this case, 56h). Note that PUSH places items on the
stack in a little endian manner. CL is in a lower address than CH. Registers are pushed onto
the stack as last-in-first-out (LIFO). The POP instruction retrieves items from the stack.
The stack pointer is incremented by 2 addresses for each POP operation. It is decremented
by 2 addresses for each PUSH operation. PUSH and POP operations are extensively used
in assembly language programming. One use is to push all pertinent registers at the beginning of a subroutine, and POP all registers just before the RET instruction.

Example 5.1

What is contained in register CX after the following code fragment is run?

```
MOV AX,F962
PUSH AX
POP CX
```

Solution   Since AX is pushed onto the stack after being set equal to F962, and CX is popped immediately after, CX will equal AX, or F962.

Example 5.2

Suppose the stack pointer = FFEE before the code fragment in Example 5.1 is run. What will be the value in addresses FFEC and FFED after the program is run?

Solution   This program will place 62 in address FFEC and F9 in address FFED.

FIGURE 5.2   Stack
Operations

Sample Stack for 80x86 Processor

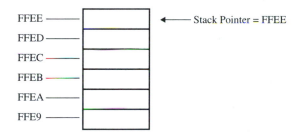

Sample Stack after Execution of PUSH

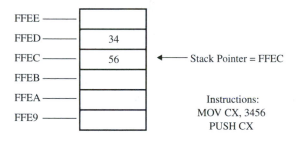

Sample Stack after Execution of POP

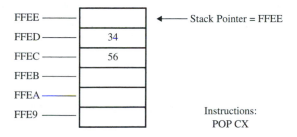

Example 5.3

Write a DEBUG assembly language subroutine that exchanges two 16-bit registers. Do not use the XCHG instruction. Have the subroutine start at address 117h.

Solution

```
100 B3EE       MOV    BL,EE       ;Load BL with EE.
102 B0FF       MOV    AL,FF       ;Load AL with FF.
104 E81000     CALL   0117        ;Call EXCHANGE subroutine.
107 CD20       INT    20          ;Terminate program
...
...
117 52         PUSH   DX          ;EXCHANGE sub begins here, save DX.
118 50         PUSH   AX
119 53         PUSH   BX
11A 58         POP    AX
11B 5B         POP    BX
11C 5A         POP    DX          ;Restore DX.
11D C3         RET                ;Return.
```

You will need to enter

A117

before entering the EXCHANGE subroutine. This ensures the routine will start at address 117.

Notice how the subroutine begins and ends. The DX register is pushed because it becomes a temporary storage location in the subroutine. It is popped before the RET is issued. In this way, the contents of the DX register in the calling program have not been altered.

Pushing and Popping the Flag Register

There are two stack instructions that operate off the flag register, **PUSHF** and **POPF.** PUSHF pushes the flag register onto the stack, and POPF pops the flag register from the stack. Pushing and popping the flag register allow the contents to be saved while in a routine. All interrupt routines use PUSHF and POPF, as described in Chapter 10.

Flag Instructions

Shown below are a series of instructions that can be used to set or clear the 80x86 flags. These instructions are given as reference here, and are used later in the text.

Carry Flag

CLC   Clears Carry Flag (Carry flag = 0.)
STC   Sets Carry Flag (Carry flag = 1.)

Direction Flag

CLD   Clears Direction Flag (Direction flag = 0.)
STD   Sets Direction Flag (Direction flag = 1.)

Interrupt Flag

CLI   Clears Interrupt Flag (Interrupt flag = 0.)
STI   Sets Interrupt Flag (Interrupt flag = 1.)

SEGMENTED ARCHITECTURE

All 80x86 microprocessor systems have data, stack, and code segments. The segments are each 16-bit registers and are named **SS** (stack segment), **DS** (data segment), **CS** (code segment), and **ES** (extra segment). The ES register is used as an extra DS.

It is important to know how the microprocessor converts a segment and an offset (or instruction pointer) to a physical address. The physical address is an actual address interfaced to a memory chip, as shown in Figure 5.3. The memory chip does not recognize a segment and offset because these registers are internal to the CPU. To compute the physical address, a decoder in the CPU multiplies the segment by 10h and adds the offset, as shown below:

Segment*10h
+ offset
physical address

You may wonder why Intel chose to use segmented architecture. The reason goes all the way back to the 8088 microprocessor. This chip had 20 address lines, but 16-bit registers. This made it impossible for a register to contain an entire physical address. Intel solved this problem by splitting the absolute address into two registers, the segment register and the offset, or instruction pointer, register.

FIGURE 5.3 8086 Address
Bus

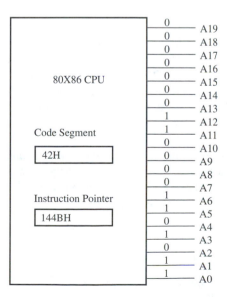

0	A19
0	A18
0	A17
0	A16
0	A15
0	A14
0	A13
1	A12
1	A11
0	A10
0	A9
0	A8
0	A7
1	A6
1	A5
0	A4
1	A3
0	A2
1	A1
1	A0

80X86 CPU

Code Segment

42H

Instruction Pointer

144BH

Example 5.4

Calculate the physical address in Figure 5.5 for an instruction at code segment 42h and offset 144Bh.

Solution

42h * 10h = 420h

```
  0420h
+ 144Bh
  0186Bh = 0000 0001 1000 0110 1011 binary
```

The physical address is 0186Bh. This is the actual address in memory containing this instruction. The binary equivalent is placed on the address bus as shown below:

A19	A18	A17	A16	A15	A14	A13	A12	A11	A10	A9	A8	A7	A6	A5	A4	A3	A2	A1	A0
0	0	0	0	0	0	0	1	1	0	0	0	0	1	1	0	1	0	1	1

Example 5.5

What is the offset if the segment equals 120h and the physical address equals FB45h?

Solution   First multiply the segment 120h by 10h to get 1200h. Next subtract FB45h – 1200h to get E945h. This is the offset address.

STRUCTURE OF .EXE FILES

PC-based microprocessor systems allow for two different types of programs, .COM and .EXE files. So far, only .COM files have been covered. .EXE programs are more complex than their .COM equivalent. The .EXE format allows the data segment, code segment, and stack segment to reside in different 64K segments of memory. Therefore, the code segment itself can be as large as 64K. This is quite an improvement over .COM files, which place all segments in the same 64K block. A comparison of .COM and .EXE files is shown in Table 5.1.

The last statement has to do with the physical appearance of the .ASM file. Usually the stack and data segments are defined before the code segment. Shown below is a typical .EXE shell program. This program will compile into a .EXE file, but will do nothing. It can be used as a core for writing .EXE programs.

EXESHELL.ASM

```
Constant equ 0

;Stack Segment
_stack segment para stack 'stack'
        dw 100h dup(?)
```

```
_stack ends

_data segment word public 'data'
        ;PLACE DATA HERE
_data ends

_text segment word public 'code'
assume CS:_text
assume DS:_data

main proc near
START:
        mov AX,_data
        mov DS,AX

        ;PLACE CODE HERE

        mov ah,4ch
        INT 21h

main endp
_text ends
end start
```

This code appears quite different from a .COM file. This example starts with the **equ** pseudo-op. EQU allows you to name a constant and set it equal to a value. When the program is compiled, the constant name is replaced with the value. The constant cannot be changed anywhere else in the program. A pseudo-op is an assembly instruction that has no machine language counterpart.

Note that each segment is identified, whether it is the code, data, or stack. The **segment** and **ends** (end segment) directives enclose the segment. Each segment has a name. Although you can name them anything you like, **_data** is commonly used for the data segment, **_stack** for the stack segment, and **_text** for the code segment. Each segment is

TABLE 5.1 Comparison of .COM and .EXE Files

.COM Files	.EXE Files
Smaller, more compact code.	Both assembly code and compiled machine language equivalent are larger than a .COM file with the same instructions.
Only one 64K block allowed.	Separate blocks can be allocated for data, stack, and code segments.
No intermediate files produced when compiling.	.OBJ file produced. A separate Link procedure must be invoked to produce an .EXE file.
Takes up less memory, loads faster.	Can link with other modules.
Terminates program with INT 20H.	Terminate with AH = 4Ch, INT 21H.
Code begins at offset 0100H.	Code begins at offset 0000H (unless specified otherwise).
Data usually placed after code.	Data appears in separate segment.

also defined in terms of boundary locations. The choices are **byte, word, dword** (double word), **para** (paragraph), and **page.** The boundary location indicates where the segment begins in memory. For example, if para is included, the segment will begin on a paragraph (16 bytes). If page is selected, the segment will begin on a page (256 bytes). The stack segment is usually defined by a paragraph boundary, whereas the code and data segments are defined on word boundaries.

The **public** directive indicates that the segment is combined with all other segments of the same name when the file is compiled. As will be seen later, it is possible to have multiple subroutines (now called procedures) defined within a _text public segment. All of these subroutines are combined into the same segment when the program is compiled if the public directive is used.

An .EXE file normally uses procedures **(proc)** to separate different routines in the code segment. Although it is not necessary, the first procedure is usually called **main.** Procedures terminate with a **endp** (end procedure) statement. Note that endp does not actually terminate the program, but serves to help organize your code. Procedures are defined as **near** or **far.** When calls are made to the procedure, the compiler knows whether to issue a near or far call, and a near or far return upon exiting. Normally it is best to use near, unless the procedure is unusually long. The LINK compiler allows you to call procedures not in your program and combine them as OBJ files with your program to produce the final .EXE file. This is covered later in the chapter.

Another unusual statement in .EXE programs is the **assume** directive. Assume is an indicator for the compiler as to where the code segment (CS) and data segment (DS) are assigned.

The data segment must still be loaded into DS at the beginning of the code segment. Since there is no MOV instruction to load DS directly with the data segment name, it must first be routed through AX with the statements:

```
mov ax,_data
mov ds,ax
```

There is also an **END** statement used in .EXE files. This statement not only tells the compiler where the program ends, but also where it begins. The label immediately following END indicates the starting point for the program when it is loaded from DOS.

The stack segment needs to have a specific area reserved for it. The **DW** and **DB** directives allocate storage for words and bytes. In EXESHELL, 100h is reserved by using the **DUP** operator. This command duplicates whatever is to the right of DUP the number of times indicated to the left of it. Since 100h is to the left, this is how much memory is reserved. The compiler will take care of assigning the stack to absolute addresses. If (?) is indicated to the right, no data is filled in immediately. It is expected the program will fill in the data later. The DUP operator can be used in data segments as well as stack segments.

Comments begin with the semicolon and extend to the end of the line. If you are using MASM, you can enter the EXESHELL example in a text editor. One of the easiest to use is EDIT, available in DOS 6.0 and higher. All numbers in MASM are assumed to be decimal (unlike DEBUG, which assumes all numbers are hex). You must explicitly state if a number is hex or binary by placing an h (hex) or a b (binary) after the number. Letters in MASM are not case-sensitive. The compiler will translate:

```
MOV
```

or

```
Mov
```

or

```
mov
```

in the same manner.

In order to produce an .EXE file from this code, you will need to complete a two-step process. First, compile the code to an .OBJ file by entering

```
MASM filename.ASM
```

then

```
LINK filename
```

to produce an .EXE file.

The MASM procedure produces a file with an **.OBJ** extension. The file with this extension contains a machine language equivalent of the program, but is not executable. In order to produce an executable file, you must LINK the .OBJ file to produce an .EXE file. The LINK procedure is very powerful. Using this utility, you can combine other .OBJ or .LIB files to produce a single .EXE file. Let's try a simple example. Enter the EXESHELL.ASM program and save it as

```
EXESHELL.ASM
```

Now copy the file using the COPY utility in DOS. Copy the file to DOLLAR.ASM, as shown below.

```
COPY EXESHELL.ASM DOLLAR.ASM
```

Now use a text editor (such as EDIT) to view DOLLAR.ASM. Enter the following code where 'PLACE CODE HERE appears in the program.

```
MOV AH,2
MOV DL,36
INT 21H
```

Save the file and compile it by entering

```
MASM DOLLAR.ASM
```

and

```
LINK DOLLAR
```

Press RETURN until the program compiles.
Now enter

```
DOLLAR
```

You should see a $ printed to the screen.

Alternatively, the value of DL could have been defined in the data segment as a variable. Look at a revised DOLLAR.ASM shown below:

```
_stack segment para stack 'stack'
        dw 100h dup(?)
_stack ends
```

```
_data segment word public 'data'
        ;Define variable.
        ShowCharacter db '$'
_data ends

_text segment word public 'code'
assume cs:_text
assume ds_data
main proc near
START:

        mov ax,_data
        mov ds,ax

        ;Display character to screen.
        mov ah,2
        mov dl,ShowCharacter
        int 21h

main endp

_text ends

end START
```

In this case, a variable in the data segment called ShowCharacter is created. It is defined as a byte (using DB) and set equal to $. In the code segment, the variable is assigned to a register, as shown below:

```
mov dl,ShowCharacter
```

Also note the use of **comment** statements in the program. A comment statement is always preceded by a semicolon and takes up the rest of the line. It does not continue onto the next line.

Example 5.6

Write an .EXE assembly language program to print the entire ASCII table to the screen.

Solution   The ASCII table is printed using the following code. Note that ShowCharacter can be incremented just like a register.

```
_stack segment para stack 'stack'
        dw 100h dup(?)
_stack ends

_data segment word public 'data'
        ShowCharacter db 0
_data ends

_text segment word public 'code'
```

```
main proc near
assume cs:_text
assume ds:_data
START:

        mov ax,_data
        mov ds,ax
        mov ah,2
        mov cx,255
CONT:
        mov dl,ShowCharacter
        int 21h
        inc ShowCharacter
        loop CONT
        mov ah,4ch
        int 21h
main endp

_text ends

end START
```

This example uses a **label** (CONT) to indicate an address. This is much more powerful than the way addresses have to be explicitly listed in DEBUG. The exact value of an address need not be known. Just refer to it by a label and let the compiler determine the absolute address needed to fit the label. MASM accomplishes this by using a two-pass compiler. The first pass lists the labels in a table, and the second inserts addresses in place of the labels. A label can be any phrase you choose, but must not be a reserved keyword and cannot contain spaces. A label always terminates with a colon.

The CBW and CWD Instructions

Now that you have looked at some of the MASM directives, let's study more 80x86 instructions. The first two instructions in this chapter are rather simple. CBW (convert byte to word) fills AH with the contents of bit 7 in AL. Two examples are shown below:

```
MOV AL,0Fh
CBW
```

AH now contains 00h.

```
MOV AL,80H
CBW
```

AH now contains FFH, since 80h = 10000000 binary. (Note that bit 7 equals 1.) This instruction is particularly useful for extending a sign bit.

CWD (convert word to double word) performs in a similar manner, except that it extends the uppermost bit in AX to all of DX.

Example 5.7

What will DX equal after the following instructions are executed?

```
MOV AX,B2
CWD
```

Solution   B2 = 0000000011010010 binary (remember AX is a 16 bit register). Since the uppermost bit (bit 15) is 0,

```
DX = 00h
```

THE MULTIPLEXED 8086 BUS

Figure 5.4 shows the address bus of the 8086. It may seem logical that the data bus occupies 16 pins separate from the address bus. Actually the 8086 and 8088 processors (used in early PCs) contain a multiplexed address and data bus. This means that the address and data bus are on the same pins, but appear at different times. A partial pinout of an 8086 system showing a latched and buffered bus is shown in Figure 5.4.

The data bus (shown at the top of the figure) has a latch between it and the processor. The latch stores the previous values sent through it. Thus, when the processor places an address on A0–A15, the data that previously appeared on the same bus is stored at the output of the latch. When the latch enable is held low, data passes through the latch. The Data ENable (DEN) pin is active low and is connected to the latch enable. When DEN goes low, valid data is present on the bus and is transferred to the output of the latch to be stored. The latch serves to separate the data from the address bus as shown in Figure 5.5.

The address bus (shown to the right of Figure 5.4) has a buffer between it and the processor. This buffer allows memory and port chips to be connected to the address bus without overloading the processor. The buffer chip has its enable tied to the Address Latch Enable (ALE) pin. ALE is active high. When ALE goes high, a valid address is on the address bus. The address is transferred through the buffer to the output pins.

Note the address bus is 20 pins wide (A0–A19), and the data bus is 16 pins wide (D0–D15). The upper 4 address pins (A16–A19) have no data bus associated with them and are tied to the processor through a buffer.

The control bus partially consists of 3 pins: M/IO, RD, and WR. The M/IO pin is used by the processor to select between memory and port I/O. If the pin is high, memory is selected; if low, I/O is selected. Thus, an IN or OUT instruction will set the pin low, and MOV register,[BX] will set the pin high.

The RD pin is active low. It goes low when a read operation occurs. The WR pin is also active low. It goes low when a write operation occurs. On the PC, M/IO, RD, and WR are tied to a decoder to obtain IOR (I/O read), IOW (I/O write), MEMR (memory read), and MEMW (memory write). These four decoder outputs are active low and partially describe the 80x86 control bus.

FIGURE 5.4   Address/Data Demultiplexing of the 8086

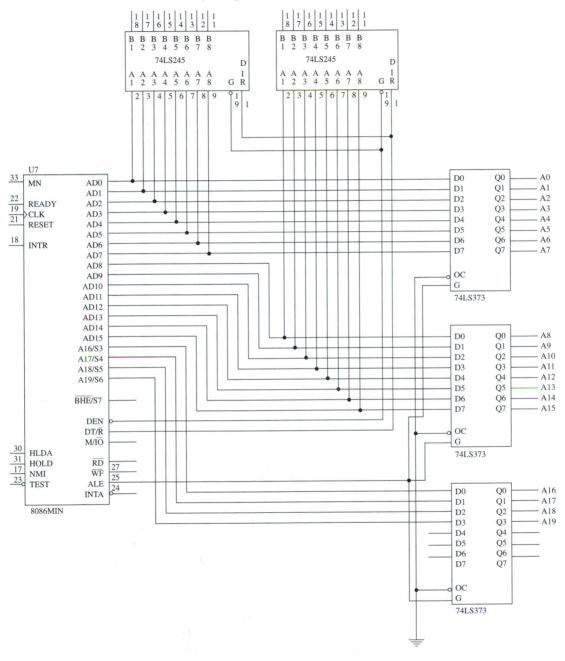

Memory and port chips are tied to the 80x86 bus through the address, data, and control bus as shown in Figure 5.6.

Note that the address bus is connected to a decoder on each of the chips in Figure 5.6. Each chip has a unique address associated with it, and it is the decoder that identifies when

FIGURE 5.5   Data Latch

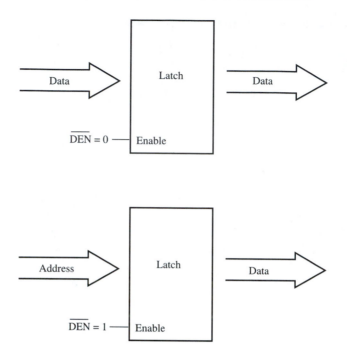

this address is on the address bus. Normally the decoder is a separate chip connected to the ROM, RAM, or port.

The ROM BIOS chip has a read enable on it. A ROM (read only memory) chip can be read from, but not written to. Since the ROM partially contains the operating system for the PC, it is imperative that its instructions not be altered. The ROM Read Enable (RE) pin is wired to the MEMR pin on the 80x86 bus.

The memory chip has both write enable and read enable pins. Memory is most often a RAM (random access memory). This type of chip allows data transfer in both directions. Note that the Read and Write pins on the RAM are referenced to the 80x86. In other words, a READ operation sends data from memory to the 80x86. A WRITE operation sends data from the 80x86 to memory. The MEMR and MEMW pins are connected to the RE and WE pins.

The port chip is similar to the memory chip except that the IOR and IOW pins are connected to the RE and WE pins on the port chip. The other major difference is that the 80x86 only allows address pins A0–A15 to be used for port addressing.

8086 Bus Cycle

The 8086 bus cycle has some similarities to the Easy4 timing cycle in Chapter 2. Due to the multiplexed nature of the bus, more timing is needed to ensure the address/data bus is in its proper configuration before an operation occurs. Figure 5.7 shows a partial description of an 8086 read bus cycle.

The bus cycle is split into four distinct T states. Each T state is one clock period long. During T1, a valid address appears on the address/data bus after ALE goes high. During T2, both DEN and RD go low. Valid data appears on the data bus during T3. During T4, all control signals return to their deactivated state.

FIGURE 5.6   Memory and Port Addressing

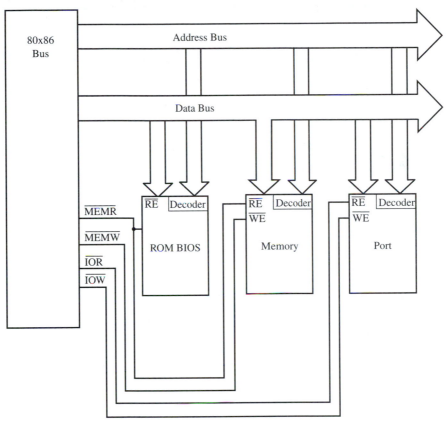

FIGURE 5.7   Partial Description of an 8086 Read Bus Cycle

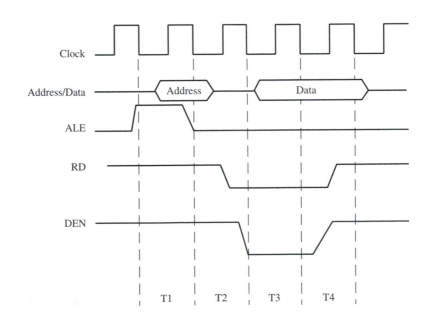

TABLE 5.2   PC ISA Bus

Section	Pin	Section	Pin
Interrupt	IRQ7	DMA	DACK1
	IRQ6	(cont.)	DRQ1
	IRQ5		DACK0
	IRQ4		T/C
	IRQ3	System	OSC
	IRQ2		ALE
	CLK		RESET
Segment	A19-A16		AEN
Address	A15-A0		I/O CHRDY
Control	IOR		I/O CHK
	IOW	Power	−5V
	MEMR		−12V
	MEMW		+12V
Data	D7-D0		+5V
DMA	DACK3		+5V
	DRQ3		GND
	DACK2		GND
	DRQ2		GND

PC ISA Bus

Many of the pins described in the last section appear on the ISA bus. This is the oldest and still one of the most popular bus designs for PCs. The bus is split into eight different sections, as shown in Table 5.2.

The interrupt section (IRQ2–7) is described in Chapter 10. These pins handle interrupt requests from external devices such as the mouse, printer, and disk drives. The CLK pin contains the system clock, which has a frequency of 200 Mhz on a 200Mhz Pentium. It has a 33% duty cycle. A 33% duty cycle means the clock is high during one-third of the period. The OSC pin has three times the frequency of the CLK pin. It has a 50% duty cycle.

The AEN pin is called Address ENable. Direct memory access (DMA) transfers can take place when this pin is high. DMA transfers are direct transfers between I/O ports and memory that use special chips to bypass the 80x86. When the AEN pin is low, the 80x86 is in control of the bus. The DMA section of the bus has DRQ and DACK pins. The DRQ pins are used by peripherals to request a DMA transfer. The DACK pins are used to acknowledge a request. The DRQ pins are active high, the DACK pins are active low.

A0–A19, D0–D7, MEMR, MEMW, IOR, and IOW are discussed earlier in this chapter. Low-cost plug-in breadboards are available for experimenting with the PC bus. A series of laboratory experiments using a breadboard and the ISA bus appear in Appendix H.

CHAPTER 5 PROBLEMS

1. Explain the difference between CBW and CWD.
2. Explain the difference between CBW and MOV AH,0.

3. Suppose SP = F432 before the following code is executed:

```
MOV CX,1234
PUSH CX
MOV DX,5678
PUSH DX
POP CX
POP AX
```

   a. What are the contents of AX, CX, and DX after the code is run?

   b. What are the contents of memory address F42F?

4. List three reasons why the .EXE file structure is better than the .COM structure.

5. Explain why the segment and ends directives are used.

6. Why are the PROC and ENDP directives needed?

7. Why does a segment require the byte, word, or para directives? What does para mean? How many bytes does it take up? How many bytes does a page take up?

8. Write an .EXE program that prints your name to the screen. Use the interrupts described in Chapter 3.

9. Write an .EXE program that loads BL with 64h and prints it to the screen. Use the hex output program in Figure 4.2 of Chapter 4.

   Hint: You will need to replace some of the addresses with labels.

10. Suppose a program contains the Equate statement:

```
Dos_Int     equ     21h
```

Can the program alter the DOS_INT label at a later point in the program?

CHAPTER 6

Linking Object Files and the .ASY Library

NEW INSTRUCTIONS IN THIS CHAPTER

Mnemonic: **LDS**
LDS *16 bit register, source*

Description: Transfers a word from source into any 16-bit register. Transfers a word into DS from source+2.

Example: LDS AX,LABEL   (Sends the contents of LABEL into AX and LABEL+2 into DS.)

Flags Affected: None

Mnemonic: **LES**
LES *16 bit register, source*

Description: Transfers a word from source into any 16-bit register. Transfers a word into ES from source+2.

Example: LES AX,LABEL   (Sends the contents of LABEL into AX and LABEL+2 into ES.)

Flags Affected: None

LINKING .OBJ AND .LIB FILES

This chapter introduces library (.LIB) files. LIB files allow you to compile separate procedures and use them in another program without having to include them as part of the assembly language code. .OBJ and .LIB files can be combined into a single .EXE file. In fact, a .LIB file is simply a collection of .OBJ files combined by using the .LIB utility supplied with the MASM compiler. This book comes with a .LIB file called **ASY.LIB.** This utility provides some frequently used I/O functions that allow you to read, display, and print decimal, hex, and string data. This library contains the procedures listed in Table 6.1, all of which may be called by your program. All of the functions must first be declared with the **EXTRN** keyword. This is necessary whenever an external procedure is called. External procedures are those not listed in the file, but are compiled by using LINK. Example 6.1 shows how to use the EXTRN keyword.

TABLE 6.1 The ASY.LIB Library/ASY.LIB Functions

GETCHAR	Gets a character from the keyboard into AX.
Example:	Call GETCHAR
Notes:	Character from keyboard is sent to AX. Toggle keys such as NUM LOCK, CAPS LOCK, SHIFT, and CTRL are not recognized. See Chapter 7 for accessing these keys.
SCANCODE	Gets the scancode from the keyboard into AX.
Example:	call SCANCODE
Notes:	Each key on the keyboard has its own scancode. This is not the same as the ASCII code. The scancode from the keyboard is sent to AX when a key is pressed. Toggle keys such as NUM LOCK, CAPS LOCK, SHIFT, and CTRL are not recognized. See Chapter 7 for accessing these keys.
GETDEC	Gets a decimal value from the keyboard into AX.
Example:	call GETDEC
Notes:	Decimal number from the keyboard is sent to AX when carriage return is pressed. Number cannot exceed 65535.
GETHEX	Gets a hexadecimal value from the keyboard into AX.
Example:	call GETHEX
Notes:	Hexadecimal number from keyboard is sent to AX when carriage return is pressed. Number cannot exceed FFFFh.
GETSTRING	Gets string pointed to by BX from the keyboard.
Example:	MOV BX,offset Message call GETSTRING
Note:	Message is any variable defined in a data segment. The carriage return is not saved as part of the string, but is replaced by a binary 0. The size of the string is returned in AX.
OUTCHAR	Sends a character from AX to the screen.
Example:	MOV AX,'B' call OUTCHAR
Note:	The character B is sent to the screen.
OUTDEC	Sends a decimal value from AX to the screen.
Example:	MOV AX,567 call OUTDEC
Note:	The decimal number 567 is sent to the screen.

(continued on next page)

TABLE 6.1   (continued)

OUTHEX	Sends a hexadecimal value from AX to the screen.
Example:	MOV AX,7EB2h call OUTHEX
Note:	The hexadecimal number 7EB2 is sent to the screen.
OUTSTRING	Sends a string pointed to by BX to the screen.
Example:	_data segment word public 'data' Message DB 'This is a string',0 _data ends _text segment word public 'code' ... MOV BX,offset Message call OUTSTRING _text ends
Notes:	Message is any variable defined in a data segment. A binary 0 must appear at the end of the string.
CRLF	Sends a carriage return–line feed combination to the screen.
Example:	call CRLF
Note:	A carriage return and line feed are sent to the screen. No registers are affected.
pDEC	Sends a decimal value from AX to the printer.
Example:	MOV AX,567 call pDEC
Note:	The decimal number 567 is sent to the printer.
KBHIT	Checks for keypress.
Example:	call KBHIT
Notes:	This procedure scans the keyboard for a keypress and passes to the next instruction. It does not suspend the program waiting for an input. If a key is pressed, it is returned into AX.
pHEX	Sends a hexadecimal value from AX to the printer.
Example:	MOV AX,7EB2h call pHEX
Note:	The hexadecimal number 7EB2 is sent to the printer.
pSTRING	Sends a string pointed to by BX to the printer.
Example:	MOV BX,offset Message call pSTRING
Notes:	Message is any variable defined in a data segment. The carriage return is not saved as part of the string, but is replaced by a binary 0.
PAUSE	Suspends program operation by the time specified in AX. Time is indicated in tenths of a second.
Example:	MOV AX,50 ;AX set to 0.5 second. call PAUSE
Note:	Any time can be used in AX from 0.1 second (AX=1) to 10 minutes (AX = 6000).

Shown below are some examples using the ASY.LIB library.

Example 6.1

Write an assembly language program using ASY.LIB to convert total seconds to minutes and seconds.

Solution   You can convert total seconds to minutes and seconds by dividing by 60. The integer result is the minutes and the remainder is the seconds. The .EXE file is shown below.

```
_stack segment para stack 'stack'
        dw 100h dup(?)
_stack ends

_data segment word public 'data'
        ;Define constant.
        MinToSec db 60

        ;Define screen messages.
        Mess1 db 'Enter total seconds',0
        Mess2 db 'Total Minutes = ',0
        Mess3 db 'Total Seconds = ',0
_data ends

EXTRN outstring:NEAR
EXTRN getdec:NEAR
EXTRN crlf:NEAR
EXTRN outdec:NEAR

_text segment word public 'code'
main proc near
assume cs:_text
assume ds:_data
START:
        mov ax,_data
        mov ds,ax
        mov bx,offset Mess1     ;Print first message to screen.
        call outstring
        call getdec             ;Get total seconds from keyboard.
        mov cl,MinToSec
        div cl                  ;Divide by 60.
        mov dx,ax               ;Save result.
        and ah,0h               ;Clear remainder, leave quotient (or total minutes).
        call crlf
        mov bx,offset Mess2     ;Print second message.
        call outstring
        call outdec             ;Print total minutes.
        call crlf
        xchg dx,ax              ;Restore AX.
```

```
        and al,0               ;Clear quotient, leave remainder (total seconds).
        xchg ah,al             ;Put remainder in AL.
        mov bx,offset Mess3    ;Print third message.
        call outstring
        call outdec            ;Print total seconds.
        call crlf
        mov ah,4ch             ;Exit program.
        int 21h
main endp
_text ends
end START
```

This program reads the total seconds from the keyboard, divides by 60 to obtain the total minutes, and saves the result to DX. This leaves the remainder with the total seconds, and the quotient with the total minutes. The results are then separated and printed to the screen.

Note the use of the EXTRN keyword. Since the original procedures in ASY.LIB were all declared as NEAR, they must be listed as such by EXTRN.

Example 6.2

Write a hex to decimal converter. Have the program ask for a hex value and print the decimal equivalent to the screen.

Solution

```
_stack segment para stack 'stack'
        dw 100h dup(?)
_stack ends

_data segment word public 'data'
        ;Define screen mesages
        Mess1 db 'Enter hex value',0
        Mess2 db 'Decimal equivalent = ',0
_data ends

EXTRN outstring:NEAR
EXTRN outdec:NEAR
EXTRN crlf:NEAR
EXTRN gethex:NEAR

_text segment word public 'code'
main proc near
assume cs:_text
assume ds:_data

START:
        mov ax,_data
```

```
        mov ds,ax
        mov bx,offset Mess1
        call outstring

        call gethex        ;Get hex character.
        call crlf
        mov bx,offset Mess2
        call outstring
        call outdec        ;Send out same character as decimal to screen.
        call crlf
        mov ah,4ch         ;Exit program
        int 21h
main endp
_text ends
end START
```

The number stored in AX is in binary. The functions that read in hex and output in decimal take care of the conversion process.

ASSIGNING VARIABLES TO A PREDEFINED ADDRESS

Variables can be assigned to a particular address by creating a data segment that points to the address segment and using the **ORG** directive to assign the starting offset. An example is shown below.

```
_memory segment at 0

ORG 417h
Key db ?

_memory ends
```

The address pointed to by Key is segment 0, offset 417h. The **at** keyword in the segment definition defines the numerical value of the start of the assigned segment.

USING THE SCANCODE FUNCTION IN ASY.LIB

The ASY.LIB library contains a routine that returns the scancode of a key into AL. Most keys on the keyboard have a scancode assigned to them. Keys such as the function keys and PageUp, Home, and the arrow keys do not have an ASCII number assigned to them. Table 6.2 shows the scancode for some common keys that are not defined by an ASCII value. Each can be accessed by calling the SCANCODE routine.

TABLE 6.2   Commonly Used Scan Codes

Key Description	Scancode (in Decimal)	Key Description	Scancode (in Decimal)
F1	59	Ctrl F1	94
F2	60	Ctrl F2	95
F3	61	Ctrl F3	96
F4	62	Ctrl F4	97
F5	63	Ctrl F5	98
F6	64	Ctrl F6	99
F7	65	Ctrl F7	100
F8	66	Ctrl F8	101
F9	67	Ctrl F9	102
F10	68	Ctrl F10	103
Ins	82	Alt F1	104
Home	71	Alt F2	105
PageUp	73	Alt F3	106
Delete	83	Alt F4	107
End	79	Alt F5	108
PageDown	81	Alt F6	109
Up Arrow	72	Alt F7	110
Left Arrow	75	Alt F8	111
Down Arrow	80	Alt F9	112
Right Arrow	77	Alt F10	113

Example 6.3

Write a program that remains in an infinite loop until the F1 function key is pressed.

Solution

```
_stack segment para stack 'stack'
        dw 100h dup(?)
_stack ends

_data segment word public 'data'
        Mess1 db 'Press the F1 function key ',0
        Mess2 db 'F1 has been pressed ',0
_data ends

EXTRN scancode:NEAR
EXTRN crlf:NEAR
EXTRN outstring:NEAR

_text segment word public 'code'
main proc near
assume cs:_text
assume ds:_data

START:
        mov ax,_data
```

```
        mov ds,ax
        mov bx,offset Mess1
        call outstring
        call crlf

        cont:              ;Start loop.
        call scancode      ;Get scancode.
        cmp al,59          ;Check if key pressed = F1.
        je EXIT
        jmp cont           ;Jump to start of loop.

EXIT:

        mov bx,offset Mess2
        call outstring
        call crlf
        mov ah,4ch
        int 21h
main endp

_text ends

end START
```

This program simply reads the keyboard buffer for the scancode and checks if it is equal to 59 (or the F1 key). If not, it loops back for another reading.

MEMORY OPERATIONS WITH THE PTR OPERATOR

The PTR operator was briefly described in Chapter 3 for near and far jumps. It is also used to correct ambiguities concerning byte or word memory operations. For example, consider the following instruction:

```
MOV [BX],10h
```

How does the compiler know whether you want to place 10h in a byte memory address or a word memory address (e.g., two consecutive addresses)? If you had specified a word (such as FF10H) to be transferred to [BX], it would be obvious. For this reason, the compiler will return an error. You need to explicitly state if the number is a byte or word. You can do this with the **byte** and **word ptr** operation.

```
MOV WORD PTR [BX], 10h
```

specifies that 10h is a word (or 0010h) and is placed in 2 consecutive bytes of memory starting at the address pointed to by BX.
Similarly,

```
MOV BYTE PTR [BX], 10h
```

specifies that 10h is a byte and is placed in memory starting at the address pointed to by BX.

THE LDS AND LES INSTRUCTIONS

The **LDS** (Load Data Segment) and **LES** (Load Extra Segment) instructions provide a quick method of loading the DS and ES registers. Both instructions work like the MOV instruction, except they load a 16-bit register from the source operand and the DS or ES register from the source operand+2. An example using LDS is shown below:

LDS.ASM

```
_stack segment para stack 'stack'
        dw 100h dup(?)
_stack ends

_data segment word public 'data'
        LoadAX DW 1234H
        LoadDS DW 5678h
_data ends

EXTRN outhex:near
EXTRN crlf:near

_text segment word public 'code'

main proc near
assume cs:_text
assume ds:_data

START:
        mov ax,_data
        mov ds,ax

        ;Load AX with 1234h and DS with 5678h.
        lds ax,DWORD PTR LoadAX

        ;Save DS.
        mov bx,ds

        ;Print AX.
        call outhex
        call crlf

        ;Print DS.
        mov ax,bx
        call outhex
        call crlf

        ;Exit.
        mov ah,4ch
        int 21h
```

```
        main endp
_text ends
end START
```

The example above uses LDS to load 1234h into AX and 5678h into DS, since 5678 immediately follows 1234 in the data segment. Note that a double-word (32-bit) PTR operator is used to perform the operation. This is necessary because a double word is needed by LDS, but LoadAX is defined as a word. DWORD PTR takes care of this ambiguity. The DS register is saved in BX, and later transferred back to AX to be printed to the screen with the OUTHEX procedure.

THE STACK AND THE BP REGISTER

The stack, SP register, and PUSH and POP operations are described in Chapter 5. The BP register also is linked to the stack. It is mostly used for searching the stack. In this sense, it is much like the BX register, which is used for indirect memory operations. Usually at some point, BP is set equal to SP and an indexed search of the stack is performed. Shown below is a program that pushes three registers onto the stack and uses BP to obtain the contents of an offset from SP. The contents of BP are printed to the screen. Note that you do not have to POP a register to view the contents of the stack. The program has to be linked with ASY.LIB when compiling.

BP.ASM

```
_stack segment para stack 'stack'
        dw 100h dup(?)
_stack ends

_data segment word public 'data'
_data ends

EXTRN outhex:near
EXTRN crlf:near
_text segment word public 'code'
main proc near
assume cs:_text
assume ds:_data

START:
        mov ax,_data
        mov ds,ax

        ;Push 1234H.
        mov dx,1234h
        push dx

        ;Push 5678H.
```

```
                    mov dx,5678h
                    push dx

                    ;Push 9ABCH.
                    mov dx,9abch
                    push dx

                    ;BP=SP.
                    mov bp,sp

                    ;Save BP.
                    mov cx,bp

                    mov bx,2
                    mov ax,0

        CONT:
                    ;Move contents of offset BP to AX.
                    mov ax,[bp]

                    ;Print AX.
                    call outhex

                    ;Print CRLF.
                    call crlf

                    ;Increment BP to next 16-bit register location on stack.
                    inc bp
                    inc bp

                    ;Subtract new BP from old BP.
                    mov dx,cx
                    sub dx,bp

                    cmp dx,-6
                    jne CONT

                    pop dx
                    pop dx
                    pop dx

                    mov ah,4ch      ;Exit program.
                    int 21h
                    main endp

        _text ends

         end START
```

This program starts by pushing a series of numbers to the stack. Then BP is set to SP, or the current position in the stack. It is then saved to CX. The statement

```
MOV AX,[BP]
```

moves the contents of the stack pointed to by BP to the AX register. This register is then printed to the screen with the OUTHEX procedure. BP is then incremented two 1-byte positions on the stack with the INC instruction. This is necessary because the stack is read in groups of 2 bytes, but INC only increments BP by 1 byte.

The statements

```
mov dx,cx
sub dx,bp
```

restore the original contents of BP and subtract from it the current contents of BP. Since the current contents of BP will be greater than the original (remember, you have been using the INC instruction), the subtraction produces a negative number. There are 6 bytes that you want to get from the stack and print. The statement

```
cmp dx,-6
```

compares the current difference between the beginning of the stack and BP to the number. If greater, the program exits and returns to DOS. This ensures that only 6 bytes from the stack are printed to the screen.

CHAPTER 6 PROBLEMS

1. Suppose CS = 0F20 hex and IP = 0035 hex. What is the physical address?
2. Write a valid segment and offset address for physical address FFFF0.
3. Repeat problem 2 for physical address 0417h.
4. Give five reasons that make an .EXE file more useful than a .COM file.
5. Write a program that takes total inches and converts them to total feet and inches.
6. Write a program that prints the ASCII table to the screen in reverse order.
7. Write a decimal to hex converter. Enter a decimal number and have the program print the result in hex.
8. Write a program that prints the name of the function key when it is pressed. For example, if F1 is pressed, the program prints.

    ```
    F00001
    ```

    Have the program exit when the ESCAPE key is pressed.
9. Explain how the program BP.ASM works. Why did it compare DX with –6?
10. Write a program to print the contents of offset addresses 20h through 30h in the current segment to the screen in hex.

CHAPTER 7

Advanced Memory and Port I/O

There are many operations that can be performed once the basics of .EXE files are known. This chapter focuses on memory and I/O operations, including

- Operating toggle keys such as SCROLL LOCK, NUM LOCK, and CAPS LOCK directly from a program.
- Accessing a timer that is updated 18.2 times per second.
- Obtaining a pseudorandom number.
- Writing directly to screen memory.
- Plugging the keyboard buffer.
- Creating tones on the speaker.
- Writing directly to the printer ports.

Any of the above procedures can be added to the ASY.LIB file to build a customized Assembly language library. Later, Assembly language functions that can be used by the C language are covered.

THE KEYBOARD FLAG REGISTER

The keyboard flag is located at segment 40, offset 17h. Each bit at this address is attached to one of the keyboard toggle keys, as shown in Figure 7.1.

For example, the NUM LOCK key can be turned on by setting bit 5 to 1. Alternately, it can be turned off by placing a 0 in bit 5. Note that the other keys should not be disturbed while setting NUM LOCK. A program to toggle the NUM LOCK key is shown below. This program uses an XOR on bit 5. When a bit is XOR'd with 1, it inverts to its opposite state.

FIGURE 7.1 Keyboard Flag
Register

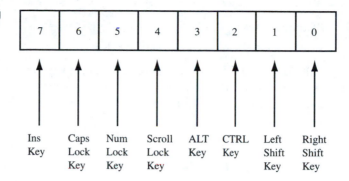

```
                        NUM.ASM
_stack segment para stack 'stack'
dw 100h dup(?)
_stack ends
_data segment at 40h
ORG 17h
keyboard db ?

_data ends


_text segment word public 'code'


main proc near
assume cs:_text
assume ds:_data

START:

mov ax,_data
mov ds,ax
mov al,keyboard        ;Load key toggle byte into AX.
XOR al,00100000b       ;Invert bit 5. Do not change other bits.
mov keyboard,al        ;Load result in key toggle byte.

mov ah,4ch
int 21h
main endp


_text ends

end START
```

　　　　Note the use of XOR in this example. Recall the XOR truth table from Chapter 4. If
you XOR any bit with 0, the bit does not change. Therefore, all bits other than 5 are XOR
with 0. If a bit is XOR with 1, it inverts its current state. Bit 5 must be XOR'd with a 1.

Example 7.1

Write a program to turn the CAPS LOCK key on.

Solution   The CAPS LOCK key is bit 6 in the keyboard flag. In order to turn this bit on, OR it with 1. Whatever the previous state, the new state will be 1. All other bits are OR'd with 0 to preserve their current state.

CAPS.ASM

```
_stack segment para stack 'stack'
dw 100h dup(?)
_stack ends

_data segment at 40h
ORG 17h
keyboard db ?

_data ends

_text segment word public 'code'

main proc near
assume cs:_text
assume ds:_data

START:

mov ax,_data
mov ds,ax
mov al,keyboard      ;Move keyboard flag into AL.
OR al,01000000b      ;OR the keyboard flag to turn bit 6 on.
mov keyboard,al      ;Move OR'd AL into keyboard flag.

mov ah,4ch
int 21h
main endp

_text ends

end START
```

THE INTERNAL PC TIMER

All PCs have an internal 4-byte timer that is updated 18.2 times per second (or about once every 55 milliseconds). Each update is called a tick. This timer is interfaced to memory at segment 40, offset 6Ch. To access this timer, simply create a data segment to point to it, then move it into a register. The 4-byte resultant represents the number of ticks since midnight.

TICKS.ASM

```
_stack segment para stack 'stack'
dw 100h dup(?)
_stack ends


_data segment at 40h
ORG 6Ch

tim dw ?              ;Point to first 2 bytes of timer.
tim1 dw ?            ;Point to second 2 bytes of timer.


_data ends

EXTRN outdec:NEAR

_text segment word public 'code'

TIMER PROC near

assume cs:_text
assume ds:_data

START:

mov ax,_data
mov ds,ax

mov AX,tim           ;Load LSB of timer into AX.
mov BX,tim1          ;Load MSB of timer into BX.

call outdec          ;Print LSB of timer.
xchg ax,bx           ;Exchange LSB and MSB of timer.
call outdec          ;Print MSB of timer.

mov ax,4ch
int 21h

TIMER endp

_text ends

end START
```

Usually it is sufficient to use the LSW (least significant word). If the MSW (most significant word) increments, it should be included in the total time. To get total seconds, divide the number by 18.2 (this is almost the same as multiplying the number by 55). The example below counts from 0 to 65535 one hundred times and displays the elapsed time.

TIMECNT.ASM

```
_stack segment para stack 'stack'
dw 100h dup(?)
_stack ends

_time segment at 40h
org 6Ch

tim dw ?
tim1 dw ?

_time ends

_data segment word public 'data'
Mess1 db 'Time to complete = milliseconds : ',0
_data ends

EXTRN outstring:NEAR
EXTRN outdec:NEAR
EXTRN crlf:NEAR
_text segment word public 'code'

TIMER PROC near

PUBLIC TIMER

assume cs:_text
assume ds:_time

START:

mov ax,_time
mov ds,ax
mov ax,tim              ;Get initial time.
push ax
mov cx,100              ;Load a loop counter equal to 100 into CX.
cont:
mov dx,0                ;Load DX with 0.
cont1:
inc dx                  ;Increment DX from 0 to 65535.
cmp dx,0                ;If greater than 65535, DX has started over at 0.
jne cont1               ;If DX = 0, stop count.
loop cont               ;Decrement CX and count again.
mov bx,tim              ;Get final time.
mov ax,bx
pop ax
sub bx,ax               ;Subtract initial time minus final time.
xchg bx,ax
push ax
```

```
assume ds:_data        ;Make DS point to data segment to print message.
mov ax,_data
mov ds,ax

mov bx,offset Mess1    ;Print message.
call outstring

pop ax
mov cx,55              ;Multiply time difference by 55 so result is in
                        milliseconds instead of ticks.
mul cx

call outdec            ;Print time difference.
call crlf              ;Print carriage return and line feed.

mov ah,4ch
int 21h

TIMER endp

_text ends

end START
```

This program took about 3.4 seconds (or 3400 milliseconds) on an 80486DX at 33Mhz. Note that you can make DS point to another data segment. The message variable is not included in the _time segment because segment 0 is reserved for special functions that cannot be written over. The instruction

```
MOV CX,55
MUL CX
```

is used to convert ticks to milliseconds, using the formula

1000 milliseconds = 18.2 ticks.

Therefore,

1 tick = 1000/18.2 milliseconds = ~55 milliseconds

Function **AH=2CH, INT 21H** can also be used to get the time. This interrupt returns the time in the following manner:

CH = Hour
CL = Minute
DH = Seconds
DL = Hundredths of second

This routine is more convenient if the current time is desired. However, if a time differential is needed, the tick method is easier because the time is not split into hours, minutes, and seconds. The pause procedure described in Chapter 6 uses the timer to provide a suspend operation in tenths of a second.

Obtaining Pseudorandom Numbers

Random numbers are used in many programs, from games to engineering applications. Fortunately, there is an easy way to get a pseudorandom number from the 8253 timer chip in the PC. This chip is used for timing operations for the disk drives, and its registers are usually not modified. However, you can use it to read a timer at channel 0. This 8253 channel is located at port 40h. First, write a 0 to port 43h to set up the 8253 so that channel 0 is latched in binary mode (see Appendix D). Then read in port 40h twice to get a pseudorandom number between 0 and 255.

RAND.ASM

```
_stack segment para stack 'stack'
dw 100h dup(?)
_stack ends


_data segment word public 'data'

_data ends

EXTRN outdec:NEAR
EXTRN crlf:NEAR

_text segment word public 'code'

main proc near
assume cs:_text
assume ds:_data

START:

mov ax,_data
mov ds,ax
mov ax,0
out 43h,al        ;Send control word equal to 0 to port 43h.
in al,40h         ;Read in port 40h twice.
in al,40h

call outdec
call crlf

mov ah,4ch
int 21h
main endp


_text ends

end START
```

Example 7.2

Write a random number generator procedure that can be called from other programs. Name the procedure **RANDOM.** Link it and place it in the ASY.LIB library.

Solution   The exit procedure (AH=4ch, INT 21h) needs to be replaced with a RET statement. AL will be used as the register to return the random number.

```
_text segment word public 'code'

main proc near
assume cs:_text

START:

mov ax,0
out 43h,al      ;Send control word equal to 0 to port 43h.
in al,40h       ;Read in port 40h twice.
in al,40h

ret             ;Return to calling procedure.
main endp

_text ends

end START
```

Once this program is entered, name it RANDOM.ASM and compile it by entering

```
MASM RANDOM
```

Now add RAMDOM.OBJ to the library file by entering:

```
C:\MASM\BIN>lib

Microsoft (R) Library Manager Version 3.18
Copyright (C) Microsoft Corp. 1983-1991. All rights reserved.

Library name: asy.lib
Operations: random.obj
List file:
Output library:
```

SCREEN I/O

There are a few different ways to get and place characters on the screen. INT 10H is reserved for screen I/O (including text and graphics). It is easy to use this interrupt to access the screen. One of the most common screen tasks is to clear the screen. Up to now, no

TABLE 7.1   Register BH Attributes for INT 10h

Bit 7 = Blink Bit	Sets to 1 for blink. Sets to 0 to turn-off blink.
Bits 6, 5, 4 = Background color	
Bits 3, 2, 1, 0 = Foreground color	

TABLE 7.2   Foreground Attribute Colors

0	Black	8	Gray
1	Blue	9	Light blue
2	Green	10	Light green
3	Cyan	11	Light cyan
4	Red	12	Light red
5	Magenta	13	Light magenta
6	Yellow	14	Brown
7	White	15	Bright white

method has been shown that can do this. One function of INT 10H is AH=6, which is defined in Appendix A as Clear Screen. You can use this function to clear a window or the entire screen (79 columns and 24 rows). The registers that need to be set upon entry into INT 10H to clear the screen are shown below:

AH = 6
AL = 0
DH = Lower right row
DL = Lower right column
CH = Upper left row
CL = Upper left column
BH = Attribute

The attribute (BH) allows us to define the foreground and background color of the text on the screen. The bits in BH are defined in Table 7.1.

The foreground color values are shown in Table 7.2. The background colors are similar except only colors 0 through 7 are available. Shown below is a program to clear the screen.

CLR.ASM

```
_stack segment para stack 'stack'
dw 100h dup(?)
_stack ends

_text segment word public 'code'
main proc near
assume cs:_text

START:
```

```
mov ah,6          ;Set AH for screen clear.
mov al,0
mov cx,0          ;Screen size.
mov dl,79
mov dh,24
mov bh,4          ;Attribute
int 10h

mov ah,4ch
int 21h

main endp
_text ends
end START
```

Try setting BH to different colors, and then recompile the program to observe how changes in BH affect the output.

Example 7.3

What will the screen output be if AH = 6, BH = 0C0H, and INT 10H is called?

Solution   Since C = 1100 binary, the blink bit is set (meaning the screen will flash off and on) and the background color is 100, or red. The foreground color is black, or 0000.

Writing Directly to Screen Memory

An alternative to using INT 10H is to write directly to screen memory. This method is always the fastest, but requires that you know the correct video segment for your monitor. Text screen memory starts at segment B000H for monochrome monitors and B800H for graphics monitors, including CGA, EGA, and VGA. The examples in this chapter assume a graphics monitor is installed. Each character on a text screen is actually assigned to a particular memory address. Segment B800H, offset 0000H defines the upper left character on the screen. Each character takes up 2 bytes of memory. The first defines the ASCII value, and the second defines the attribute for the character. The attribute is the same as described in the last section. By writing directly to screen memory, you can control the color of each character, rather than the color of an entire window on the screen. Because each character takes up 2 bytes, and there are 80 characters in each row; a total of 160 bytes resides in each row. There are 25 rows on the screen, giving a total of 4000 bytes (80*2*25). The program below writes to the background and foreground colors of the current DOS text screen, but does not alter the text.

SCRCOLOR.ASM

```
_stack segment para stack 'stack'
dw 100h dup(?)
_stack ends
```

```
_data segment at 0B800h
ScreenChar db ?

_data ends

_text segment word public 'code'

main proc near
assume cs:_text
assume ds:_data

START:

mov ax,_data
mov ds,ax
mov bx,offset ScreenChar
inc bx
mov cx,4000              ;Screen size = 80*2*25 = 4000.
mov al,0a0h             ;Load foreground and background colors.
cont:

mov [bx],al             ;Send to screen.

inc bx                  ;Increment twice to skip text character.
inc bx

loop cont
mov ah,4ch
int 21h
main endp

_text ends

end START
```

The following program saves the screen in memory, clears it, and restores the screen when the ESCAPE key is pressed. This program uses the DS segment to point to the screen and the ES segment to point to an area in memory to save the screen. The program copies the screen byte by byte to the _data segment.

SCREEN.ASM

```
_stack segment para stack 'stack'
dw 100h dup(?)
_stack ends

_screen segment at 0B800h
ORG 1
ScreenChar db 4000 dup (?)

_screen ends
```

```
_data segment word public 'data'
Copy db 4000 dup (?)
_data ends

EXTERN random:NEAR
EXTERN kbhit:NEAR
EXTERN outdec:NEAR
EXTERN crlf:NEAR


_text segment word public 'code'

main proc near
assume cs:_text
assume ds:_screen
assume es:_data
START:

mov ax,_data
mov es,ax
mov ax,_screen
mov ds,ax

mov bx,0
nxt:
mov ax,[bx+offset ds:ScreenChar]        ;Load byte from screen into AX.
mov [offset es:Copy+bx],ax              ;Send AX to the _data segment.
inc bx
cmp bx,4000                             ;Entire screen is 80*2*25 = 4000 bytes.
jl nxt

mov ah,6                                ;Routine to clear the screen.
mov al,0
mov cx,0

mov dl,79
mov dh,24
mov bh,4
int 10h
cont:
call kbhit                              ;Wait for keypress.
cmp al,27
jne cont

EXIT:

mov bx,0
nxt1:
mov ax,[bx+offset es:Copy]              ;Restore screen from ES to DS segment.
mov [offset ds:ScreenChar+bx],ax
inc bx
```

```
cmp bx,4000
jz exit1
jmp nxt1
exit1:

mov ah,4ch
int 21h
main endp


_text ends


end START
```

PLUGGING THE KEYBOARD BUFFER

There is an area of memory that stores keystrokes prior to being captured by INT 9. This area begins at segment 0, offset 41A. The data structure of the buffer is described in Table 7.3.

The keystroke storage area can store up to fifteen usable keystrokes. This area is a circular buffer, meaning the keys are cycled around the buffer area. The next key that is eligible to be retrieved is pointed to by the Head of Buffer. The next available space in the buffer is pointed to by Tail of Buffer. The buffer can be cleared by setting Head of Buffer equal to Tail of Buffer. Each keystroke in the buffer needs 2 bytes to store the ASCII value and scancode. For keys with no ASCII value, a 0 is inserted and the scancode immediately follows. Plugging is the method of forcing characters into the keyboard buffer. A program that demonstrates keyboard plugging is shown below:

KEYPOKE.ASM

```
SizeBuffer equ 12

_stack segment para stack 'stack'
dw 100h dup(?)
_stack ends

_data segment at 0

org 41ah
StartBuff db ?

org 41ch
EndBuff db ?
HeadBuff db 20 dup (?)

_data ends

_text segment word public 'code'
```

```
main proc near
assume cs:_text
assume ds:_data

START:

mov ax,_data
mov ds,ax

mov bx,1

mov al,'d'
call StuffBuffer

mov al,'i'
call StuffBuffer

mov al,'r'
call StuffBuffer

mov al,'/'
call StuffBuffer

mov al,'w'
call StuffBuffer

mov al,13
call StuffBuffer

mov al,1Eh
add al,SizeBuffer
mov EndBuff,al

mov al,1Eh
mov StartBuff,al

mov ah,4ch
int 21h
main endp

StuffBuffer proc near
mov [bx+HeadBuff],al
inc bx
inc bx
ret
StuffBuffer endp

_text ends

end START
```

TABLE 7.3   Keyboard Buffer Data Structure

Offset Address	Operation
41Ah	Head of buffer
41C	Tail of buffer
41D	Start of keystroke storage area

This program causes a **DIR/W** DOS command to be executed whenever the KEY-POKE.EXE program is loaded. Because 2 bytes are needed for each keystroke, the size of buffer is equal to the number of keys entered times 2. In the KEYPOKE example, 5 keys were reserved for DIR/W, plus an extra key for the carriage return for a total of 6 keys. These 6 keys are multiplied by 2 to get 12, which the constant SizeBuffer. This constant will have to be changed if a different number of keys is used. The maximum value of SizeBuffer is 30 (15 keystrokes times 2). SizeBuffer is added to 1Eh and inserted into Tail of Buffer. Also note that bx is incremented twice in the StuffBuffer procedure.

Plugging the keyboard is especially useful when combined with a terminate and stay resident (TSR) program. This is covered in a later chapter.

CREATING TONES ON THE SPEAKER

The PC has an internal speaker. This speaker is connected to ports 61h, 42h, and 43h. Port 43h initializes an internal oscillator circuit that creates the tone, and 42h sets the period of the output tone. The equation to calculate the period from the frequency is shown below:

Period = 120000h/Frequency

To initialize the speaker, first send B6 out to port 43h. Port 42h uses a double byte to specify the period; first the LSB is sent out, then the MSB. Bits 0 and 1 on port 61h turn the speaker off and on. A 1 sent to bits 0 and 1 turns the speaker on, while a 0 to bits 0 and 1 turns the speaker off. Shown below is an example program that creates a tone for 2 seconds. It uses the PAUSE function described in Chapter 6. *Note:* There is only limited control of the speaker through the microprocessor. Once the speaker is turned on, it must be turned off through port 61h. Otherwise, it will stay on even after you exit the program.

TONE.ASM

```
_stack segment para stack 'stack'
 dw 100h dup(?)
_stack ends


_data segment word public 'data'

_data ends
```

```
EXTRN pause:NEAR
_text segment word public 'code'

main proc near
assume cs:_text
assume ds:_data

START:

mov ax,_data
mov ds,ax

;Initialize oscillator circuit.
mov al,0B6h
out 43h,al

;Period of output tone in little endian order.
mov al,0cch
out 42h,al
mov al,04ch
out 42h,al

;Turn on speaker.
in al,61h
and al,0fch
or al,3
out 61h,al

;AX is in tenths of seconds;AX = 20 indicates a pause of 2 seconds.
mov ax,20
call pause

;Turn off speaker.
in al,61h
and al,0fch
out 61h,al

mov ah,4ch
int 21h

main endp

_text ends

end START
```

Example 7.4

Calculate the frequency of the tone in the program TONE.ASM. Also determine how long the tone is sounded.

128   CHAPTER 7   ADVANCED MEMORY AND PORT I/O

Solution   The frequency can be calculated as:

Frequency = 120000h/Period

From the program, the LSB of the period = CCh and the MSB = 4Ch. This gives a period of 4CCCh.

Frequency = 120000h/4CCCh =3Ch, or 60 decimal

The frequency is therefore 60 Hz. Frequencies and periods for three octaves of musical notes are shown in Table 7.4

TABLE 7.4   Frequency Table for Musical Notes

Note	Frequency (Hz)	Period (Hex)	
C	131	232C	
C#	139	2126	
D	149	1EED	
D#	156	1D89	
E	165	1BED	
F	175	1A54	
F#	185	18E8	
G	196	1782	
G#	208	1627	
A	220	14F2	
A#	233	13C6	
B	247	12A7	
C	262	1196	(Middle C)
C#	277	10A2	
D	294	0FAC	
D#	311	0ED1	
E	330	0DF6	
F	349	0D34	
F#	370	0C74	
G	392	0BC1	
G#	415	0B1A	
A	440	0A79	
A#	466	09E3	
B	494	0953	
C	523	08CF	
C#	554	0851	
D	587	07D9	
D#	622	0768	
E	659	06FE	
F	698	069A	
F#	740	063A	
G	784	05E0	
G#	831	058B	
A	880	053C	
A#	932	04F1	
B	988	04A9	

WRITING DIRECTLY TO THE PRINTER PORT

Chapter 4 introduced the concept of writing directly to the printer through the parallel printer ports. Shown below is an example using MASM that prints a line feed to the printer port. Knowing how to write directly to the printer port provides a gateway from the computer to the outside world. With a little more work, you could send information from the computer to your own peripherals connected to the DB25 printer connector on back of the computer.

Example 7.5

Print a line feed to the printer using the IN and OUT instructions.

Solution   The key to printing information to the printer is to first load the base port with the character to be printed. Next, check to be sure the printer is ON, then check the Busy pin to ensure the printer is ready, and finally send a negative-going pulse to the Strobe pin in port 3 to print the character. The MASM program below prints a line feed on the printer. It assumes port 378h is the base address of LPT1. You can check segment 40, offset 8 to find the actual printer port for your computer. This program will not work on a laser jet or some ink-jet printers.

```
;Writing a line feed to the printer port
_STACK SEGMENT PARA STACK 'STACK'
DW 100h DUP(?)
_STACK ENDS

_DATA SEGMENT WORD PUBLIC 'DATA'

LineFeed db 10
_DATA ENDS

_TEXT SEGMENT WORD PUBLIC 'CODE'

MAIN PROC NEAR
ASSUME CS:_TEXT
ASSUME DS:_DATA

START:

MOV AX,_DATA
MOV DX,AX

;Check if printer is on.
MOV DX,379H
IN AL,DX
AND AL,10H
CMP AL,10H
JNZ EXIT
```

```
;Send line feed (ASCII 10) to the printer buffer at port 378h.
MOV DX,378H
MOV AL,10
OUT DX,AL

;Check for busy signal from printer.
MOV DX, 379H
CONT:IN AL,DX
AND AL,80H
CMP AL,80H
JNZ CONT

;Produce a negative-going pulse on the Strobe pin.
MOV DX,37AH
IN AL,DX
OR AL,1
OUT DX,AX
DEC AL
OUT DX,AL
EXIT:
MOV AH,4cH
INT 21H
MAIN ENDP

_TEXT ENDS

END START
```

CHAPTER 7 PROBLEMS

1. Write a program that checks to see if the SCROLL LOCK key is on. If it is, have the program print 'ON'; if not, print 'OFF'.
2. Use the RANDOM procedure to help write a program that "scrambles" a text screen. Have the program randomly obtain a character from screen memory and randomly position it somewhere else on the screen. The program should restore the original screen when the ESCAPE key is pressed.
3. Use the RANDOM procedure to help write a program that randomly changes the background and foreground colors on a text screen.
4. Write a program called CSCREEN.ASM that plugs the keyboard buffer with CLS. Try the program in DOS to see if it clears the screen.
5. Write a program that plugs the keyboard buffer to load the EDIT program in DOS and a file called BP.ASM, or

   ```
   EDIT BP.ASM
   ```

6. Write a program to play the chorus of "Jingle Bells" on the speaker. Use the pause routine in ASY.LIB.
7. Write a program to print your name to the printer by writing directly to the printer port.

CHAPTER 8

String Operations

NEW INSTRUCTIONS IN THIS CHAPTER

Mnemonic:	**MOVSB**
Description:	Moves string of bytes. Copies the byte of memory at DS:SI into the byte at ES:DI and automatically increments or decrements SI and DI. It is equivalent to

```
MOV       byte ptr ES:[DI], DS:[SI]
INC       SI
INC       DI
```

This instruction is normally used with the repeat prefix described in this chapter.

Example:	MOVSB
Flags Affected:	None

Mnemonic:	**MOVSW**
Description:	Moves string of words. Copies the word of memory at DS:SI into the word at ES:DI and automatically increments or decrements SI and DI. It is equivalent to

```
MOV       byte ptr ES:[DI], DS:[SI]
INC       SI
INC       DI
```

This instruction is normally used with the repeat prefix described in this chapter.

Example:	MOVSW
Flags Affected:	None

Mnemonic:	**CMPSB**
Description:	Compares string of bytes. Compares the byte located at DS:SI to the byte located at ES:DI and increments or decrements SI and DI. It is equivalent to
	CMP byte ptr DS:[SI], ES:[DI]
	INC or DEC SI
	INC or DEC DI
	Performs the operation (DS:[SI] - ES:[DI]) and sets the flags accordingly. If DF = 0, DI and SI are incremented. If DF = 1, DI and SI are decremented.
	This instruction is normally used with the repeat prefixes described in this chapter.
Example:	CMPSB
Flags Affected:	Overflow, Sign, Zero, Auxiliary, Parity, Carry

Mnemonic:	**CMPSW**
Description:	Compares string of words. Compares the word located at DS:SI to the word located at ES:DI and increments or decrements DI and SI. It is equivalent to
	CMP word ptr DS:[SI], ES:[DI]
	INC or DEC SI
	INC or DEC DI
	Performs the operation (DS:[SI] - ES:[DI]) and sets the flags accordingly. If DF = 0, DI and SI are incremented. If DF = 1, DI and SI are decremented.
Example:	CMPSB
Flags Affected:	Overflow, Sign, Zero, Auxiliary, Parity, Carry

Mnemonic:	**CLD**
Description:	Clears direction flag.
Example:	CLD
Flags Affected:	Direction

Mnemonic:	**STD**
Description:	Sets direction flag.
Example:	STD
Flags Affected:	Direction

Mnemonic:	**REP**
	REP *string instruction*

Description: Executes *string instruction* the number of times specified by CX. It is used with the MOVSB and MOVSW instructions.

Example: MOV   CX, 5
REP   MOVSB
Move 5 bytes starting at memory location DS:[SI] to memory location ES:[DI].

Flags Affected: Per string instruction

Mnemonic: **REPE**
REPE *string instruction*

Description: Executes *string instruction* the number of times specified by CX as long as the zero flag is set. Used with the CMPSB and CMPSW instructions.

Example: MOV   CX, 5
REPE   MOVSB
Compare the 5 bytes starting at DS:[SI] to the 5 bytes starting at ES:[DI], stopping if the zero flag is cleared.

Flags Affected: Per string instruction

Mnemonic: **REPNE**
REPNE *string instruction*

Description: Executes *string instruction* the number of times specified by CX as long as the zero flag is clear. Used with the CMPSB and CMPSW instructions.

Example: MOV   CX, 5
REPNE   MOVSB
Compare the 5 bytes starting at DS:[SI] to the 5 bytes starting at ES:[DI], stopping if the zero flag is set.

Flags Affected: Per string instruction

CHARACTER STRINGS

A string is a continuous sequence of memory bytes. Each character is stored in a single byte using the ASCII coding scheme described in Appendix F. String functions must know the length of the string. Length information is stored in addition to the character codes. There are two popular methods for representing strings and their lengths: ASCIIZ and bounded length.

An ASCIIZ string is a string of ASCII characters terminated by a byte containing 0. This is the string type used in C. A fixed amount of memory is allocated for the data and the 0 byte is added to indicate end of the string. The length of the string is determined by counting the number of characters before the 0 (or NUL character).

```
string1    db    "An ASCIIZ string",0
```

A bounded-length string allocates a fixed amount of memory using the first byte to indicate the length or number of characters actually stored in the string. The string size is usually limited to 255 characters, since a single byte is used to store the length. This is the method used by the Pascal language.

```
string2    db    23, "A bounded length string"
```

Fixed-length strings can be declared as shown below.

```
strSize    equ   20
sourceStr  db    strSize dup(?)
destStr    db    strSize dup(?)
```

The DI and SI Registers

A string must be copied one character at a time. Fortunately, there are some built-in 80x86 instructions to help do this. They use the DI and SI index registers to move through the strings and the DS and ES segment registers to indicate the addresses of the operands in the string instructions. SI is the offset of the source string relative to DS. DI is the offset of the destination string relative to ES. The source and destination operands of the string instructions are assumed to be DS:SI and ES:DI.

DS: SI   Source Index. Starting address of source operand.

ES: DI   Destination Index. Starting address of destination operand.

The registers may be initialized as follows. Note that the DS and ES registers often point to the same segment. Also DS and ES must be initialized through AX.

```
;initialize the segment registers
MOV    AX, _DATA
MOV    DS, AX                   ;Make DS and ES point to same segment.
MOV    ES, AX

                                ;Initialize the index registers.
MOV    SI, offset sourceStr     ;SI points to first address of source string.
MOV    DI, offset destStr       ;DI points to first address of destination string.
```

THE DIRECTION FLAG

When copying each character of a string, the pointer can move forward or backward. The direction flag (DF) specifies the direction of the transfer.

DF = 0   Increasing address order (DI and SI are incremented).

DF = 1   Decreasing address order (DI and SI are decremented).

The CLD and STD instructions are used to clear and set the DF and control the direction of the string operations. CLD sets the string pointer to increment. STD set the string pointer to decrement. An example is shown below:

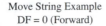

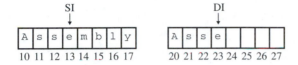

SI points to character in existing string.
DI points to character in new string.

Prior to the transfer, SI points to
Address 10. DI points to Address 20.

Move String Instructions

The move string instructions copy a string a byte or a word at a time from the source location DS:SI to the destination location ES:DI. To move a string from one location to another, set up DS:SI to the segment:offset address of the source and ES:DI to the segment:offset address of the destination, load the length of the string into CX, clear the direction flag, and use the move string instruction in a loop. The following code fragment will copy 5 bytes from sourceStr to destStr.

```
        CLD
        MOV       SI, offset sourceStr
        MOV       DI, offset destStr
        MOV       CX, 5
Loop1:
        MOVSB
        loop Loop1
```

The STRCPY.ASM program shown below implements the string copy function for bounded-length strings.

```
;STRCPY.ASM
;String copy function using bounded-length strings.

_STACK SEGMENT para stack 'stack'
      dw 100h dup (?)
_STACK ENDS

_DATA SEGMENT word public 'data'
      sourceStr  db 5, "Hello"
      destStr    db 10 dup (?)
_DATA ENDS
```

```
        EXTRN   OutString:NEAR
        EXTRN   crlf:NEAR
        EXTRN   outdec:NEAR

        _TEXT SEGMENT word public 'code'
                main proc near
                assume CS: _TEXT
        START:
                mov     ax, seg _DATA
                mov     ds, ax
                mov     es, ax
                assume ds: _DATA

                cld
                mov     si, offset sourceStr
                mov     di, offset destStr

                mov     cx, 0
                mov     cl, sourceStr
                inc     cx

        loop1:
                movsb
                loop    loop1

                mov     byte ptr ES:[DI], 0
                mov     ax, 0
                mov     al, destStr
                call    outdec
                call    crlf
                mov     bx, offset destStr
                inc     bx
                call    OutString
                call    crlf

                ;Exit to DOS.
                mov     ah, 4ch
                mov     al, 00
                int     21h

                main endp

        _TEXT ENDS
        END START
```

String Comparison Instructions

The string comparison instructions compare two strings a byte or a word at a time. The source string located at address DS:SI is compared to the destination string located at ES:DI.

The CMPSB and CMPSW instructions subtract the source operand from the destination operand and set the flags according to the difference. The string compare instructions then increment or decrement the DI and SI registers based on the DF and the size of the operands.

The CMPSTRIN.ASM demonstrates the use of the CMPSB instruction.

```asm
;CMPSTRIN.ASM
;Program to compare strings.
_STACK SEGMENT para stack 'stack'
     dw 100h dup (?)
_STACK ENDS

_DATA SEGMENT word public 'data'
sourceStr      db 5, "Skunk"
destStr        db 5, "Harry"
_DATA ENDS

EXTRN crlf:NEAR
EXTRN outdec:NEAR

_TEXT SEGMENT word public 'code'
     main proc near
     assume CS: _TEXT
Start:
     mov     ax, seg _DATA
     mov     ds, ax
     mov     es, ax
     assume ds: _DATA

     cld
     ;Find shorter length.
     mov     cx, 0
     mov     cl, sourceStr
     cmp     cl, destStr
     jle     Continue
     mov     cl, destStr
Continue:
     mov     di, offset destStr
     inc     di
     mov     si, offset sourceStr
     inc     si
loop1:
     ;While cx > 0 and sourceStr[si] == destStr[di].
     cmp cx, 0
     je endLoop1
     cmpsb
     jne endLoop1
     dec cx
     jmp loop1
endLoop1:
```

```
        dec     di
        dec     si
                                ;if sourceStr[si] == destStr[di]
        cmpsb                   ;if length(sourceStr) == length(destStr)
        jl      elseLess        ;AX = 0
        jg      elseGreater     ;else if length(sourceStr) >length(destStr)
                                ;AX = -1
        mov     ax, 0           ;else
        mov     al, sourceStr   ;AX = 1
        cmp     al, destStr     ;else if sourceStr[si] < destStr[di]
        jl      elseLess        ;AX = -1
        jg      elseGreater     ;else
        mov     ax, 0           ;AX = 1
        jmp     exit
elseLess:
        mov     ax, -1
        jmp     exit
elseGreater:
        mov     ax, 1
exit:
        call    outdec
        mov     ah, 4ch
        mov     al, 00
        int     21h
        main    endp
_TEXT ENDS

END Start
```

Repeat Prefixes

The repeat prefixes are used to repeat a string instruction for each byte or word in a string. The CX register and optionally the zero flag are used to control the number of repetitions.

REP   The unconditional repeat prefix, REP, is used with the MOVSB and MOVSW instructions. The instruction is executed the number of times indicated in CX. The CX register must first be loaded with the number of bytes or words in the string. After each execution, the CX register is decremented (without affecting the flags). Execution stops when CX reaches 0. For example, the following code fragment will copy 5 bytes from sourceStr to destStr. The REP prefix replaces the loop in the previous string copy example.

```
CLD
MOV                 SI, offset sourceStr
MOV                 DI, offset destStr
MOV   CX, 5
REP MOVSB
```

REPE and REPNE   The conditional repeat prefixes, REPE and REPNE, are used with the CMPSB and CMPSW instructions. The instruction is executed the number of times indicated in CX or until the zero flag is set (REPE) or cleared (REPNE).

The CX register must be loaded with the number of bytes or words in the string. After each execution of the string instruction, the zero flag is set if the bytes are equal and cleared if the bytes are not equal and the CX register is decremented (without affecting the flags). When CX reaches 0 or the zero flag is set (REPNE) or cleared (REPE), the repetition stops.

The following code fragment compares two bounded strings for equality.

```
        MOV       SI, offset sourceStr
        MOV       DI, offset destStr
        ;Find shorter string.
        CLR       CX
        MOV       CL, sourceStr
        CMP       CL, destStr
        JL        DO
        MOV       CL, destStr
DO:
        REPE      CMPSB
        JNE       notEqual
        CMP       CX, 0
        JNE       notEqual
        MOV       AX, 0
        JMP   Continue
        MOV       AX, 1
Continue:
```

CHAPTER 8 PROBLEMS

1. Write string length functions for ASCIIZ strings. Your functions will be passed the string as an input parameter and will return the count of the number of characters in AX.
2. Write string length functions for bounded-length strings. Your functions will be passed the string as an input parameter and will return the count of the number of characters in AX.
3. Rewrite the string compare function of CMPSTRIN.ASM using the repeat prefixes.
4. Rewrite the string compare function of CMPSTRIN.ASM for ASCIIZ strings.
5. Write a program to copy data from segment FFFF,offset 0 through segment FFFF,offset F to a string called HIMEMORY. Print the string to the screen in a hex and an ASCII table.
6. Write a program that displays the first sixteen entries in the interrupt vector table to the screen. Use string instructions to first move the vectors into a buffer prior to displaying on the screen in hex.

CHAPTER 9

80x87 Floating Point Operations

THE 80X87 MATH COPROCESSOR

The 80x87 floating point coprocessor contains a stack that is similar to the HP calculator stack. Memory locations are pushed onto the stack. Once on the stack, various mathematical operations are performed. Unlike the conventional 80x86 stack, stack entries are accessed by referring to their place on the stack, not via a stack pointer. Values can be popped off the stack into memory. It is important to note that the coprocessor is separate from the CPU and operates independently. There is a complete set of instructions for the 80x87. The 80x87 stack is outlined below:

```
ST(7)      Bottom
ST(6)
ST(5)
ST(4)
ST(3)
ST(2)
ST(1)
ST(0)      Top
```

The top entry, ST(0), is also referred as ST. Operations are performed between stack members, or stack members and memory. Each stack member has a width of 10 bytes. Values are entered by pushing them onto ST(0). Previous entries are moved up one position. For example, an entry that was at ST(0) is moved to ST(1) when a new value is pushed. Because of the limited number of entries on the stack, care must be taken not to push more than the available stack space.

FRACTIONAL BINARY NOTATION

Before attempting any operations with floating point numbers, you should first understand how fractional binary numbers are stored. When working with real numbers, the column value is a multiple of 2. Fractional binary columns are multiples of $1/2$, as shown below:

Binary Fractions

```
3  2  1  0    –1 –2 –3 –4  ◄———— Powers
2  2  2  2     2  2  2  2  ◄———— Column Weights
1  1  1  1  .  1  1  1  1  ◄———— Binary Values
```

CONVERTING FRACTIONAL BINARY TO DECIMAL

Converting fractional binary to decimal is accomplished by multiplying each binary digit times its column weight and adding them together. For example,

```
101.1101 = 1*2² + 1*2⁰ + 1*2⁻¹ + 1*2⁻² +1*2⁻⁴ = 5.8125
```

There is no need to include the columns where the binary digit is 0, since the outcome of that column does not contribute to the answer.

CONVERTING DECIMAL NUMBERS TO FRACTIONAL BINARY

Converting decimal numbers to fractional binary is more difficult. One of the most common methods used is the successive approximation method, as described below.

Procedure for Converting Decimal to Fractional Binary

1. Isolate the whole number and convert it separately, using the techniques described in Chapter 1.
2. Begin with the 2^{-1} column and compare this value with the decimal fraction. If 2^{-1} is greater than the fraction, put a 0 in this column, else insert a 1.
3. Move to the 2^{-2} column. Assume a 1 is in it, and add it to the value calculated for the 2^{-1} column. If the answer is greater than the fraction, put a 0 in this column, or insert a 1.
4. Continue moving to the next column and following the same procedure until either the binary fraction exactly equals the decimal fraction, or the maximum number of binary columns is filled with 1s or 0s.

Example 9.1

Convert .4165 decimal to binary. Use five columns for the binary fraction.

Solution   Begin be comparing 2^{-1} = .5 to .4165. Since .5 > .4165, insert a 0 in this column.

2^{-1}	2^{-2}	2^{-3}	2^{-4}	2^{-5}
0				

Next compare 2^{-2} = .25 to .4165. Since .25 < .4165, insert a 1 in this column.

2^{-1}	2^{-2}	2^{-3}	2^{-4}	2^{-5}
0	1			

Moving to the next column, compare 2^{-2} + 2^{-3} = .25 + .125 = .375. You must include the 2^{-2} column since a 1 was inserted here in the last step. Since .375 < .4165, put a 1 in this column.

2^{-1}	2^{-2}	2^{-3}	2^{-4}	2^{-5}
0	1	1		

For the next column, compare 2^{-2} + 2^{-3} + 2^{-4} = .25 + .125 + .0625 = .4375. Since .4375 > .4165, insert a 0 in this column.

2^{-1}	2^{-2}	2^{-3}	2^{-4}	2^{-5}
0	1	1	0	

For the last column compare 2^{-2} + 2^{-3} + 2^{-5} = .25 + .125 + .03125 = .40625. Since .40625 < .4165, place a 1 in this column.

2^{-1}	2^{-2}	2^{-3}	2^{-4}	2^{-5}
0	1	1	0	1

Notice that the closest the result comes to .4165 is .40625. There is a round-off error because the answer is limited to five columns. The 80x87 single precision processor uses 24 columns to store decimal numbers. Needless to say, this produces a high level of accuracy!

FLOATING POINT DATA

The 80x87 supports three basic types of data transfer: BCD, floating point, and signed-integer. Floating point data is stored in the 80x87 in either single (4-byte) or double (8-byte) precision. Only single precision floating point operations are covered in this chapter. Single precision uses a 1-bit sign, an 8-bit exponent, and a 23-bit mantissa. This adds up to 32 bits, or 4 bytes. Floating point numbers are stored in the IEEE 754 format. A brief description of each field in the single precision structure is shown in Table 9.1.

Although single precision takes up only 4 bytes of conventional memory, the number is converted to a 10-byte representation when loaded onto the 80x87 stack. The

TABLE 9.1   IEEE 754 Format for Single Precision Numbers

Field	Number of Bits	Description
Sign	1	Determines if the number is positive or negative.
Exponent	8	Contains the power of 2 that must be multiplied times the mantissa to obtain the number.
Mantissa	23	Contains the number in fractional form.

method that MASM uses to store four-byte single precision numbers in memory is known as IEEE-754. The mantissa representation can seem a bit tricky at first. It actually stores a 24-bit number in 23 bits! This is accomplished by leaving off an implied (hidden) MSB. For example, 15 = 1111 binary. An exponential format can be represented as

1.111×2^3 (Equation 1)

Since all numbers greater than 0 will have an MSB = 1, the mantissa leaves this bit off. Also, the exponent is added to the number 127. The exponent then contains 127 + 3 = 130, or 10000010. The mantissa contains the fractional part of Equation 1, or

```
1110000 00000000 00000000
```

Shown below are two examples:

Example 9.2

Convert 22.5 to IEEE 754 format.

Solution $22.5 = 10110.1$, or 1.01101×2^4 binary. Strip off the leading 1 and represent the mantissa as

```
0111010 00000000 00000000
```
(remember the mantissa takes up 23 bits).

Now add the exponent (in this case, 4) to the base number 127 to get 131. The exponent equals 131 decimal, or 10000011 binary.

Finally, the sign bit is 0, since the number is positive. The entire number is packed in memory using 4 bytes (32 bits), as shown below:

Sign bit	Exponent	Mantissa		
Bit 32	Bits 31–24	Bits 23–0		
0	10000011	0111010	00000000	00000000

Example 9.3

Convert –.046875 to binary.

Solution

```
.046875 = 2⁻⁵ + 2⁻⁶ = .000011b
```

```
.000011b = 1.1 x 2⁻⁵
```

The stored exponent $= 127 - 5 = 122$, or 01111010b.

The mantissa $= 1000000\ 00000000\ 00000000$ (remember to leave off the leading 1). Since the number is negative, the sign bit $= 1$. The entire 32-bit field for this number is:

```
1 01111010 10000000000000000000000
```

s exponent   mantissa

```
s = sign bit
```

FLOATING POINT OPERATIONS

So far this chapter has covered the floating point stack and how the stack stores numbers. This section covers 80x87 instructions, focusing on instructions related to single precision floating point numbers. Other 80x87 instructions are covered in the *Macro Assembler Programmers Guide* that comes with MASM. The floating point instructions covered here are described in Table 9.2.

TABLE 9.2   Floating Point Instructions

Instruction	Description
FLD	Load real numbers from memory into source.
FILD	Load 16-bit integers from memory into source.
FTSP	Pop real number into memory.
FXCH	Exchange registers.
FLDZ	Push 0 into ST(0).
FLD1	Push 1 into ST(0).
FLDPI	Push π into ST(0).
FLDL2E	Push the value of $\log_2 e$ into ST(0).
FLDL2T	Push the value of $\log_2 10$ into ST(0).
FLDLG2	Push the value of $\log_{10} 2$ into ST(0).
FLDLN2	Push the value of $\log_e 2$ into ST(0).
FADD	Add the source and destination.
FSUB	Subtract the source from destination.
FSUBR	Subtract the destination from source.
FMUL	Multiply the source times the destination.
FDIV	Divide the destination by the source.
FDIVP	Divide the destination by the source. Pop the stack.
FDIVR	Divide the source by the destination.
FABS	Compute the absolute value ST(0).
FCHS	Change sign of ST(0).
FSQRT	Find the square root of ST(0).
FSCALE	Multiply ST(0)*$2^{ST(1)}$.
FPREM	Calculate the remainder of ST(0) divided by ST(1).
FPTAN	Calculate the tangent of ST(0).
FPATAN	Calculate the arctangent of ST(0).
FFREE	Empty the source.

Shown below are some operand examples, with explanations.

Instruction	Operand	Description
FADD	ST,ST(0)	Adds ST(0) to itself. Remember ST = ST(0).
FADD	ST,ST(1)	Adds ST(0) to ST(1)
FLD	Memory	Pushes memory data onto address

The first instruction adds ST(0) to itself, effectively multiplying it times 2. The second example adds ST(0) to ST(1). The third example takes a single precision number (identified in the data segment with the DD directive) and pushes it onto the 80x87 stack. Shown below is a short code fragment that shows how to push two single precision numbers from memory onto the floating point stack, add them together, and push the result back into memory.

```
.286
.287
_stack segment para stack 'stack'
dw 100h dup(?)
_stack ends

_data segment word public 'data'

X dd ?
Y dd ?
Number dd ?
_data ENDS

_text segment word public 'code'

ASSUME CS:_text,DS:_data
MAIN PROC FAR

MOV AX,_data
MOV DS,AX

FLD X
FLD Y
FADD, ST,ST(1)
FSTP Number
FWAIT

MOV AH,4CH
INT 21H
MAIN ENDP

_text ENDS
END main
```

The .286 and .287 directives at the top of the program tell MASM that the program contains code compatible with the 80286 and 80287 processors, and also to use 16-bit segments. Notice that the data segment contains a new data type in it. The **dd** data type is reserved for a single precision 4-byte floating point number. When you enter a number into a variable of type dd, the number is automatically converted to IEEE 754 format. The code segment in the above example contains the following 80x87 instructions:

```
FLD X
FLD Y
FADD, ST,ST(1)
FSTP Number
FWAIT
```

The FLD X instruction pushes X onto the floating point stack. Next, the FLD Y instruction first moves ST(0) (or the value of X) to ST(1). Then Y is pushed onto ST(0). The instruction FADD ST,ST(1) adds ST and ST(1) [it is common to refer to ST(0) as ST]. Next, the single precision sum is popped back into memory with the FSTP number instruction. FSTP stands for Floating point STore and Pop. The variable number now contains the sum. The final instruction causes the 80x87 to wait. This ensures that the 80x87 is ready for the 80x86 processor to read the next instruction. Remember, the 80x86 and 80x87 are two separate processors. FWAIT eliminates the chance that the 80x86 may continue before the 80x87 is finished; FWAIT simply pauses before returning to 80x86 code. It is necessary to do this on the 8088 and 8086 processors. It is optional on the 80286, 80386, 80486, and Pentium.

The preceding examples showed how to retrieve and store floating point numbers in memory. This is of little use if you compile the program and cannot see the results. Even if DEBUG is used, the data will appear in IEEE 755 format, and each number must be converted to decimal. For these and other reasons to be discussed later, C is used in this chapter to read in and print floating point numbers. The _asm command can be used to switch between C and assembly. This command is covered in Chapter 11. The above example can be rewritten in C as shown below:

```
void main()
{
int X;
int Y;
        _asm{
        FLD X
        FLD Y
        FADD, ST,ST(1)
        FSTP Number
        FWAIT
        }
}
```

Example 9.4

Write a program that calculates capacitive reactance, given frequency and capacitance.

Solution   The formula for capacitive reactance (Xc) is

$Xc = 1/(2\pi fC)$

where Xc is the capacitive reactance, f is the frequency in hertz, and C is the capacitance in farads.

First multiply the denominator, then take its reciprocal.

```c
#include <stdio.h>

main()
{

//Define variables

float Cap = 0.000001;      //Capacitor = 1 microfarad.
float f   =  60.0;         //Frequency = 60 hertz.
float Xc;                  //Xc is filled in by program.
float TWO=2;               //Define the number 2.

//Switch to assembly for floating point calculations.

        _asm{

        fldpi                   ;Load PI onto stack.
        fld TWO                 ;Load TWO onto stack. PI moves to ST(1).
        fmul st,st(1)           ;Multiply 2*π.
        fld Cap                 ;Load capacitance onto stack.
        fmul st,st(1)           ;Multiply 2π*C.
        fld f                   ;Load frequency onto stack.
        fmul st,st(1)           ;Multiply 2π C*f.
        fld1                    ;Push the number 1 onto stack.
        fdiv st,st(1)           ;Divide 2π Cf into 1.
        fstp Xc                 ;Store into Xc.
        FWAIT                   ;Pause.
        }
//Print result.
printf ("Xc = %f\n",Xc);
}
```

The above example could have been done completely in C, but the purpose of these examples is to demonstrate floating point in assembly. Also, assembly language is faster than C. For purposes such as real-time data acquisition using floating point, a combination of C and assembly is often the best choice.

Example 9.5

Write an 80x86 assembly language program to load a word-length integer and store it as a single precision floating point number.

Solution   The instruction FILD loads a word-length integer into memory. Remember, all numbers are stored as 10 bytes on the stack. The number can be saved into a single precision number by using FSTP. An example is shown below:

```
.286
.287
_stack segment para stack 'stack'
dw 100h dup(?)
_stack ends


_data segment word public 'data'

Xword dw 5
Xsingle dd ?

_data ENDS

_text segment word public 'code'

ASSUME CS:_text,DS:_data
MAIN PROC FAR

MOV AX,_data
MOV DS,AX

CALL WordToFloat

mov ah,4Ch
int 21h
main endp


WordToFloat PROC NEAR

fild Xword      ;Load word...Note Xword contains an integer.
fstp Xsingle    ;Save as single precision into Xsingle.
fwait           ;Pause to give 80x86 time to catch up.
ret
WordToFloat ENDP

_text ENDS
END main
```

TRIGONOMETRIC FUNCTIONS

The 80x87 can take the tangent of angles between 0 and $\pi/4$ (45°). The tangent is stored as a fraction with the numerator in ST(1) and the denominator in ST(0). You must divide

ST(1) by ST(0) to obtain the true tangent. An assembly code routine that takes the tangent of a number and performs the proper division is shown below:

```
fptan
fdiv st(1),st
```

The 80387 and up coprocessors are also capable of taking the sine (using FSIN) and cosine (using FCOS) of an angle in radians. Since these instructions are not supported in real mode, they are not covered here. How then does one take the sine or cosine of an angle? You might remember from algebra that the tangent of an angle is related to the sine and cosine through half-angle formulas, as shown below:

$$\sin\alpha = 1/[(1/\tan(\alpha/2))-(1/\tan\alpha)]$$
$$\cos\alpha = 1/[(\tan\alpha/\tan(\alpha/2))-1]$$

Of course, transcendental operations are included in most C compilers. If the header file

```
math.h
```

is included, you have access to the following functions:

```
sin()        //sine function
cos()        //cosine function
tan()        //tangent function
asin()       //arc sine function
acos()       //arc cosine function
atan()       //arc tangent function
```

Example 9.6

Write a C program that uses assembly code to take the sine of 39°. Also use the sin() function included in math.h to take the sine of 39°. Compare the results.

Solution   The program shown below uses a newly created function named sine() to use the floating point coprocessor. The conventional sin() function is also used. Note that math.h has been included.

```
#include <stdio.h>
#include <math.h>
float sine();
main()
{
float angle=39.0;          //Set angle to 39°.
angle/=57.3;               //Convert 39° to radians by dividing by 57.3, or 180/π.

float TanAngle;
float TanAngle1;

TanAngle=sine(angle);      //Use our sine function to take the sine.
TanAngle1=sin(angle);      //Use C.
printf("%f\n",TanAngle);
printf("%f\n",TanAngle1);
```

```
}

float sine(xangle)
float xangle;              //xangle = angle.
{

float xtemp,TWO=2.0;

_asm{
fld xangle               ;Load angle onto ST(0).
fld TWO                  ;Load the constant TWO onto ST(0). Angle moves to ST(1).
fdivp st(1),st           ;Divide angle by TWO to create the half angle.
fptan                    ;Compute the tangent.
fdivp st(1),st
fld1                     ;Take inverse of tangent.
fxch
fdivp st(1),st
fstp xtemp               ;Store inverse in dummy variable.
fld xangle               ;Re-load angle into ST(0).
fptan                    ;Compute the tangent.
fxch
fdivp st(1),st
fld1                     ;Take inverse of tangent.
fdivp st(1),st
fld xtemp                ;Load dummy variable.
fxch
fsubp st(1),st           ;Subtract [1/tan(α/2)]-(1/tanα).
fld1                     ;Take inverse.
fdiv st,st(1)
fstp xangle              ;Store result in xangle.
FWAIT                    ;Tell 80x86 to wait until 80x87 is finished.
}
return xangle;

}
```

Both the sine() and sin() functions return .629281 as the sine of 39°.

Example 9.7

Write a C program to convert rectangular coordinates to polar. Have the program prompt for rectangular, then use assembly to calculate the magnitude and angle.

Solution   The C program shown below converts from rectangular to polar. The equations used in the program are also described.

```
#include <stdio.h>
main()
{
float Real,Imaginary,Magnitude,Angle;
float CircleDegrees=180.0;
puts("Enter real number");
```

```
scanf("%f",&Real);
puts("Enter imaginary number");
scanf("%f",&Imaginary);

//Equation to convert rectangular to polar.
//                  2 2 1/2
//Magnitude = (x + y )
//Angle = tan-1(y/x)

        _asm{
        fld Real              ;Load Real value into ST(0).
        fmul st,st(0)         ;Square Read value.
        fld Imaginary         ;Load Imaginary value into ST(0).Real moves to ST(1).
        fmul st,st(0)         ;Square Imaginary value.
        fadd st,st(1)         ;Add squared values.
        fsqrt                 ;Find the square root of added values.
        fstp Magnitude        ;Pop ST(0) onto Magnitude variable.

        fld Imaginary         ;Load Imaginary onto ST(0).
        fld Real              ;Load Real onto ST(0).Imaginary moves to ST(1).
        fpatan                ;Find Arctan(Imaginary/Real).
        fld CircleDegrees     ;Load 360 into ST(0).
        fmul st,st(1)         ;Multiply ST(0)*ST(1).
        fldpi                 ;Load PI onto ST(0).
        fdivr st,st(1)        ;Divide PI into number.
        fld1                  ;Load number 1.0 onto ST(0).
        fdivr st,st(1)        ;Divide 1 into number.
        fstp Angle            ;Store ST(0) onto Angle.
        }

printf("%f, %f\n",Magnitude,Angle);
}
```

The above program solves the equation

$$\text{Magnitude} = \sqrt{(\text{Real}^2 + \text{Imaginary}^2)}$$
$$\text{Angle} = \text{atan}(\text{Imaginary}/\text{Real})$$

The angle is calculated in radians and is converted to degrees by multiplying it by $180/\pi$.

FLOATING POINT EMULATION

If your PC does not have a coprocessor chip, you can still process floating point instructions through an emulator supplied with the compiler. When you are ready to compile the program, enter

```
cl /FPi filename.c
```

if you are using Quick-C, enter qcl instead of cl.

CHAPTER 9 PROBLEMS

1. Convert the following binary numbers to decimal.
   a. 1011.0111
   b. 11010100.011111
   c. 10101010.11001011
2. Convert the following decimal numbers to 8-bit binary.
   a. .625
   b. 0.6928
   c. 76.159
3. Convert 36.0625 to 4-byte IEEE 754 format.
4. Decode the following 4-byte IEEE 754 number into decimal:
   ```
   10111111010000000000000000000000
   ```
5. Write a C program using 80x87 floating point instructions written in assembly that finds the cube of a number.
6. Write a C program using 80x87 floating point instructions written in assembly that takes the log of a number to the base 10.
7. Write a C program using 80x87 floating point instructions written in assembly that solves the equation for a sine wave.

   $v = Vp \sin(\theta)$

   where Vp = the peak voltage, θ = the angle, and v = an instantaneous voltage as a function of the angle.

   Have the program request Vp and θ. After receiving input for the angle and peak voltage, process the equation, and print the value of v.

CHAPTER 10

Interrupts and I/O

WHAT ARE INTERRUPTS?

Interrupts have traditionally been included in the hardware control section of the microprocessor. When a signal level is applied to a certain pin on the processor, a number is read from the data bus, which is then translated to an interrupt address, as shown in Figure 10.1.

After the INT pin is activated and the interrupt number is read from the data bus, the current CS and instruction pointer are pushed, as well as the contents of the flag register. The INT pin pushes the registers in the following order:

- Push flag register.
- Push CS register.
- Push IP.

Next, CS and IP are loaded with the interrupt address. When the interrupt is executed, the STI instruction is used to set the interrupt flag. This flag must be set to 1 before the next interrupt can be executed. When an interrupt is finished, it executes an IRET instruction. This instruction:

- Pops the offset address into the IP.
- Pops the segment address into CS.
- Pops the flag register.

Note that IRET is the same as a far RET (used with a far CALL instruction), except it also pops the flag register. Intel extended the use of interrupts in the 80x86 family to include software access. When the interrupt number is specified with the INT instruction, the interrupt is executed, just as if the processor received the number from the data bus after the INT pin was set.

FIGURE 10.1   When the interrupt (INT) pin is high, a binary number corresponding to the interrupt number is sent through the data bus to the processor.

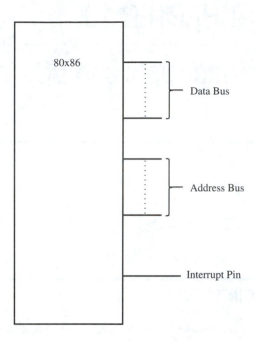

THE INTERRUPT VECTOR TABLE

Residing at the very bottom of memory is the interrupt vector table. Vectors are pointers, or a series of numbers indicating a memory address. The vector table is actually a series of far addresses specifying the segment and offset of various routines used by the BIOS and DOS. All of the interrupts are in the physical address range from 00000h to 003FFh. There are 256 available interrupts on the PC, although not all are used. The corresponding vector for each interrupt number can be calculated as shown below:

```
Interrupt Number * 4 = Vector Entry Address
```

For example, find the location of the vector entry for INT 21h.

```
21h * 4 = 84h
```

Beginning at 84h, a little endian representation of the INT 21h memory address is stored, as shown below:

84h	LSB of offset (IP)
85h	MSB of offset (IP)
86h	LSB of segment (CS)
87h	MSB of segment (CS)

A partial PC interrupt vector table is shown in Table 10.1

Although it is not recommended, interrupt vectors can be accessed by the CALL instruction. Example 10.1 demonstrates this procedure.

TABLE 10.1   Interrupt Vector Table

Interrupt	Function	Interrupt	Function
0	Divide by 0	12	Memory Ccheck
1	Single step	13	Disk I/O
2	Nonmaskable interrupt (NMI)	14	RS232 interrupt
3	Breakpoint	15	Unused
4	Overflow	16	Keyboard
5	Print screen	17	Printer
6	Reserved	18	ROM BASIC
7	Reserved	19	Boot strap load
8	Timer (18.2 times per second)	1A	Time of day
9	BIOS keyboard interrupt	1B	Control on keyboard break
A	Reserved	1C	Control on timer interrupt
B	Reserved	1D	Video initialization table pointer
C	Reserved	1E	Disk parameter table pointer
D	Reserved	1F	ASCII character generator table pointer
E	Disk interrupt	20	Return to DOS interrupt
F	Reserved	21	DOS interrupt
10	Video interrupt	33	Mouse interrupt
11	Equipment check		

Example 10.1

Use the CALL instruction to emulate INT 21h.

Solution   Since the vectors stored in the interrupt table change with different machines, the vectors must first be determined. The INT 21h is at address 84h (21*4). A disassembled listing (using the d command) for a particular PC might give:

```
0000:0084     45 1E B2 54
```

Since the segment and offset addresses are in little endian order, the segment = 54B2 and the offset = 1E45. A DEBUG routine emulating INT 21h based on these addresses is shown below.

```
311A:0100 MOV AH,2
311A:0102 MOV DL,54
311A:0104 PUSHF
311A:0105 CALL 54B2:1E45
311A:010A INT 20
311A:010C
```

Upon execution of the G command, DEBUG returns:

```
T
Program terminated normally
```

The ASCII code for T is 54, or the contents of DL.

VIDEO INT 10H

This interrupt allows you to clear the screen, as shown in Chapter 7. It can also perform other needed functions such as setting and getting the cursor position, setting the screen mode, and plotting pixels on the screen. Appendix A shows the functions of INT 10h.

Example 10.2

Use INT 10h to set the screen mode to VGA 16 colors.

Solution   From Appendix A, the following code fragment will set the screen to VGA 16 colors:

```
MOV AX, 12h        ;Set AH=0, AL=12h
INT 10h
```

Pixels can be plotted on a graphics screen with **AH = 12d, INT 10h.** The DX register must first be set to the desired row location, and CX to the column location. There are 640 horizontal (0–639), and 480 vertical (0–479) pixels on a 16-color standard VGA screen. The following code fragment plots a pixel on the center of a VGA screen. It is assumed the mode has already been set.

```
MOV DX, 240        ;480/2
MOV CX, 320        ;640/2
MOV AH,12d
INT 10h
```

Example 10.3

Use INT 10h to draw a moving diagonal line on the screen. If the line hits an edge of the screen, have it "bounce" off in the other direction.

Solution   The BOUNCE.ASM program shown below produces a moving line on the screen. You must have a VGA monitor to run this program.

BOUNCE.ASM

```
_stack segment para stack 'stack'
        dw 100h dup(?)
_stack ends

_data segment word public 'data'
        Left DW 0
        Top DW 0
        Bottom DW 479
        Right DW 639
        XX DB 1
        YY DB 1
```

```
_data ends

EXTRN kbhit:NEAR

_text segment word public 'code'
main proc near
assume cs:_text
assume ds:_data
        START:
                mov AX,_data
                mov ds,AX
                mov AX,12h
                int 10h

                ;Row 20, Column 100
                mov DX,20
                mov CX,100
        cont:

                ;Plot pixel.
                mov ah,12
                mov al,10
                int 10h

                ;Increment CX and DX for diagonal line.
                inc CX
                inc DX

                ;If the line has bounced off right edge, subtract 1 by
                 decrementing CX twice.
                cmp XX,0
                jne incx
                dec CX
                dec CX
        incx:

                ;If the line has bounced off the bottom of screen, subtract 1
                 by decrementing DX twice.
                cmp YY,0
                jne incy
                dec DX
                dec DX
        incy:

                ;Hit bottom of screen?
                cmp DX,Bottom
                jne next2
                mov YY,0
        next2:

                ;Hit right Side of screen?
```

```
        cmp CX,Right
        jne next3
        mov XX,0

next3:
        ;Hit top of screen
        cmp DX,Top
        jne next4
        mov YY,1
        next4:

        ;Hit left side of screen?
        cmp CX,Left
        jne next5
        mov XX,1
next5:

        ;Check for keyboard press.
        call kbhit
        cmp AX,27
        jne cont
        mov ah,4ch
        int 21h


main endp
_text ends
end START
```

This program first uses the data segment to define the TOP, LEFT, RIGHT, and BOTTOM positions on the screen in terms of pixels. The starting pixel is defined as row 20, column 100. The program checks for a keyboard press using **kbhit** in ASY.LIB.

THE MOUSE INTERRUPT

The mouse interrupt uses INT 33h to check for mouse movement and button presses. Appendix B shows the register contents on return from the interrupt. Note that mouse movements are returned in a relative displacement, or the distance traveled since the last INT 33h call. The program below checks mouse movement and button presses and displays them on the screen. The mouse driver must first be loaded before running this program.

MOUSEDET.ASM

```
_stack segment para stack 'stack'
        dw 100h dup(?)
_stack ends

_data segment word public 'data'
```

```
            dummy dw ?
            LeftB db 'Left Button',0
            RightB db 'Right Button',0
            Up db 'Up',0
            Down db 'Down',0
            Left db 'Left',0
            Right db 'Right',0
_data ends

EXTRN outstring:near
EXTRN kbhit:near
EXTRN crlf:near
EXTRN outdec:near

_text segment word public 'code'
main proc near
assume cs:_text
assume ds:_data
        START:
                mov AX,_data
                mov ds,AX

        cont1:
                call mouse
                call kbhit
                cmp al,27
                jne cont1
                mov ah,4ch
                int 21h
main endp

mouse proc near
                mov AX,3
                int 33h
                and BX,1
                cmp BX,1
                jne move
        cont:
                mov AX,3
                int 33h
                and BX,1
                cmp BX,1
                mov BX, offset LeftB
                call outstring
                call crlf
                je cont
        move:
                mov AX,3
                int 33h
                and BX,2
```

```
                cmp BX,2
                jne exit
        cont2:
                mov AX,3
                int 33h
                and BX,2
                cmp BX,2
                mov BX, offset RightB
                call outstring
                call crlf
                je cont2
        exit:
                ;Mouse move interrupt.
                mov AX,11
                int 33h

                ;Check for no up-down movement.
                cmp DX,0
                je cont5

                ;If DX negative, upward movement.
                mov dl,0
                and dh,10000000b
                cmp DX,0
                je cont4
                mov BX,offset Up
                call outstring
                call crlf
                jmp cont5
        cont4:
                ;Mouse movement must be down.
                mov BX,offset Down
                call outstring
                call crlf
        cont5:
                ;Check for no left-right movement.
                cmp CX,0
                je cont6
                mov cl,0

                ;If CX negative, left movement.
                and ch,10000000b
                cmp CX,0
                je cont7

                ;CX negative, move must be left.
                mov BX,offset Left
                call outstring
                call crlf
                jmp cont6
```

```
        cont7:

                ;CX positive, move must be right.
                mov BX,offset Right
                call outstring
                call crlf
        cont6:
                ret
mouse endp
_text ends
end START
```

The mouse buttons are checked with **AX = 3, INT 33h.** If a 1 is returned from this interrupt, the left button has been pressed. If a 2 is returned, the right button has been pressed. Mouse movements are detected by **AX = 11, INT 33h.** If CX is negative, the movement is left; if positive, a right movement is detected; if 0, no movement in the horizontal direction is found. If DX is negative, the movement is up; if positive, a down movement is detected; if 0, no movement in the vertical direction is found.

FILE I/O

Reading and writing ASCII files to disk is fairly easy, thanks to INT 21h. Appendix B shows the DOS interrupts necessary to create, open, read, write, and close a file. They are repeated here.

Create File Function

AH = 3Ch
DS:DX = address of ASCIIZ string
CX = file attribute
INT 21h

This interrupt exits with the carry flag = 0 if no error exits, and AX is equal to the file handle. If CF = 1, an error has occurred, and AX indicates the error code. The file attribute used on entry controls the type of file to be created, as shown in Figure 10.2.

FIGURE 10.2 File Attribute

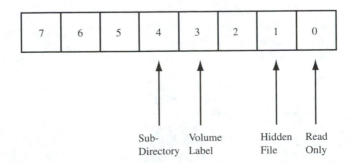

If CX = 1, a Read Only file is created.

If CX = 2, a Hidden File (one that cannot be seen by DIR) is created.

If CX = 8, a Volume Label is created. A volume label can only be written to if it does not already exist.

If CX = 16, a subdirectory is created instead of a file.

The file handle is a number assigned to the file by DOS. In this way, DOS can access the file using a number instead of an entire filename.

Open File Function

AH = 3Dh
DS:DX = address of ASCIIZ string
AL = access code
INT 21h

The Open File function uses ASCIIZ strings, just as Outstring and Getstring did in ASY.LIB. AL represents an one of three access codes, as shown in Table 10.2.

Opening a file for only reading or writing helps prevent mistakes when writing the program. It could be disastrous if you wrote to a file that you only intended to read from. Upon exiting the interrupt, the carry flag is used to indicate an error. If the carry flag = 1, an error has occurred and AX indicates the error code; if not, AX indicates the file handle.

Read File Function

AH = 3Fh
BX = file handle
DS:DX = address of ASCIIZ string
CX = number of bytes to read
INT 21h

If the carry flag = 0, AX = the number of bytes actually read. If the carry flag = 1, AX indicates an error code. The Read File function works much like midlevel file I/O in C (e.g., the read() function). The function inserts a "block" of code from the disk into the DS:DX string. The size of the block is defined by CX. If the remainder of the file is less than the size specified by CX, only the remaining portion is brought into the string. AX specifies the size of the remaining portion.

Write File Function

AH = 40h
BX = file handle
DS:DX = address of ASCIIZ string
CX = number of bytes to write
INT 21h

Table 10.2 File Access Codes

AL = 0	Read Only
AL = 1	Write Only
AL = 2	Read/Write

If the carry flag = 0, AX = the number of bytes actually read. If the carry flag = 1, AX indicates an error code. The Write File function behaves much like the write() function in C. The functions sends a "block" of code from the DS:DX string to the disk. The size of the block is defined by CX.

Close File Function

AH = 3Eh
BX = file handle
INT 21h

The Close File function closes a file specified by the file handle in BX. Once again, the carry flag = 1 if an error occurs. If an error occurs, AX = the error code.

Example 10.4

Write a program named READFILE.ASM that reads an ASCII file from disk and prints it to the screen. Have the program prompt for the filename.

Solution   The READFILE.ASM program is shown below. It uses the file functions described in this chapter.

READFILE.ASM

```
_stack segment para stack 'stack'
        dw 100h dup(?)
_stack ends

_data segment word public 'data'
        FileHandle dw ?
        Message db 0dh,0ah,'Enter Filename',0
        FileName db 50 dup(?)
        db 0
        FileBuffer db 1000 dup(?)
_data ends

EXTRN outstring:near
EXTRN getstring:near
EXTRN crlf:near

_text segment word public 'code'
main proc near
assume cs:_text
assume ds:_data

        START:
                mov AX,_data
                mov ds,AX

                ;Print 'Enter Filename' message.
                mov BX,offset Message
                call outstring
```

```
        ;Get Filename.
        mov BX,offset Filename
        call getstring
        call crlf

        ;Open File.
        mov DX,offset Filename
        mov al,0
        mov ah,3dh
        int 21h
        mov FileHandle,ax
CONT:
        mov bx,FileHandle
        ;Read in 1000 characters into FileBuffer.
        mov CX,1000
        mov DX,offset FileBuffer
        mov ah,3fh
        int 21h

        ;If no characters read in, must be at end of file. Go to exit.
        cmp AX,0
        je exit
        push BX

        ;Print to screen number of characters read in.
        mov CX,AX
        mov BX,offset FileBuffer
next:

        ;Print character from FileBuffer to screen.
        mov ah,2
        mov dl,[BX]

        ;Check for Ctrl-Z, if so jump to exit.
        cmp dl,1ah
        je exit
        int 21h

        ;Increment to next position in FileBuffer.
        inc BX
        loop next
        pop BX
        jmp cont
exit:
        mov ah,4ch
        int 21h


main endp
_text ends
end START
```

Example 10.5

Write a program named WRITFILE.ASM that writes

`The quick brown fox jumps over the lazy dog.`

contained in a string pointed to by DS:DX to disk. Have the program prompt for the file-name.

Solution   The WRITFILE.ASM program is shown below. It uses the write file function described in this chapter.

```
                          WRITFILE.ASM
_stack segment para stack 'stack'
         dw 100h dup(?)
_stack ends

         _data segment word public 'data'
         FileHandle dw ?
         Message1 db 0dh,0ah,'Enter Filename',0
         String db 0dh,0ah,'The quick brown fox jumps over the lazy dog.',13,10,0
         StringSize dw 47
         FileName db 50 dup(?)
         db 0
         FileBuffer db 80 dup(?)
_data ends

EXTRN outstring:near
EXTRN getstring:near
EXTRN crlf:near

_text segment word public 'code'
main proc near
assume cs:_text
assume ds:_data
         START:
                 mov ax,_data
                 mov ds,ax.
                 ;Print 'Enter Filename' message.
                 mov bx,offset Message1
                 call outstring

                 ;Get Filename.
                 mov bx,offset Filename
                 call getstring
                 call crlf

                 ;Open File.
                 mov dx,offset Filename
                 mov cx,0
                 mov ah,3ch
```

```
                int 21h

                ;Save FileHandle.
                mov FileHandle,ax

                ;Place FileHandle in bx.
                mov bx,FileHandle

;Set dx to String address and write to disk.
                mov dx,offset String
                mov cx,StringSize
                mov ah,40h
                int 21h
        exit:
                mov ah,4ch
                int 21h
main endp
_text ends
end START
```

INTERRUPT SERVICE ROUTINES ON THE PC

The PC uses the 8259 programmable interrupt controller chip to send interrupt requests (IRQs) to the 8088. This controller chip resides at ports 20h and 21h. IRQs 2, 3, 4, 5, 7, 10, 11, and 12 are available, although only 2–4 are frequently used. Before attempting to generate an IRQ, an inquiry should be made as to whether a particular IRQ is being used as a COM port (e.g., for a mouse). Software is available (such as Norton's Utilities) to help analyze the IRQs.

IRQS IN THE PC

IRQs 0–7 are outlined below:

IRQ0	System timer
IRQ1	Keyboard
IRQ2	I/O channel
IRQ3	COM 2
IRQ4	COM 1
IRQ5	I/O channel, available for use
IRQ6	I/O channel disk controller (do not use)
IRQ7	Parallel printer

Structure of an Interrupt Service Routine

In order to generate an interrupt on a PC, an interrupt service routine (ISR) should first be written. A simple example is shown below. The ISR should first set up the port and timer chips. The remainder of the steps are outlined below:

1. Read 8259 interrupt mask (port 21h) and enable the appropriate interrupt bit. The bit assignments are shown below:

```
        D7    D6    D5    D4    D3    D2    D1    D0
IRQ     7     6     5     4     3     2     1     0
```

A 0 in any bit position enables an IRQ, a 1 disables it. For example, if port 21h is read into AL, the instructions

```
IN AL,21H
AND AL,0EFH
OUT 21H,AL
```

are executed, IRQ4 is enabled.

2. When an interrupt is being serviced, the software will need to inform the 8259. Simply executing the instruction

```
OUT 20H,20H
```

will perform this task.

3. The ISR must be stored in memory and the PAGE 0 interrupt vector table must be set to point to the ISR. This is handled automatically by INT 21h, function 25. For this function, DS must point to the ISR code segment, DX must point to the ISR offset, and AL must point to the Page 0 address for the location of the interrupt vector. Shown below are some of the addresses for IRQs.

```
IRQ3    0A
IRQ4    0C
IRQ5    0E
IRQ7    12
```

For example, IRQ4 would set AL to 0Ch before executing INT21h, function 25. Upon termination of the program, the 8259 interrupt mask should be reset. In other words, the selected IRQ should be reset to 1. For IRQ4 this could be accomplished by ORing 10h at port 21h with a 1.

As for hardware connections, you will need to set the appropriate IRQ high to activate it, and have the hardware available to perform the task. Experiment 6 in Appendix H shows the actual implementation of an ISR.

CHAPTER 10 PROBLEMS

1. Use the CALL instruction to emulate AH=1, INT 21h. Write the routine in DEBUG.
2. Modify the BOUNCE.ASM example so that the line changes color whenever a hex number from 1 to F is entered from the keyboard.

3. Rewrite the MOUSEDET.ASM example to return cursor keys scan codes when the mouse is moved. If the left button is pressed, have a carriage return (ASCII 13) returned. If the right button is pressed, have an Escape returned (ASCII 27).

4. Write an assembly language program that allows you to type in a sequence of characters into a buffer, then save the buffer to disk in a file named TEST.DOC. Have the program check for errors in each file function.

5. Format a blank disk. Do not include a volume label on it. Write an assembly language program that prompts for a string, then writes it to the volume label on the disk. *Note:* A volume label can only be written once to a disk.

6. Write an assembly language program that reads in a disk file and prints it the screen backwards. The file created in Example 10.5 would be printed as:

```
.god yzal eht revo spmuj xof nworb kciuq ehT
```

7. Describe how an assembly language program could be written that reads port 528h when IRQ3 is activated.

CHAPTER 11

Assembly Language and C

DISASSEMBLY OF C PROGRAMS

.EXE files written in assembly language were covered in previous chapters. The disassembled .EXE files written in C look somewhat different than compiled assembly programs. C is more complex, and therefore creates larger .EXE files than assembly does. Also, C typically does more stack manipulations than a program written in assembly. You can learn a lot about the structure of C by studying the programs shown below, even if you don't compile them. Let's start with a simple program written in Microsoft C.

```
#include <stdio.h>
main()
{
int x;
x=6;
x++;
printf("x=%d\n",x);
}
```

The above program could be compiled in Microsoft C, QuickC, or Visual C++. Because Turbo-C links differently than Microsoft products do, it is not covered in this chapter. An assembly language listing can be produced with the C file by entering

```
qcl -Fa file.c
```

for QuickC, or

```
cl -Fa file.c
```

for all other Microsoft C compilers.

The equivalent assembly file will have an .ASM extension. The above program sets the integer x equal to 6, increments it, and prints the result.

Shown below is the same program's .ASM file compiled with the -Fa switch using Microsoft Visual C++. You may get slightly different results with QuickC.

```
;File ex1.c
;Line 3
_main:
        push    bp
        mov     bp,sp
        mov     ax,OFFSET L00178
        call    __aNchkstk
        push    si
        push    di
;x = fffc
;Line 4
;Line 5
        mov     WORD PTR -4[bp],OFFSET 6
;Line 6
        add      WORD PTR -4[bp],OFFSET 1
; Line 7
        push     WORD PTR -4[bp]
        mov      ax,OFFSET L00177
        push     ax
        call     _printf
        add      sp,OFFSET 4
;Line 8
;Line 8
L00175:
        pop     di
        pop     si
        mov     sp,bp
        pop     bp
        ret     OFFSET 0
```

The above .ASM file may seem strange at first. Instead of declaring

```
mov     WORD PTR [bp-4], 6
```

it uses

```
mov     WORD PTR -4[bp],OFFSET 6
```

Both of these instructions are the same. In fact, if the C .EXE file is loaded into DEBUG and unlisted with the U command, the instruction would appear as the familiar

```
mov WORD PTR [bp-4],6.
```

The OFFSET is another way of saying the same thing.

DESCRIPTION OF .ASM FILE CREATED BY C

C begins by setting up the stack. First, the existing base pointer (BP) is pushed onto the stack. Next, BP is loaded with the contents of the stack pointer (SP). Then, a subroutine (in this case, **CALL _aNchkstk** is called to set up the stack. This CALL routine also checks to ensure there is enough room on the stack for all of the variables.

AX is then loaded with the size of all variables declared in the program, plus the return address. Since the only variable is an integer (2 bytes), AX = the integer plus the return address, or AX = 4. Next, the SI and DI registers are pushed. Then, the stack address of x is shown as the commented line x = fffc.

Next comes the program. You might expect the assembly program to follow the C program, which sets the variable x equal to 6. The variable x could be translated as a register, but it isn't. Remember that the **CALL _aNchkstk** routine is used to reserve variables on the stack. All variables in C are on the stack. To reference a variable, C uses the BP pointer. The integer x is 4 bytes up on the stack (at BP–4). *Note:* Some C compilers place the x integer 2 bytes up on the stack. For the examples that follow, it is assumed that x is four bytes into the stack. The instruction:

```
mov WORD PTR -4[bp],OFFSET 6
```

is equivalent to:

```
x=6;
```

Next, the instruction

```
add WORD PTR -4[bp],OFFSET 1
```

is equivalent to:

```
x++;
```

You may have thought C would use something like:

```
inc WORD PTR -4[bp],OFFSET 1
```

for x++, because x++ seems like it would be tied in with the INC instruction. Instead, C uses the ADD instruction. What if x++ is changed to x = x + 1 ? The result is shown below:

```
/* C version*/

#include <stdio.h>
main()
{
int x;
x=6;
x=x+1;
printf("x=%d\n",x);
}

;.ASM version of C file
;Line 3
_main:
        push    bp
        mov     bp,sp
        mov     ax,OFFSET L00178
        call    __aNchkstk
        push    si
```

```
          push    di
;x = fffc
;Line 4
;Line 5
          mov     WORD PTR -4[bp],OFFSET 6
;Line 6
          mov     ax,WORD PTR -4[bp]
          add     ax,OFFSET 1
          mov     WORD PTR -4[bp],ax
;Line 7
          push    WORD PTR -4[bp]
          mov     ax,OFFSET L00177
          push    ax
          call    _printf
          add     sp,OFFSET 4
;Line 8
;Line 8
L00175:
          pop     di
          pop     si
          mov     sp,bp
          pop     bp
          ret     OFFSET 0
```

This time C used:

```
mov     ax,WORD PTR -4[bp]
add     ax,OFFSET 1
```

instead of:

```
add     WORD PTR -4[bp],OFFSET 1
```

The end result is that even though **x++** is not translated to an INC assembly instruction, less code is used for **x++** than **x = x + 1.** Finally, the instructions

```
mov     ax,OFFSET L00177
push    ax
call    _printf
add     sp,OFFSET 4
```

are equivalent to the printf instruction. Obviously, the CALL and MOV AX statements take care of printing information to the screen. The ADD SP is inserted to recover from the PUSH instruction appearing immediately before the printf routine.

What if there are two integers defined in C? A disassembled example is shown below:

Example 11.1

Disassemble a C program that contains two integers. Locate the two integers in the disassembled file.

Solution

```c
/*C Program*/
#include <stdio.h>
main()
{
int x,y;
x=5;
y=6;
printf("x=%d\n, y=%d\n",x,y);
}
```

```asm
;.ASM version of C file
;Line 3
_main:
        push    bp
        mov     bp,sp
        mov     ax,OFFSET L00179
        call    __aNchkstk
        push    si
        push    di
;y = fffc
;x = fffa
;Line 4
;Line 5
        mov     WORD PTR -6[bp],OFFSET 5
;Line 6
        mov     WORD PTR -4[bp],OFFSET 6
;Line 7
        push    WORD PTR -4[bp]
        push    WORD PTR -6[bp]
        mov     ax,OFFSET L00178
        push    ax
        call    _printf
        add     sp,OFFSET 6
;Line 8
;Line 8
L00175:
        pop     di
        pop     si
        mov     sp,bp
        pop     bp
        ret     OFFSET 0
```

Note that BP–4 references the integer **y,** and BP-6 references the integer **x.** The statement:

```asm
mov     WORD PTR -6[bp],OFFSET 5
```

sets x equal to 5, and the statement

```asm
mov     WORD PTR -4[bp],OFFSET 6
```

sets y equal to 6.

Example 11.2

Translate a C program containing a **for** loop.

Solution   Shown below is a C program with a for loop translated into assembly:

```
/*C Program*/
#include <stdio.h>
main()
{
int x;
for(x=1;x<=5;x++)
printf("x=%d\n",x);
}
```

```
;.ASM version of C file
;Line 3
_main:
        push    bp
        mov     bp,sp
        mov     ax,OFFSET L00182
        call    __aNchkstk
        push    si
        push    di
;x = fffc
;Line 4
;Line 5
        mov     WORD PTR -4[bp],OFFSET 1
        jmp     L00180
L00177:
;Line 6
        push    WORD PTR -4[bp]
        mov     ax,OFFSET L00181
        push    ax
        call    _printf
        add     sp,OFFSET 4
L00178:
        add     WORD PTR -4[bp],OFFSET 1
L00180:
        cmp     WORD PTR -4[bp],OFFSET 5
        jle     L00177
L00179:
;Line 7
L00175:
        pop     di
        pop     si
        mov     sp,bp
        pop     bp
        ret     OFFSET 0
```

The offset addresses and machine op-codes are included in the DEBUG example because of the jump statements. The C loop

```
for(x=1;x<=5;x++)
```

begins by setting x equal to 1. The assembly equivalent occurs at address 001B as:

```
mov     WORD PTR -4[bp],OFFSET 1
```

The x++ statement in the for loop is translated at address 0030 as:

```
add     WORD PTR -4[bp],OFFSET 1
```

Finally, the x<=5 section of the for loop is translated as:

```
cmp     WORD PTR -4[bp],OFFSET 5
jle     L00177
```

INTERFACING C WITH ASSEMBLY LANGUAGE

At first it may seem that there is no need to use assembly language in C, because C emulates so much of what assembly does. Even interrupts are used in C. There are a few advanced topics that C cannot do and that must be done in assembly. A sample is listed below:

- Assessing the stack or base pointer registers.
- Setting some segment registers.
- Performing PUSH and POP operations (particularly the flag register).
- Performing real-time operations where speed is important. This could be reading and writing to an I/O port or writing graphics to the screen.

These topics become important when writing advanced operations such as terminate and stay resident (TSR) programs, device drivers, and interrupt service routines.

IN-LINE ASSEMBLY

In-line assembly is accomplished through the _asm command. It was covered briefly in Chapter 9. You can use _asm as a one-line command:

```
_asm mov dl,4
```

or as a multiline function:

```
_asm{
mov ah,2
mov dl,2
int 21h
}
```

By the way, this small routine prints a happy face (ASCII 2) to the screen. If you are using Borland or Turbo-C, enter asm instead of _asm. Suppose you want to obtain the current address of the base of the stack. The stack pointer will provide this information. The program below returns **sp** into a variable called StackPointer.

```
#include <stdio.h>
void main()
{
unsigned StackPointer;
_asm
{
        mov StackPointer,sp
}
        printf("StackPointer = %u",StackPointer);

}
```

The small program hints at the true power of in-line assembly. You can create variables in C (such as StackPointer) and use these variables in the _asm function with 80x86 registers.

LINKING ASSEMBLY LANGUAGE PROGRAMS WITH C

Separate assembly language functions can be created and linked with C. This allows for modular programs that are easier to understand. Variables are passed to the assembly function through a temporary stack. The last variable in the list is the first that is popped. The first variable is at location BP+4 (below this is the offset of the return address). The second integer variable is at BP+6, the third at BP+8, etc. While in a function called from C, you can obtain values from the stack, but cannot alter values in it. This is because the stack is only used for passing information to the function. Upon exiting, the function destroys the stack. See Chapter 14 for more information on temporary stacks.

Character variables are returned in AL. Integer variables are returned in AX, and long variables are returned in AX and DX. Shown below is a simple program that complements (inverts) a number. The complement function must be compiled to an .OBJ file with MASM.

COMP.C

```
/*C Program*/
main()
{
/* c = 55 hex */
                char c=0x55;
                c=complement(c);
                printf("The complement of 55 hex is %x",c);
}
```

COMPLMT.ASM

```
;MASM subroutine
_text segment word public 'code'
_complement proc near
PUBLIC _complement
assume cs:_text
      push bp
      mov bp,sp
      mov ax,[bp+4]
      xor ax,0FFFFh
      pop bp
      ret
_complement endp
_text ends
end
```

To compile the above functions using C and MASM, do the following: For the C code, assuming the file is named comp.c and the compiler is QuickC, enter the following:

```
qcl -c comp.c
```

If Microsoft C is used, compile the program as shown below.

```
cl -c comp.c
```

This -c operation compiles the program to an .OBJ file, but not an .EXE file. For the assembly code, assume it is called COMPLMT.ASM. Enter

```
masm complmt.asm
```

Now place both .OBJ files in the C directory and enter

```
link comp+complmt
```

Assuming no errors, the COMP.EXE file is now produced. Enter

```
COMP
```

to test the program. The output should be the inverse of 55h, or AAh.

BUILDING TERMINATE AND STAY RESIDENT PROGRAMS IN MICROSOFT C

Terminate and stay resident (TSR) programs are loaded like normal programs, but remain resident in memory after returning to DOS. They are event-triggered, meaning they run when a predefined condition occurs, usually a certain key combination or a time on the clock. Creating a TSR program in C is no easy task. Fortunately, Microsoft C provides some tools that are a great help. Among these are such functions as _dos_getvect(), _dos_setvect(), _chain_intr(), and _asm{}. When creating a function that remains resident, certain rules must be adhered to:

• If the TSR function uses the keyboard interrupt to trigger it, the function itself should not use the interrupt, because it will call itself. Other techniques are available for accessing the keyboard.

- The TSR should not interrupt a disk operation.
- The program should restore the code used by the keyboard interrupt upon returning to DOS.

A TSR utility program can be created from the following steps:

1. Obtain the current values of the stack segment and stack pointer. This can be done in assembly language using the _asm statement.
2. Assuming a keyboard hot key is used to activate the TSR, get the address of the code that currently accesses keyboard INT 9. In the **key.c** example below, the address is returned in OldInt.
3. Set INT 9 to point to your TSR function.
4. Set the zero divide interrupt. This is accomplished using the _aintdiv function (a standard zero divide interrupt handler in Microsoft C).
5. Exit the program, keeping the TSR portion reserved in memory. This is accomplished using the _doskeep function.

Now that INT9 is transferred to your program, you need to write the code to properly handle INT 9, and also run your program. To do this, have your TSR function perform the following:

6. Provide some sort of check to be certain that an INT 9 has not been generated while you are inside the routine. In the key.c program below, InsideInt is set to 1 if you are currently in the program; otherwise, it is 0. An if statement is used to only allow entry to the TSR if a copy of it is not presently running.
7. Check for a hot key press. The status of the ALT, CAPS, CTRL, and SHIFT keys is contained in the byte at segment 40h, offset 17h. This can be used to determine if one of these keys have been pressed. Table 11.1 shows the key combinations for the hot keys.
8. If you are using the keyboard in your INT routine, call the original INT 9 from your TSR routine.

When inside the TSR function, there are certain things that must not be done. First of all, since INT 9 has been corrupted, you cannot use it to intercept keystrokes. Unfortunately, all of the common C functions such as **scanf** and **getc** use this interrupt. Since the

TABLE 11.1   Bit Combinations
for TSR Hot Keys

Key Name	Bit Number
INS	7
CAPS LOCK	6
NUM LOCK	5
SCRL LOCK	4
ALT	3
CTRL	2
LEFT SHIFT	1
RIGHT SHIFT	0

TABLE 11.2   Single Key Scancodes

Key	Scancode	Key	Scancode	Key	Scancode
Escape	1	e	18	j	36
~	41	r	19	k	37
1	2	t	20	l	38
2	3	y	21	;	39
3	4	u	22	'	40
4	5	i	23	Enter	28
5	6	o	24	z	44
6	7	p	25	x	45
7	8	[	26	c	46
8	9	]	27	v	47
9	10	\	43	b	48
0	11	a	30	n	49
-	12	s	31	m	50
=	13	d	32	,	51
BackSpace	14	f	33	.	52
Tab	15	g	34	/	53
q	16	h	35	Space	57
w	17				

keyboard is tied directly to port 60h, each keystroke can be intercepted by reading in this port. This port returns a scancode (not an ASCII code) when the key is pressed. Scancodes were first covered in Table 6.1. The scancode is a number assigned to the key by the keyboard. It is this number (not the ASCII code) that is sent from the keyboard. Table 11.2 shows some common scancodes other than those shown in Table 6.1.

Note that the scancodes are more aligned with the position of the key on the keyboard than the position of the letter in the alphabet. In the **key.c** example listed below, a check is made to see if the ALT and Left Shift keys are pressed. This can be accomplished by using GET_MEM to obtain the value of segment 40h, offset 17h, masking out the ALT and Left Shift keys, and determining if they have been pressed. The binary combination for the shift keys is 00001010, or decimal 10 (note that a 1 is inserted for the desired hot key). The key.c program scrambles the text screen when the hot keys are pressed. To restore the screen, press Escape. Of course you will need to compile this program in DOS.

KEY.C

```
#pragma check_stack(off)
#include <dos.h>
#include <time.h>
#include <stdio.h>
#include <conio.h>
#include <stdlib.h>

#define GET_MEM(seg,off) (*(char far *)((long)(seg)<<16|(off)))
#define PUT_MEM(seg,off,byte) GET_MEM(seg,off)=byte
#define ProgramSize 2080
```

```c
static void (interrupt far *OldInt)(void);
static void interrupt far NewInt(void);
extern void (interrupt far *_aintdiv)(void);
extern void key(void);
int ProgramStackSegment,ProgramStackPointer;
int InterruptStackSegment,InterruptStackPointer;
unsigned v;
int x;
void main()
{

        /*Save Stack Pointer and Stack Segment*/
        _asm{
        mov ProgramStackPointer,sp
        mov ProgramStackSegment,ss
}

/*Get old value of Int 9*/

OldInt=_dos_getvect(9);

/*Set New value of INT 9 to point to our interupt handling routine*/

_dos_setvect(9, NewInt);
_dos_setvect(0, _aintdiv);

/*Keep enough memory reserved for program*/

_dos_keep(0, ProgramSize);
}

void interrupt far NewInt()
{
_asm CLI

/*Check for hot key press*/

if((GET_MEM(0x40,0x17)&10)==10){

_asm{

/*Save current stack*/
mov InterruptStackSegment,ss
mov InterruptStackPointer,sp

/*Set stack to interrupt*/

mov ss,ProgramStackSegment
mov sp,ProgramStackPointer

}
```

```
/*Call your function.You can replace key() with your own function here*/
key();

_asm{

/*Restore stack segment*/

mov ss,InterruptStackSegment;
mov sp,InterruptStackPointer;

}

}

_chain_intr(OldInt);
_asm STI

}
char p[2000];

void key()
{
int x,y,b;
int a;
a=0;

/*Save original text screen*/

for(x=0;x<=25*80*2;x+=2)
p[a++]=GET_MEM(0xb800,x);

/*Scramble screen until escape is pressed*/
while(1)
{
        y=rand()/16;
        y*=2;
        a=GET_MEM(0xb800,y);
        y=rand()/16;
        y*=2;
        PUT_MEM(0xb800,y,a);
        for (y=0;y<=6500;y++);
        /*Read keyboard port*/
        b=inp(0x60);

        /*Transfer control to original interrupt 9*/
        (*OldInt)();

        /*Clear keyboard buffer*/
        PUT_MEM(0,0x41a,GET_MEM(0,0x41c));

        /*Check for Escape key*/
```

```
        if(b==1) break;
        }

a=0;
/*Restore original text screen*/

for(x=0;x<=25*80*2;x+=2)
PUT_MEM(0xb800,x,p[a++]);


}
```

You can compile this program by entering:

```
CL KEY.C
```

Try this program on a text screen. The original screen is saved when the hot keys are pressed and restored when the Escape key is pressed. Suppose you have information on your computer that you don't want anyone else to see, and would rather not turn the computer off and reload the software. With this TSR, you can scramble the screen with the touch of the hot keys, making it impossible for anyone to see what was there. When you return, simply press Escape and return to what you were doing. Unfortunately, this program can only scramble a text screen. If you are in a graphics screen (such as Microsoft Windows) nothing will happen when the hot keys are pressed. A sample screen before and after the screen is scrambled is shown in Figure 11.1.

The first line of KEY.C

```
#pragma check_stack(off)
```

turns off stack checking when compiling. This is needed because some of the interrupt routines used later, although perfectly functional, alter the stack in a manner that is unfamilar to the C compiler.

The next two #define statements allow you to read and write anywhere in memory by converting segments and offsets to physical addresses. The #define macros are shown below:

```
#define GET_MEM(seg,off) (*(char far *) ( (long) (seg)<<16 |(off)) )
#define PUT_MEM(seg,off,byte) GET_MEM(seg,off)=byte
```

As can be seen from the GET_MEM macro, the segment is shifted left 16 bits (remember a long is 32 bits, which is another way of saying 2 words). It is then OR'd with the offset (this has the same effect as adding the offset to the shifted segment). The segment is always in the upper word and the offset in the lower, as shown below:

	Upper 16 bits	Lower 16 bits
Segment	Seg value	0
Offset	0	Off value
Segment OR'd with offset	Seg value	Off value

It may seem strange to store a segment and offset in this manner. Remember, in assembly the segment is multiplied by 10h and added to the offset. In C, the method shown above must be used. The compiler takes care of determining the correct physical address

FIGURE 11.1   KEY.C Program Description

```
[BIN]        [WIN]        [QD5]        [CDSTUFF]     [J]
[CAD]        [JUNK]       [TXT]        [MS-SETUP.T]  [ACCESS]
[RECT]       [PBRUSH]     [SWTDEMOS]   [TC]          [FFT]
[QDOS]       [MSOFFICE]   [WINWORD]    [TT_TOOLS]    W.BAK
DOS.BAT      [VB.WIN]     [EXCEL]      [WRITE]       COMMAND.COM
WORD.BAT     WORD.BAK     JUNK1        A.BAT         ADDRESS.DAT
ATBRDS.CFG   AUTO00.OLD   AUTOEXEC.D   AUTOEXEC.DOS  AUTOEXEC.OLD
AUTOEXEC.ORC AUTOEXEC.BAK C.BAT        CONFIG.D      CONFIG.BAK
CONFIG.ORC   CONFIG.S     CONFIG.SYS   CONFIG.WIN    CONVERT.BAS
D.BAT        DISKPARK.COM DO_CACHE.EXE EPH.DWG       FILELIST.EXE
FS.BAK       QDOS.LOG     MARS128.SYS  MARSTEK.SYS   MASM.BAT
MOUSE.BAT    NO_CACHE.EXE NUM.COM      ORC.BAT       [COASTER]
SCAN.BAT     TC.BAT       TEMPLATE.SCH TOM.SCH       TSR.EXE
AUTOEXEC.B   WINDOWS.BAT  WP.BAT       FILE.NAM      AUTOEXEC.000
EMM386.EXE   HIMEM.SYS    AUTOEXEC.ACE CONFIG.ACE    ACES.BAT
PAPER        LAB6         CLASS        AUTOEXEC.NEW  READ.ME
FS.BAT       AUTOEXEC.JNK CONFIG.JNK   EPH           CONFIG.DOS
SMARTDRV.EXE AUTOEXEC.BAT AUTOEXEC.WIN [VB]          KEY.EXE
VB.BAT       AUTOEXEC.BAT R.BAT        [A86]         [ESI]
ELEM.MAK     W.BAT
    112 file(s)      401,612 bytes
                13,053,952 bytes free


C:\>
```

Scrambled Screen After Hot Key is Activated

```
[BIN   S  C  [WTN]       RE [MD5] S   E  L[ DSTUF ]   K[   O
[CA FF     B  JUNK] U   A . [TL ]  A    M  [M  ETUA ] . [ CE S ] M E  A
[B K ]        [PBRUSH] [ E  J [SW DE OS]E A   ] C]  X   TS N.FFT]K
FQDO          MSOF IPE]   [[IMWORD]  E  TT EOOLSO     W B K       .
DOS.BA       [VB. IN]  S  RF [VXDEU]C    [ RXN    b   OMEA D.COM
 O,D  T  S   WOR .BAK  C   VBNK1 TE  C D  AAA T D      ADD EBK.D  C
AT RDS CAG  Q  A.KO0]E LDWM    FTO XEC TG  X AU OEXR .D U S   U ] XU . L  B
A TOEXE .OSC   A .EX C]BAA  . VAAT.   E  CONII..D    AANFIGC    B
CONFIG.YRB    CODKLG.SV TE  EONFI . Y   E C N MG. IM   OUS NVNR  TS L
D.BA  9]    TISKPA K.COM  EDOMC CHE. XE  EDH.DW        EE]KTsEXX
FSABA       QDOS.L G    MAES1 8. Y[C  MASST[KSS S    ([ .BAT
 O  E.Q A   y  NO ACHE C E    UMDCO    AED .O J.    E   [C ASTER]
SCAN BA    DA  C.CAT    T   TEMP A E.S H D TOM.S[H    D TSRTEXE   O
AU  XDC.B   WWRN WSDB T   W .B S      8F]L VNAMM A D  ATT EXEC.0FE[
 B MX  EXE   HIME . .S  E  U .X C.A E   ONF GG .   ] A  S.B T      C
PAPER    B LAB6     E  CLA   A  E AUTOEX .N W ] REe   S
S. AT  A D   AU  E EK.    TO  IL.JNK    EPi     N]C QNIG. S
 bRTDRVHTXE,  AUTOEEET.OAT   A TOU EC..IN  ][V CT.   A  TD AE .GNE A
VB.BATT   A   AUMEOXEC FAT   . ATL  T   [ ]      T [ESIA
EL M MtK9   IW BE.  C     R   . ME  S B   R JX E
 D  9  12A CleJs)  . 491 612 byt sS    [  .    B D      A K
 O   IR  T      13,053,9] b tes  ee A     S
     .            M  N SN .        S   M    0   6
  A  .            U  M DC   D          B  . B
```

from the 32-bit word. This word is cast as a far character pointer. The first * at the left obtains the value of the pointer, not the address. The PUT_MEM command simply places the value of "byte" into the memory position being pointed to by seg and off.

The interrupt keyword used in:

```
static void (interrupt far *OldInt)(void);
static void interrupt far NewInt(void);
extern void (interrupt far *_aintdiv)(void);
```

indicates that the following function is an interrupt handler. The compiler treats these functions like an interrupt. C pushes all registers, including the flag register, before calling the function. Upon exiting, C issues an IRET instead of a RET.

Note that OldInt is treated as a far pointer. Because it is a pointer, interrupt vectors can be stored in it. NewInt, rather than being a pointer, is an actual function used in the program.

Upon entering function main(), the stack pointer and stack segment are saved. Next, the OldInt pointer is loaded with the contents of INT 9 by the statement:

```
OldInt = _dos_getvect(9);
```

Next, the _dos_setvect function is used to store the NewInt function address into the INT 9 position at the bottom of memory using the instruction:

```
_dos_setvect(9,NewInt);
```

Because C has its own zero divide handling routine (called aintdiv), it is also necessary to store the address of the routine at INT 0 (the divide by zero interrupt). You can do this with:

```
_dos_setvect(0,_aintdiv)
```

Now the program is stored in memory and exited to DOS. This is done with the _dos_keep function, as shown below.

```
_dos_keep(0,ProgramSize);
```

ProgramSize is a number representing the length of the program in paragraphs. Remember from Chapter 1 that a paragraph is 16 bytes. In KEY.C, ProgramSize is declared as 2080 paragraphs (see the #define statement). This would reserve an area of memory equal to 2080*16, or 33280 bytes, which is more than enough for the program. Calculating the exact memory requirement involves subtracting the top of the stack from the bottom of the program segment prefix (this is covered in Chapter 12). Since this method does not always work, it is best to reserve too much memory than not enough.

At this point, the program is saved in memory and ready to execute. Whenever a key is pressed, INT 9 is transferred to the NewInt function. This function first clears the interrupt flag (remember CLI from Chapter 10?). This prevents another interrupt from occurring while the program is in this one. Next, get the data from segment 40, offset 17 and AND it with 10 decimal, or 1010 binary. This address contains the keyboard flag information. Using Table 11.1, it can be seen that the AND operation is masking the ALT and Left Shift keys. ALT-Left Shift will be the hot keys used to allow entry into the NewInt function.

Once in the function, the program saves the interrupt's stack segment and pointer, and loads the program's stack segment and pointer into SP and SS, respectively. Next, the key() function is called, which contains the program that scrambles the screen. After exiting the key() function, the interrupt stack segment and pointer are restored.

As stated above, the key() function scrambles the screen. The function first saves the screen in a character array by using a FOR loop. Note that the text screen segment starts at B800h. The array must be large enough to store 25 lines by 80 columns of text. Note that the FOR loop skips over every other byte. This is because intermediate bytes contain the color attributes. After the FOR loop, an infinite WHILE loop is created with the

```
while(1)
```

statement.

Next, the rand() function and GET_MEM are used to obtain a number from a random offset (position) on the screen. This character is stored in a. The character a is then inserted into another random screen position using PUT_MEM.

Now keyboard port 60h is read into variable b by using the inp (in port) C function. After reading the port, the original keyboard INT 9 is called to properly store the entry in the keyboard buffer. Next, clear the keyboard buffer, since you will not want to see multiple keystrokes after exiting the TSR.

Next b is compared with 1. Remember from Table 11.2 that this is the scancode for the Escape key. If the Escape key is pressed, the program exits the WHILE loop. After exiting, the screen is restored with the original characters.

The key() function can be replaced with one of your own. You could trap for a more difficult key combination than Escape to ensure that no one can return to your original screen by accidentally pressing the Escape key. The key function reads in port 60h and checks for a 1. Simply change the if statement to check for a different scancode to change the key.

Example 11.3

Write a TSR to plug the keyboard buffer with

```
DIR *.EXE/w
```

Solution   The solution is shown below:

```
                          KEYPOKE.C
#pragma check_stack(off)
#include <dos.h>
#include <time.h>
#include <stdio.h>
#include <conio.h>
#include <stdlib.h>

#define GET_MEM(seg,off)  (*(char far *)((long)(seg)<<16|(off)))
#define PUT_MEM(seg,off,byte)  GET_MEM(seg,off)=byte
#define ProgramSize 2080
```

```
static void (interrupt far *OldInt)(void);
static void interrupt far NewInt(void);
extern void (interrupt far *_aintdiv)(void);
extern void keypoke(void);
int ProgramStackSegment,ProgramStackPointer;
int InterruptStackSegment,InterruptStackPointer;
unsigned v;
int x;
void main()
{

_asm{
        mov ProgramStackPointer,sp
        mov ProgramStackSegment,ss
}
OldInt = _dos_getvect(9);

_dos_setvect(9, NewInt);
_dos_setvect(0, _aintdiv);
_dos_keep(0, ProgramSize);
}

void interrupt far NewInt()
{

if(InsideInt==0){
                /*Check for Left and Right Shift key press*/
                if((GET_MEM(0x40,0x17)&3)==3){
                _asm CLI
                _asm    {
                        mov InterruptStackSegment,ss
                        mov InterruptStackPointer,sp
                        mov ss,ProgramStackSegment
                        mov sp,ProgramStackPointer
                        }

                keypoke();
                _asm    {
                        mov ss,InterruptStackSegment;
                        mov sp,InterruptStackPointer;
                        }

                }
        _asm STI
        _chain_intr(OldInt);
else
        InsideInt—;
        }

#include <stdio.h>
#include <string.h>
```

```
/*Store keystrokes here*/
char k[]="dir *.exe/w\r";
void keypoke()
{
int x;
int BufferSize;

/*Size of buffer = 2 times the number of keystrokes*/
BufferSize=strlen(k)*2;
for(x=1;x<=BufferSize;x+=2)
PUT_MEM(0,0x41D+x,k[x/2]);

/*Buffer Tail = Buffer Head + Buffer Size*/
PUT_MEM(0, 0x41C, 0x1E + BufferSize);

/*Buffer Head*/
PUT_MEM(0, 0x41A, 0x1E);

/*Call Old Interrupt 9*/
(*OldInt)();
}
```

This program prints

```
dir *.exe/w
```

whenever the Left and Right shift keys are pressed. The k[] array at the top of the key-poke() function can be modified to include any keys you like. Using the scan codes in Table 11.2, you can even include function keys.

Example 11.4

Write a TSR that produces an alarm at a preset time.

Solution   In order to produce an alarm at a specific time, you will have to point to the clock interrupt rather than INT 9 (the keyboard interrupt). The clock interrupt number is 8. A specific time in ticks since midnight is obtained from segment 0, offset 46Ch in the form of a long integer. Once in the routine, the alarm sounds by turning on the speaker at a specific frequency. A short delay loop is used to keep the alarm on. The program is shown below:

ALARMCLK.C

```
#pragma check_stack(off)
#include <dos.h>
#include <time.h>
#include <stdio.h>
#include <conio.h>
#include <stdlib.h>

#define GET_MEM(seg,off) (*(char far *)((long)(seg)<<16|(off)))
#define PUT_MEM(seg,off,byte) GET_MEM(seg,off)=byte
```

```c
#define GET_MEM_LONG(seg,off) (*(long far *)((long)(seg)<<16|(off)))


#define ProgramSize 2080

static void (interrupt far *OldInt)(void);
static void interrupt far NewInt(void);
extern void (interrupt far *_aintdiv)(void);
extern void key(void);
int ProgramStackSegment,ProgramStackPointer;
int InterruptStackSegment,InterruptStackPointer;

unsigned v;
int x;
void main()
{

/*Save Stack Pointer and Stack Segment*/
_asm{
        mov ProgramStackPointer,sp
        mov ProgramStackSegment,ss
}

/*Get old value of Int 9*/
        OldInt = _dos_getvect(0x8);

/*Set New value of INT 9 to point to our interrupt handling routine*/
        _dos_setvect(0x8, NewInt);
        _dos_setvect(0, _aintdiv);

/*Keep enough memory reserved for program*/
        _dos_keep(0, ProgramSize);
}

void interrupt far NewInt()
{

_asm cli

/*Check for time*/
        if((long)((GET_MEM_LONG(0,0x46c)))==327600)

        /*Time set for 5 am, or 5 hours*3600 seconds/18.2 ticks per second*/
        {
        _asm      {

                /*Save current stack*/
                mov InterruptStackSegment,ss
                mov InterruptStackPointer,sp
```

```
                        /*Set stack to interrupt*/
                        mov ss,ProgramStackSegment
                        mov sp,ProgramStackPointer
                        }

/*Call your function.You can replace key() with your own function here*/
        alarm();
        _asm{

/*Restore stack segment*/
        mov ss,InterruptStackSegment;
        mov sp,InterruptStackPointer;


        }
}
_asm sti
_chain_intr(OldInt);


}


void alarm()
{
        int x;
        _asm{
                mov al,0B6h
                out 43h,al
                mov al,0cch
                out 42h,al
                mov al,04ch
                out 42h,al
                in al,61h
                and al,0fch
                or al,3
                out 61h,al
                mov ax,60
                push cx
                push bx
                mov bx,100
                ag1:
                mov cx,65535
                again:loop again
                dec bx
                cmp bx,0
                jg ag1
                pop bx
                pop cx
                in al,61h
```

```
        and al,0fch
        out 61h,al
    }

}
```

Using the examples above and a little practice, you can write your own TSR routines.

CHAPTER 11 PROBLEMS

1. Disassemble the program shown below and load it into DEBUG. Analyze each line of the assembly listing.

```
#include <stdio.h>
main()
{
int x;
x=1;
        while (x<=5)
        {
        x++;
        printf("x=%d\n",x);
        }

}
```

2. Write an in-line assembly program to store the message:

   C and assembly

   in a C string and send it to the screen using INT 21h. Have the program declare the string outside of main(), as shown below:

```
char string[] = "C and assembly"
void main()
```

3. Repeat problem 2, but send the message to the printer using INT 21h. (See Chapter 3 for information on sending characters to the printer.)
4. Write an external assembly language function that increments a number sent to it via the C language.
5. Write a TSR in C that will change the current text screen to a blue background with white letters whenever Alt-Ctrl is pressed.
6. Write a TSR that checks to see if the printer is turned on (use the on-line indicator) whenever Alt-S is pressed. If it is not on, sound a beep to the speaker.
7. Revise the ALARMCLK.C program to print a preset time to the screen at that precise time. You will need to write directly to screen memory.

CHAPTER 12

BIOS, DOS, COMMAND.COM, and the Program Segment Prefix

THE PC MEMORY MAP

A memory map is a sequential list of addresses and the functions assigned to them. The PC memory map is composed of six major areas. Each area has its own special purpose in the operation of the PC. The six areas are the interrupt vector table, BIOS routines, DOS program and data area, screen area, disk control area, and the ROM BIOS itself. The memory locations for the six areas are shown below:

000–3ffh	Interrupt vector area
400–6FF	BIOS routines
700–9FFFF	DOS program and data area
A0000–C0000	Screen area
C0000–D0000	Disk control area
F0000–FFFFF	System ROM BIOS

The DOS program and data area (700–9FFF) can be further divided into the following variable-length sections.

DOS interrupt area
DOS buffers
Device drivers
Resident part of COMMAND.COM
Terminate and stay resident programs
Application program area
Transient part of COMMAND.COM

Note that COMMAND.COM is split into a resident and transient part. The transient part contains such DOS directives as DIR and COPY. It can be written over by an application program. Each time a program terminates, the transient part of COMMAND.COM is again loaded from disk. The resident part of COMMAND.COM is responsible for restoring

DOS and reloading the transient part of COMMAND.COM when a program terminates, and handling system errors when a program is running.

Terminate and stay resident programs are loaded from disk and have either a .COM or an .EXE extension. Upon termination, they remain resident in memory and are reactivated by interrupts. Examples of TSR programs are discussed in Chapter 11. Device drivers are used by DOS to access external I/O. For example, a laser printer may have a device driver located in this section of memory.

A more detailed memory map is shown in Appendix C. Here the BIOS information about the PC is contained in the BIOS routine area between 400 and 6FF hex. Device drivers, buffers, and file control entries (if in low memory) reside in the program and data area between 4DB9 and 53ED. The resident portion of COMMAND.COM is located between 53F0 and 5FCF.

Example 12.1

Assume the double word beginning at address 46C = CD 06 09 00. As noted in Appendix C, this address gives the current time in ticks. Calculate the current time using the data given above.

Solution   Since data is stored in little endian notation, the hex number for the data = 906CDh. This is equivalent to 591565 decimal. This number represents the number of ticks since midnight. There are 18.2 ticks per second. Since there are 3600 seconds in an hour, the following equation produces the current time in a fractional format.

591565/(3600*18.2) = 9.0288

This gives the current hour as 9 am. The minutes can be calculated by multiplying the fraction by 60, or

0288*60 = 1.7280

The integer tells us that it is 1 minute past 9. The seconds can be calculated by again multiplying the fraction by 60.

728*60 = 43.577 seconds

The current time is 9 hours, 1 minute, and 43.577 seconds.

Example 12.2

Use DEBUG to read the ROM BIOS type.

Solution   The ROM BIOS information is contained in Appendix C, location F0000–FFFFF. In DEBUG, enter

```
-dF000:0
```

The ROM BIOS information will now appear on the right part of the screen.

THE PROGRAM SEGMENT PREFIX

Have you wondered why .COM files start at offset address 100 hex? What is located between addresses 00h and FFh? Also how does Ctrl-C or Ctrl-Break terminate a program? Where are filenames stored? The answer to these questions is the program segment prefix (PSP). The PSP stores critical information about the current program in use. In a .COM file, it stores this information in the first 256 bytes (00–FFh) of the program. In an .EXE file, the PSP is stored in a separate segment. At the start of the code segment, DS first points to the PSP. It is changed to point to the data segment by entering

```
MOV AX,_DATA
MOV DS,AX
```

If DS is saved prior to issuing the above instructions, you can gain access to the PSP segment. Example 12.6 shows an example of reading the PSP in an .EXE file. The structure of a PSP is the same in a .COM or .EXE file. Table 12.1 shows some of the information contained in a typical PSP.

Shown below are some examples of the PSP in COM files using DEBUG.

Example 12.3

Force a program termination using the PSP.

Solution   PSP location 0A locates the DOS handler for program termination. In order to simulate an interrupt, you will need to push the flag register prior to calling the vector. Using DEBUG enter

```
100   PUSHF
101   CALL [0A]
```

When the program is executed in DEBUG, it immediately stops and prints "program terminated normally."

TABLE 12.1   Addresses and Contents

Offset Location (in hex)	Use
00–01	INT 20h command. Used as a far call by .EXE programs.
02–03	Location of 1 byte past top of memory.
0A–0D	INT 22h address. This location points to a DOS routine to terminate a program.
0E–11	INT 23h address. This location points to a routine to handle Ctrl-C or Ctrl-Break.
12–15	INT 24h address. Handles disk errors.
80	Stores length of command line tail.
81–FF	Stores command line tail.

Example 12.4

Force a Ctrl-Break using the PSP.

Solution   PSP location 0E is the vector for the Ctrl-Break handler. Once again, push the flag register prior to calling the interrupt vector. Using DEBUG enter

```
100 PUSHF
101 CALL [0E]
```

When the program is executed in DEBUG, it terminates and prints the registers to the screen. Also notice that IP points to a location at the end of the Ctrl-Break routine.

Example 12.5

Write, save, and run a DEBUG program that uses the PSP to print the number of characters entered in the command line tail after the program name.

Solution   The location of the length of the command line tail is address 80h. This byte contains the number of characters entered on the command line after the program name. The space before the string is included. The program below loads the contents of address 80 into the BL register and uses the binary to hex routine from Chapter 4.

```
2620:0100  BB8000      MOV     BX,0080
2620:0103  8A07        MOV     AL,[BX]
2620:0105  86C3        XCHG    AL,BL
2620:0107  B104        MOV     CL,04
2620:0109  D2CB        ROR     BL,CL
2620:010B  88DA        MOV     DL,BL
2620:010D  80E20F      AND     DL,0F
2620:0110  80C230      ADD     DL,30
2620:0113  80FA39      CMP     DL,39
2620:0116  7D04        JGE     011C
2620:0118  80EA07      SUB     DL,07
2620:011B  80C207      ADD     DL,07
2620:011E  B402        MOV     AH,02
2620:0120  CD21        INT     21
2620:0122  D2C3        ROL     BL,CL
2620:0124  88DA        MOV     DL,BL
2620:0126  80E20F      AND     DL,0F
2620:0129  80C230      ADD     DL,30
2620:012C  80FA39      CMP     DL,39
2620:012F  7F03        JG      0134
2620:0131  80EA07      SUB     DL,07
2620:0134  80C207      ADD     DL,07
2620:0137  B402        MOV     AH,02
2620:0139  CD21        INT     21
2620:013B  CD20        INT     20
```

Enter the above program. Set BX to 0 and CX to 3C by entering

```
-RBX
0
-RCX
3C
```

Save the program to disk as TEST.COM. To do this enter

```
-NTEST.COM
-W
```

Now exit DEBUG; at the command line enter

```
test string
```

The program prints

```
7
```

to the screen. This is the length of "string" plus the space character before the string. Try running the program again with other strings.

Example 12.6

Repeat Example 12.5 for an .EXE file by using MASM.

Solution Fortunately, the OUTDEC procedure in ASY.LIB can be used to print the length of the command line tail. First, record the original value of DS into DX. Then, change DS so that it points to the current data segment. Next, push the new value of DS and restore the original (which points to the PSP). Finally, print the integer in 80h (the length of the command line tail) and the string, starting at 82h. Why 82h? The string actually starts at 81h, but there is always a SPACE character in this location (since that's what you press after the program name).

```
_stack segment para stack 'stack'
dw 100h dup(?)
_stack ends


_data segment word public 'data'

_data ends

EXTRN outdec:near
EXTRN crlf:near

_text segment word public 'code'

main proc near
```

```
        assume cs:_text
        assume ds:_data

        START:
                mov dx,ds           ;Record PSP location.
                mov ax,_data        ;Change to data segment.
                mov ds,ax
                push ds             ;Store point to data segment.
                mov ds,dx           ;Restore pointer to PSP.
                mov bx,80h          ;Set index to length of command line tail.
                mov ax,[bx]         ;Get length of command line tail.
                mov ah,0
                call outdec         ;Print length of command line tail.
                call crlf
                cmp ax,0            ;Check if no tail entered.
                je exit             ;If so, exit.
                mov bx,81h          ;Set bx to start of string.
                mov cl,'$'
                add bl,al           ;Point bx to end of string.
                mov [bx],cl         ;Moves '$' into end of string.
                mov dx,82h          ;Set dx to start of string.
                mov ah,9            ;Print string.Terminates with a $.
                int 21h
        exit:
                pop ds              ;Restore pointer to data segment.
                mov ah,4ch          ;Exit.
                int 21h
        main endp

        _text ends
        end
```

BOOTING THE PC

The PC uses the BIOS to help boot DOS from a disk into memory. BIOS stands for binary input output system. Just as it sounds, the BIOS handles communication between the PC and the outside world. When a PC is first turned on, the BIOS is used to load a series of hidden programs on the boot disk. The entire process of booting a PC begins when it is turned on. Address FFFF0 is used to locate a power on self test (POST) ROM routine. This routine looks at addresses 472 for the number 34, and 473 for the number 3412. If these locations contain the numbers, a warm boot is assumed.

The POST Test

Whenever Ctrl-Alt-Del is pressed, 1234h is first loaded into 472 and 473, and address FFFF0 is called. On a cold boot (as when the on/off switch is activated) addresses 472 and

473 contain 0. During the boot process, the POST routine looks at 472 and 473, sees 0s there, and performs a parity check on memory before continuing. All PC memory contains eight data lines plus an extra parity line. Using the parity line, the POST inserts five different combinations of data into memory, and reads each combination back along with the parity bit to check the integrity of the address.

Example 12.7

Write a DEBUG program to force a cold boot on the PC.

Solution   A cold boot can be emulated by first inserting 0s in address 472 and 473, then calling segment FFFF, offset 0. This is equal to absolute address FFFF*10h + 0 = FFFF0h. First, load DEBUG. Now in order to load zeros into 472 and 473, enter

```
-a0:472
db 0,0
```

Next, call absolute address FFFF0. This can be done by entering

```
-a100
call ffff:0
```

After entering the program, enter G to execute it. At this point, the computer will reboot and do a memory check.

The IOSYS.COM Hidden File

Once the POST, memory, and I/O routines are completed, a short beep is sounded and a BIOS initialization routine pointed to by address C8000h is started. This routine calls INT 19h. This interrupt uses the CMOS to determine if the floppy or hard disk should be loaded first. Next, the boot sector is loaded from disk. The boot record is stored in memory beginning at address 7C000h.

   Address 7C000h points to a routine that loads a hidden file. This file can have different names. The POST routine reads the boot sector of the disk to determine the name, then loads the file. The most common is IOSYS.COM. On the original PC, this file was called IBMBIO.COM. This file initializes auxiliary I/O including COM1, COM2, LPT1, and LPT2.

The MSDOS.COM and COMMAND.COM Files

After the initialization, IOSYS executes the processes in CONFIG.SYS. IOSYS loads any device drivers and sets the buffers as specified by CONFIG.SYS. It then loads and executes another hidden file named MSDOS.COM. This file was called IBMDOS.COM in the original IBM PC. MS-DOS can also have different names. It sets up a PSP and program area for COMMAND.COM. It then loads this program into its storage area and executes it. Both of these files are hidden on the boot floppy or hard drive. Next, COMMAND.COM is executed from the disk. COMMAND.COM controls the PC while DOS is running. It puts the C:> as a display prompt, interprets commands entered from the keyboard, and loads and executes application programs. It is COMMAND.COM that ensures that either the time and date are shown or the file AUTOEXEC.BAT is executed at the end of the boot process. All computers that run MS-DOS follow the above procedure.

HIGH MEMORY MODELS

Many of today's programs require huge amounts of memory to operate. The 640K supplied by DOS is no longer sufficient. Fortunately, there are methods used to extend memory beyond the 640K limit. The two most popular are expanded memory and extended memory.

The Expanded Memory Specification

The expanded memory specification (EMS), available since 1986, allows program developers to access memory above the 640K DOS limit. Since 640K memory ends at hex address A0000h, expanded memory must be higher. While it can vary from machine to machine, it is typically in the C0000–DFFFF range.

To use EMS you must have a plug-in EMS memory card. This card typically has 16 banks of memory, each with a 64Kb page frame. This means that only one 64K block is accessed at a time. In addition, each 64Kb page is further subdivided into 16Kb blocks. A switching mechanism in the expanded memory (EMM) driver locks into one 16Kb block at a time.

An EMM driver is needed to operate this board. Your application program must be able to interface with this driver to use expanded memory. The 32-bit Intel processors (80386, 80486, Pentium) support a driver that comes with DOS titled EMM386.SYS. This allows the simulated use of EMS bank switching through extended memory. Many DOS-based programs use expanded memory, such as databases, spreadsheets, and most graphics-intensive games. Neither Windows 3.1 nor Windows 95 supports the EMS. For this you will need extended memory.

The Extended Memory Specification

Rather than use a 16Kb paging system, extended memory allows the user to access huge amounts of memory at a time. In fact, the 80486 supports an additional 4Gb of memory! As with expanded memory, DOS does not inherently support extended memory. Fortunately, software is available that allows the programmer to access higher extended memory. Many CAD programs (such as AutoCad) support extended memory. In addition, Windows 3.1 also supports extended memory. Extended memory is managed though a driver called HIMEM.SYS.

Drivers and TSRs (covered in Chapters 11 and 12) can be loaded into extended memory starting at address A0000h. Device drivers normally end with a .SYS extension. They are loaded by CONFIG.SYS. You can choose to load them in high memory by entering DEVICEHIGH= before the filename. A sample CONFIG.SYS file is shown in Table 12.2.

TABLE 12.2   A Sample CONFIG.SYS File

```
DEVICE=C:\DOS\HIMEM.SYS
DEVICE=C:\DOS\EMM386.EXE RAM MIN=0 D=64
buffers=40,0
FILES=40
DOS=UMB
LASTDRIVE=Z
FCBS=16,8
DEVICEHIGH /L:1,12048 =C:\DOS\SETVER.EXE
DOS=HIGH
DEVICE=C:\WINDOWS\IFSHLP.SYS
STACKS=9,256
```

You can see how much conventional and extended memory you have by running MEM in the DOS directory. Table 12.3 shows a typical output from MEM.

The above program has 6984K free extended memory and 571K free in the DOS memory area (0–9FFFFh). If more detail is required, you can use the **/c** switch to see what drivers are loaded in high and low memory. Table 12.4 shows a sample output using MEM/C.

The output tells us that part of MSDOS (DOS), HIMEM (the extended memory driver), EMM386 (the expanded memory driver), IFSHLP (a Windows driver), COM-MAND (COMMAND.COM), and MSCDEX (a CD-ROM driver) are all located in lower memory. The remaining drivers and TSRs are loaded in upper memory.

An even more detailed memory dump can be done by using the **/d** switch. A sample output using MEM/D is shown in Table 12.5.

TABLE 12.3   A Sample MEM Output

```
Memory Type              Total   =  Used  +  Free
---------------          ------     -----     -----
Conventional              635K      64K       571K
Upper                      59K      52K        7K
Adapter RAM/ROM           261K     261K        0K
Extended (XMS)*          7237K     253K      6984K
---------------          ------     -----     -----
Total memory             8192K     631K      7561K

Total under 1 MB          694K     117K       577K

Total Expanded (EMS)                   7616K  (7798784 bytes)
Free Expanded (EMS)*                   6976K  (7143424 bytes)

* EMM386 is using XMS memory to simulate EMS memory as needed.
  Free EMS memory may change as free XMS memory changes.

Largest executable program size         570K  (584016 bytes)
Largest free upper memory block            7K  (6896 bytes)
MS-DOS is resident in the high memory area.
```

TABLE 12.4   A Sample MEM/C Output

Modules using memory below 1 MB:

Name	Total		=	Conventional		+	Upper Memory	
MSDOS	18589	(18K)		18589	(18K)		0	(0K)
HIMEM	1120	(1K)		1120	(1K)		0	(0K)
EMM386	3120	(3K)		3120	(3K)		0	(0K)
IFSHLP	3872	(4K)		3872	(4K)		0	(0K)
COMMAND	2912	(3K)		2912	(3K)		0	(0K)
MSCDEX	36224	(35K)		36224	(35K)		0	(0K)
SETVER	624	(1K)		0	(0K)		624	(1K)
PROS	6736	(7K)		0	(0K)		6736	(7K)
SJCD	6000	(6K)		0	(0K)		6000	(6K)
SCANDEVC	27456	(27K)		0	(0K)		27456	(27K)
VBEAI	12736	(12K)		0	(0K)		12736	(12K)
Free	591232	(577K)		584208	(571K)		7024	(7K)

Memory summary:

Type of Memory	Total		=	Used		+	Free	
Conventional	650240	(635K)		66032	(64K)		584208	(571K)
Upper	60576	(59K)		53552	(52K)		7024	(7K)
Adapter RAM/ROM	267264	(261K)		267264	(261K)		0	(0K)
Extended (XMS)*	7410528	(7237K)		258912	(253K)		7151616	(6984K)
Total memory	8388608	(8192K)		645760	(631K)		7742848	(7561K)
Total under 1 MB	710816	(694K)		119584	(117K)		591232	(577K)
Total Expanded (EMS)				7798784	(7616K)			
Free Expanded (EMS)*				7143424	(6976K)			

```
* EMM386 is using XMS memory to simulate EMS memory as needed.
  Free EMS memory may change as free XMS memory changes.

Largest executable program size       584016    (570K)
Largest free upper memory block         6896     (7K)
MS-DOS is resident in the high memory area.
```

TABLE 12.5   A Sample MEM/D Output

Conventional memory detail:

Segment	Total		Name	Type
00000	1039	(1K)		Interrupt Vector
00040	271	(0K)		ROM Communication Area
00050	527	(1K)		DOS Communication Area
00070	2656	(3K)	IO	System Data
			CON	System Device Driver

TABLE 12.5   *(continued)*

			AUX	System Device Driver
			PRN	System Device Driver
			CLOCK$	System Device Driver
			A: - C:	System Device Driver
			COM1	System Device Driver
			LPT1	System Device Driver
			LPT2	System Device Driver
			LPT3	System Device Driver
			COM2	System Device Driver
			COM3	System Device Driver
			COM4	System Device Driver
00116	5072	(5K)	MSDOS	System Data
00253	17056	(17K)	IO	System Data
	1104	(1K)	XMSXXXX0	Installed Device=HIMEM
	3104	(3K)	EMMXXXX0	Installed Device=EMM386
	3856	(4K)	IFSHLP	Installed Device=IFSHLP
	2080	(2K)		FILES=40
	960	(1K)		FCBS=16
	512	(1K)		BUFFERS=40
	2288	(2K)		LASTDRIVE=Z
	3008	(3K)		STACKS=9,256
0067D	80	(0K)	MSDOS	System Program
00682	2640	(3K)	COMMAND	Program
00727	80	(0K)	MSDOS	— Free —
0072C	272	(0K)	COMMAND	Environment
0073D	96	(0K)	MSDOS	— Free —
00743	36224	(35K)	MSCDEX	Program
0101B	224	(0K)	MEM	Environment
01029	88608	(87K)	MEM	Program
025CB	495424	(484K)	MSDOS	— Free —

Upper memory detail:

Segment	Region	Total		Name		Type
0C93A	1	608	(1K)	IO		System Data
		576	(1K)		SETVERXX	Installed Device=SETVER
0C960	1	6720	(7K)	IO		System Data
		6688	(7K)		THNDRII$	Installed Device=PROS
0CB04	1	5984	(6K)	IO		System Data
		5952	(6K)		MVCD005	Installed Device=SJCD
0CC7A	1	27440	(27K)	IO		System Data
		27408	(27K)		HPSCAN	Installed Device=SCANDEVC
0D32D	1	128	(0K)	MSDOS		— Free —
0D335	1	12736	(12K)	VBEAI		Program
0D651	1	6896	(7K)	MSDOS		— Free —

Memory summary:

Type of Memory	Total		=	Used		+	Free	
Conventional	650240	(635K)		66032	(64K)		584208	(571K)

(continued on next page)

TABLE 12.5   (continued)

```
Upper                   60576    (59K)      53552    (52K)       7024      (7K)
Adapter RAM/ROM        267264   (261K)     267264   (261K)          0      (0K)
Extended (XMS)*       7410528  (7237K)     258912   (253K)    7151616   (6984K)
---------------      --------------      --------------      --------------
Total memory         8388608  (8192K)     645760   (631K)    7742848   (7561K)

Total under 1 MB      710816   (694K)     119584   (117K)     591232    (577K)


Handle      EMS Name        Size
-------     --------       ------
    0                      060000

Total Expanded (EMS)                   7798784   (7616K)
Free Expanded (EMS)*                   7143424   (6976K)

* EMM386 is using XMS memory to simulate EMS memory as needed.
  Free EMS memory may change as free XMS memory changes.

Memory accessible using Int 15h              0     (0K)
Largest executable program size         584016   (570K)
Largest free upper memory block           6896     (7K)
MS-DOS is resident in the high memory area.

XMS version  3.00; driver version  3.09
EMS version  4.00
```

FLAT MEMORY MODEL

Extended memory still uses the DOS system and therefore has to jump over hoops to break the 640K barrier. Newer operating systems such as IBM's OS/2 and Microsoft's Windows 95 run in protected mode. These systems require an 80386 or higher processor. The flat memory system does not use the segmented architecture inherent in DOS. Since these processors have a 32-bit address bus and 32-bit registers, they can load an entire physical address into one register. This allows much faster and easier memory access.

While it is beyond the scope of this book to cover protected mode systems, it is important to note that, from a programmer's and user's standpoint, much is to be gained by replacing a segmented system with a flat memory model. You no longer have to deal with "conventional" and "upper" memory. All of memory is located in one continuous map.

CHAPTER 12 PROBLEMS

1. Using C, read the current time from memory and display it in hours, minutes, and seconds. Use memory address 46Ch to get the time.

2. Write a program in DEBUG to perform a warm boot.
3. Write an .EXE file in MASM to perform a cold boot.
4. Write a program using MASM to print the number of hard disks. (*Hint:* See Appendix C).
5. Write a program using MASM to print the model type (PC, XT, or AT) on the screen. (*Hint:* See Appendix C).
6. Write an .EXE program using MASM to display information about the ROM BIOS.
7. In what range of memory are the simple I/O devices (COM1, COM2, LPT1, and LPT2) located in Table 12.5?
8. Identify the starting addresses of all high memory device drivers in Table 12.5.
9. According to Table 12.5, at what address did high memory start?
10. There is a program that comes with DOS to help relocate drivers and TSRs to high memory. Read a DOS 6.0 or higher manual and determine the name of this program.
11. Use the information in Appendix D to send a file from one PC to another using the RS232.

CHAPTER 13

Advanced C Memory and I/O Routines

This chapter contains useful techniques in C related to the type of I/O and memory operations that might be performed in assembly language. You have already used the powerful **_asm** operator to switch between assembly and C. There are many more low-level operations that can be performed in C, all of which are easier than accomplishing the same task in assembly. This chapter assumes you are using Microsoft C. If Quick C is used, enter

```
qcl
```

instead of

```
cl
```

to compile programs in this chapter. If you are using Turbo-C, use

```
tcc
```

instead of

```
cl
```

to compile programs in this chapter.

WHAT TIME IS IT IN C?

You studied how to get the time in assembly in Chapter 7. There are at least twelve functions related to the date and time in Microsoft C, most of them ANSI C-compatible. This means they can be used in Turbo-C or even UNIX. Since there are only so many ways to tell time, the functions tend to be repetitive. The most common are listed below.

```
asctime
_bios_timeofday
```

```
ctime
_dos_getdate
_dos_gettime
ftime
gmtime
localtime
strdate
strtime
time
tzset
```

The _bios_timeofday function most closely represents the TICKS.ASM program in Chapter 7. It returns the number of seconds elapsed since midnight. This function is useful in cases where a length of time is to be measured in seconds. For example, you may want to see how long it takes to run a program. Simply use the _bios_timeofday function to get the time at the beginning and end of the program and subtract. The _bios_timeofday function does not return the number of seconds elapsed since midnight, but rather the number of ticks since midnight. The PC clock is updated 18.2 times a second, and each update is a tick. To get the seconds, divide the ticks by 18.2.

String representations of the current date and time are contained in a variety of functions. The date and time is stored in time.h in a structure called tm. The structure template of tm is shown below:

```
struct tm {
    int tm_sec;    // seconds after the minute - [0,59]
    int tm_min;    // minutes after the hour - [0,59]
    int tm_hour;   // hours since midnight - [0,23]
    int tm_mday;   // day of the month - [1,31]
    int tm_mon;    // months since January - [0,11]
    int tm_year;   // years since 1900
    int tm_wday;   // days since Sunday - [0,6]
    int tm_yday;   // days since January 1 - [0,365]
    int tm_isdst;  // daylight savings time flag
    };
```

To get this information, first call the time function (also defined in time.h) to return an encoded form of the date and time in a long value.

```
time_t long_time;
time(long_time);
```

Next, break the long value into the tm structure by calling localtime with the long encoded value and returning to a tm structure variable.

```
tme=localtime(&long_time);
```

The ctime function is also available. This function, although not as flexible as localtime, converts the encoded value to one long string.

```
ctime(&long_time)
```

A sample program demonstrating these function calls is shown below. The _bios_timeofday function is used to get the seconds before and after a keypress.

```
/*Time program*/

#include <time.h>
#include <bios.h>
#include <stdio.h>
#include <conio.h>

time_t long_time;
struct tm *tme;

main()
{
long i, begin, end;
bios_timeofday(_TIME_GETCLOCK, &begin);
puts("Press any key to stop");
getch();
bios_timeofday(_TIME_GETCLOCK, &end);
printf("\nElapsed time = %4.2f seconds\n",
(float)((end-begin))/18.2);
time(&long_time);
tme=localtime(&long_time);
printf("\nThe date and time is %s\n",ctime(&long_time));
printf("\nIt is %d months since January\n",tme->tm_mon);
printf("It is %d days since Sunday\n",tme->tm_wday);
printf("It is %d days since January\n",tme->tm_yday);
printf("It is day %d of the month\n",tme->tm_mday);
printf("It is %d hours since midnight\n",tme->tm_hour);
printf("It is %d minutes since the hour\n",tme->tm_min);
printf("It is %d seconds since the minute\n",tme->tm_sec);
}
```

Arguments to Main()

You might remember from Chapter 12 that the command line tail is stored in the PSP. For example, when

```
cl file.c
```

is entered on the command line, the cl program is loaded, and file.c is read into the PSP.

In C, the command line tail can be read in through the main() function. Shown below is an example of how to do this.

```
main(argc,argv)
int argc;
char *argv[];
```

The first variable, argc, specifies how many command line entries are being made, including the program name. For example:

```
cl program.c
```

has two command line entries, cl and program.c. The second variable passed to main stores each argument in a separate string, as part of a string array. Try entering the program shown below:

```
/*Program to read in entries from command line*/

#include <stdio.h>

main(argc,argv)
int argc;
char *argv[];
{
    int x;
    printf("\nThere were %d arguments entered\n",argc);
    puts("\nThe entries are\n");

        for (x=0;x<argc;x++)
        {
        printf("\n%d ->    %s\n",x,argv[x]);
        }
}
```

The first string points to the name of your program. The remaining strings point to the other arguments. For example, suppose you named the above program:

```
COMREAD.C
```

Compile the file in DOS by entering

```
cl comread.c
```

and load the program by entering

```
comread I love C.
```

The program output looks something like this:

```
comread I love C
```

There were four arguments entered. The entries are:

```
0 ->    COMREAD.EXE

1 ->    I

2 ->    love

3 ->    C
```

Using command line arguments, you can write a program to save a text screen and another to redisplay it.

```
/* Program to write text screen to disk*/

#include <stdio.h>
```

```
#define GET_MEM(seg,off) (*(char far *)((long)(seg) <<16 | (off)))
FILE *fd_out;
main(argc,argv)
int argc;
char *argv[];
{
 int x;
char c;
fd_out = fopen(argv[1],"w");
        for(x=0;x<=3999;x++)
        {
        c=GET_MEM(0xB800,x);
        fprintf(fd_out,"%c",c);
        }
fclose(fd_out);
}
```

Save the file as:

```
WRITE.C
```

Now exit C and compile the file as WRITE.C by entering

```
cl write.c
```

When running the program, enter the program name and the file that you want to save to. For example:

```
write screen.sav
```

will save the screen to a file called SCREEN.SAV.

On most PC screens, text memory is in segment address B800 hex. The offset starts at address 0 (upper left of screen) and increments to the lower right of the screen (offset address 3999 decimal).

```
/* Program to read a text screen from disk*/
#include <stdio.h>
#include <graph.h>
#define GET_MEM(seg,off) (*(char far *)((long)(seg) <<16 | (off)))
#define PUT_MEM(seg,off,byte) GET_MEM(seg,off)=byte
FILE *fd_in;
main(argc,argv)
int argc;
char *argv[];
{
int x;
char c;
_setvideomode(_TEXTC80);
fd_in = fopen(argv[1],"r");
        for(x=0;x<=3999;x++)
        {
        fscanf(fd_in,"%c",&c);
```

```
        PUT_MEM(0xB800,x,c);
        }
fclose(fd_in);
}
```

Save the file as:

```
READ.C
```

Once again, exit Microsoft C and compile the file as READ.C by entering:

```
cl read.c
```

When running the program, enter the program name and the file to be read. For example:

```
read screen.sav
```

will read the screen from a file called SCREEN.SAV.

INTERRUPTS IN C

There is a built-in interrupt function in C called int86(). This function provides a way of accessing interrupts without using _asm. You need to modify the AX, BX, CX, and DX in order to use int86(). These registers are accessed by way of the REGS union. The REGS union uses an **.x** extension to access 16-bit registers, and an **.h** extension to access 8-bit registers. For example, if the union regs is declared as:

```
union REGS regs
```

you can access the DX register by the statement:

```
regs.x.dx
```

The CL register can be accessed by:

```
regs.h.cl
```

An example that prints a '$' ASCII character to the screen using INT 21h, AH = 2, and DL = '$', is shown below:

```
#include <dos.h>
#include <stdio.h>
union REGS regs;
main()
{
int x;
regs.h.ah=2;
regs.x.dx='$';
int86(0x21,&regs,&regs);
}
```

Shelling and Chaining in C

Microsoft C contains a number of ways to execute other programs within your current program. There are generally four ways to do this:

Method 1:   Run part of a program, shell out and run another program (with the original still in memory), then return to the original program when exiting the second.

Method 2:   Run a first program and chain a second program, releasing the first from memory. When terminating the second program, the user is returned to DOS.

Method 3:   Run part of a program, then shell out to DOS. Return to the program when EXIT is entered.

Method 4:   Run part of a program, then issue a single DOS command such as COPY, RENAME, or CD.

The first method can be accomplished by using the SPAWNLP function, which uses the include file process.h. This function allows you to run one program while inside another. An example is shown below:

```
#include <process.h>
#include <stdio.h>
main()
{
char buff[20];
puts("Enter the filename of a program to run");
gets(buff);
spawnlp(P_WAIT,buff,NULL);
puts("Back in program");
}
```

Compile and run this program from DOS using qcl. It spawns a child process and returns to the original program.

The second method can be accomplished with either the EXEC() or SPAWNLP() functions. Both work about the same. If the SPAWNLP is to be used, change the P_WAIT switch to P_OVERLAY. Revise the program from method 1 as shown below:

```
spawnlp(P_OVERLAY,buff,NULL);
```

Again compile the program in DOS using qcl. Now the program does not return to the calling program when the child program terminates. A further description of spawnlp is found in the Microsoft C reference manual.

The third method again uses the SPAWNLP function. It also uses the GETENV function to return a copy of COMSPEC. This environment variable indicates the current location of COMMAND.COM. After returning the location into a string called buff, spawnlp is used to temporarily exit to DOS. Control is again passed to the program when EXIT is entered.

```
#include <process.h>
#include <stdio.h>
#include <stdlib.h>
```

```
static char buffer[64];
FILE *fp;
void main()
{
int c;
printf("Type EXIT to return to NOTE\n");
strcpy(buffer,getenv("COMSPEC"));

c=spawnlp(P_WAIT,buffer,buffer,NULL);
puts("Returned to program");
}
```

The fourth method can be done using the system() function. This function uses process.h and stdlib.h. An example is shown below:

```
#include <process.h>
#include <stdio.h>
#include <stdlib.h>
main()
{
system("COPY FIG.EXE FIG1.EXE");

}
```

This program shells out to DOS to copy a file called FIG.EXE to FIG1.EXE.

Reading a Disk Directory in C

The _dos_findfirst and _dos_findlast commands are used to read files on disk. The _dos_findfirst command must first be called to find the first instance of a filename. If one is found, _dos_findlast can be used to find other matches. You can insert the file names into a string array, so that the programs can be easily called from a menu.

In order to write a program using these commands, you must define a variable as the find_t structure template.

```
struct find_t {
   char reserved[21];    /*Reserved for DOS*/
   char attrib;          /*Attribute byte for matched pair*/
   unsigned wr_time;     /*Time stamp on file*/
   unsigned wr_date;     /*Date stamp on file*/
   long size;            /*Length of file*/
   char name[13];        /*Name of file*/
   };
```

When calling _dos_findfirst, you can pass it wildcard matches (* or ?). You must also pass it an attribute argument. The attribute arguments are shown below:

_A_ARCH   For use with DOS BACKUP.

_A_HIDDEN   Hidden file. Not shown with DIR.

_A_NORMAL   Normal read/write file.

_A_RDONLY   Read only file.

_A_SUBDIR   Subdirectory.

_A_SYSTEM   System file. Not shown with DIR.

_A_VOLID   Volume ID in root directory.

An example of _dosfindfirst is shown below.

```
struct find_t file;

_dos_findfirst("*.exe", _A_NORMAL, &file);
```

The _dos_findnext function is similar, except the file attributes have already been defined by _dos_findfirst, so you just need to pass it the find_t structure. Shown below is a program that prints the first twenty .EXE files in the current directory, and allows you to select one to execute. The program uses the system() function, which calls a child program from within the current program.

```
#include <stdlib.h>
#include <process.h>
#include <dos.h>
#include <stdio.h>
#include <string.h>
char fls[12][20];
main()
{
struct find_t file;
int x=0,a;
_dos_findfirst("*.exe", _A_NORMAL, &file);
printf("Listing of C files\n\n");
strcpy(fls[x],file.name);
strcat(fls[x++],"\0");
        while(_dos_findnext(&file)==0 && x<20)   {
        strcpy(fls[x],file.name);
        strcat(fls[x++],"\0");
                                                 }
        for(a=0;a<x;a++)
        printf("%d. %s\n",a,fls[a]);

printf("Enter a choice to execute, 0 to %d\n",a);
scanf( "%d",&a);
system(fls[a]);
```

CHAPTER 13 PROBLEMS

1. Write a C program that prints the number of seconds elapsed since midnight.
2. Write a C program to print the number of hours past since January 1 of the current year.

3. Write a C program that uses INT 21h, AH = 5 to print a C string to the screen.
4. Write a C program that reads a filename as a command line argument. Have the program open the file, print the contents to the screen, and close it.
5. Write a C program that chains another .EXE program.
6. Write a C program that shells another .EXE program.
7. Write a C program that prints the contents of the root directory of the PC you are working on.
8. Rewrite the MOUSEDET.ASM program in Chapter 10 as a C program using the INT86 function.

CHAPTER 14

80286/80386/80486 Instructions

NEW INSTRUCTIONS IN THIS CHAPTER

Mnemonic:	**PUSHA** PUSHA
Description:	Pushes all registers onto the stack. Used with POPA. For 80286 and higher machines. Must use the .286 or higher directive.
Example:	PUSHA (Push all registers onto the stack.) POPA
Flags Affected:	None

Mnemonic:	**POPA** POPA
Description:	Pops all registers from the stack. Used with PUSHA. For 80286 and higher machines. Must use the .286 or higher directive.
Example:	PUSHA POPA (Pop all registers from the stack.)
Flags Affected:	None

Mnemonic:	**ENTER** ENTER *bytes,level*
Description:	Creates a temporary stack frame for use with procedures. Used with LEAVE. For 80286 and higher machines. Must use the .286 or higher directive.

Example:	ENTER 4,0 (Create 4-byte stack. BP is located at top of stack. SP is at bottom of stack.)
	LEAVE
Flags Affected:	None

Mnemonic:	**LEAVE**
	LEAVE
Description:	Restores BP and SP to original position, effectively destroying stack. Used with ENTER. For 80286 and higher machines. Must use the .286 or higher directive.
Example:	ENTER 4,0
	LEAVE (Restores BP and SP to original positions.)
Flags Affected:	None

Mnemonic:	**Extended MOV**
	MOV *extended destination,extended source*
Description:	Transfers an extended register from source to destination. The source can be an extended register, an immediate number, or an address. The destination can be an extended register or an address. For 80386 and higher machines. Must use the .386 or higher directive.
Examples:	MOV EAX,13 (Copy 13- to 32-bit EAX.)
	MOV EAX,EBX (Copy 32-bit EBX to EAX. EBX is not changed.)
	MOV ECX, [BX] (Copy 4 bytes beginning at the address pointed to by BX to EBX.)
Flags Affected:	Carry, Overflow, Parity, Sign, Zero

Mnemonic:	**Extended MOVSX**
	MOV *extended destination,source*
Description:	Loads source into extended destination. Remaining bits in extended source are filled with sign bit. For 80386 and higher machines. Must use the .386 or higher directive.
Example:	MOVSX EAX,BL (Moves BL into AL; remaining EAX bits equal AL sign bit.)
Flags Affected:	None

Mnemonic:	**Extended MOVZX**
	MOV *extended destination,source*
Description:	Loads source into extended destination. Remaining bits in extended source are filled with zero. For 80386 and higher machines. Must use the .386 or higher directive.
Example:	MOVZX EAX,BL (Moves BL into AL; remaining EAX bits equal 0.)
Flags Affected:	None

Mnemonic:	**BTC, BTR, BTS**
	BTC *destination,source*
	BTR *destination,source*
	BTS *destination,source*
Description:	Tests destination with bit position indicated by source, starting with 0 as LSB. Carry flag affected as result of test. Selected bit also complemented (BTC), set (BTS), or reset (BTR). For 80386 and higher machines. Must use the .386 or higher directive.
Example:	BTC AL,4 (Test and complement bit number 4 in AL.)
	BTR AL,4 (Test and reset bit number 4 in AL to 0.)
	BTS AL,4 (Test and set bit number 4 in AL to 1.)
Flags Affected:	None

Mnemonic:	**BSF, BSR**
	BSF *destination,source*
	BSR *destination,source*
Description:	Scans source for first (BSF) or last (BSR) location of a 1 in destination. Position stored in destination. For 80386 and higher machines. Must use the .386 or higher directive.
Example:	BSR AL,DL (Find first 1 in DL and store position number in AL.)
	BTR AL,DL (Find first 1 in DL and store position number in AL.)
Flags Affected:	None

Mnemonic:	**SETB, SETZ, SETS**
	SETB *destination*
	SETZ *destination*
	SETS *destination*
Description:	Inserts the appropriate flag into bit 0 of the destination register. SETB checks the carry flag, SETZ checks the zero flag, and SETS checks the sign flag. For 80386 and higher machines. Must use the .386 or higher directive.
Example:	SETB AL (Bits 7 through 1 of AL = 0, bit 0 equals carry flag.)
	SETZ AL (Bits 7 through 1 of AL = 0, bit 0 equals zero flag.)
	SETS AL (Bits 7 through 1 of AL = 0, bit 0 equals sign flag.)
Flags Affected:	None

COMPILING 80286 AND HIGHER INSTRUCTIONS

Up until now, 8088/8086 instructions have been covered. There are also many instructions that exist only in 80286 and higher processors. In its default mode, MASM only recognizes the 8088/8086 instructions. In order to compile 80286 and higher instructions, you must use the .286 or .386 directives. For 80286 instructions, simply place this directive as the first line in your file. 80386 instructions also require the USE directive described later in this chapter.

Let's look at an example using two 80286 instructions. When working with the stack, you may have wanted an instruction that automatically pushed all registers, and another to pop all registers. These instructions exist in 80826 and higher processors as PUSHA (push all) and POPA (pop all). This is especially useful before and after a subroutine is called, as shown below:

```
.286
_stack segment para stack 'stack'
dw 100h dup(?)
_stack ends

_data segment word public 'data'
_data ends

_text segment word public 'code'
main proc near
assume cs:_text
assume ds:_data

START:
      mov ax,_data
      mov ds,ax
      pusha              ;Push all registers.
      call subroutine    ;Call subroutine.
      popa               ;Restore registers.
      mov ah,4ch
      int 21h

main endp
_text ends
end START
```

Note the .286 directive at the top of the program. By pushing all registers before a subroutine and popping all registers after, you can be sure that the subroutine will not alter the register values. Of course, it is assumed that the subroutine procedure doesn't return anything, or POPA would erase whatever was returned.

ENTER AND LEAVE INSTRUCTIONS

The 80286 provides even more useful stack manipulation tools, designed primarily for calling procedures. The ENTER instruction creates a stack frame bounded by BP at the top and SP at the bottom, as shown in Figure 14.1.

When using the ENTER instruction, state the size of the stack and access individual elements using BP (much as with the C language in Chapter 11). SP is not altered. The

FIGURE 14.1   Four-byte
stack frame created with
ENTER 4.0

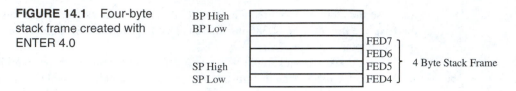

second entry on the ENTER instruction is the level number. In DOS you are always at
level 0.

The LEAVE instruction returns BP and SP to the original positions, effectively de-
stroying the stack. The stack created with ENTER is only intended to be a temporary
storage area. It provides a handy method of data transfer for procedures and subroutines.
Shown below is an example using ENTER and LEAVE.

Example 14.1

Write a program that uses ENTER and LEAVE to load and display "abc" on the temporary
stack.

Solution   The program shown below creates a 6-byte stack, and loads "abc" on it:

```
.286
_stack segment para stack  'stack'
      dw 100h dup(?)
_stack ends

_data segment word public  'data'
_data ends

_text segment word public  'code'
main proc near
assume cs:_text
assume ds:_data
START:
      mov ax,_data
      mov ds,ax
      ENTER 3,0        ;Create 6 byte stack.
      mov ax,'a'
      mov [bp-1],al    ;Move 'a' into bp-1, the first position.
      mov ax,'b'
      mov [bp-2],al    ;Move 'b' into bp-2, the second position.
      mov ax,'c'
      mov [bp-3],al    ;Move 'c' into bp-3, the third position.
      call OutStack    ;Subroutine to display stack in ASCII.
      Leave            ;Restore BP and SP to previous values.
      mov ah,4ch
      int 21h
main endp
```

```
OutStack proc near
      pusha               ;You can push here without affecting ENTER stack.
      MOV AH,2
      mov dl,[bp-1]       ;Display 'a'.
      INT 21H
      mov dl,[bp-2]       ;Display 'b'.
      INT 21H
      mov dl,[bp-3]       ;Display 'c'.
      INT 21H
      popa
      ret
OutStack Endp
_text ends
end START
```

Data is referenced by BP, as in BP-2 or BP-4. You cannot use PUSH or POP on the ENTER stack, since SP is not at the top of the ENTER stack. Also, since the ENTER stack is temporary, all data stored in it is lost after the LEAVE instruction is executed. Note the PUSHA statement in the OutStack routine. Since SP points to the bottom of the ENTER stack, PUSHA pushes the registers below the ENTER stack.

COMPILING 80386 AND HIGHER INSTRUCTIONS

When using 80386 or above instructions, you will need to include the .386 directive. Beginning with the 80386, a series of 32-bit registers were introduced, along with a 32-bit address and a data bus. Because of this, the .386 directive assumes 32-bit segments. Unfortunately, DOS still emulates 16-bit segments. In order to ensure compatibility, the statement USE 16 must be included when declaring segments.

Four of the 32-bit registers are named EAX, EBX, ECX, and EDX; these registers are supersets of the AX, BX, CX, and DX registers. Most of the operations available with the lower registers are also present here. For instance, data can be moved into EAX by the following instruction:

```
MOV EAX, 0FFFFh
```

Note that this instruction also puts FFFFh in AX. Since this is a 32-bit instruction, the statement

```
MOV EAX,0FFFFFFFFh
```

is valid. This would fill all 32 bits in EAX with 1s.

You can also transfer 32-bit registers, as in the following statement:

```
MOV EDX,ECX
```

This statement transfers the contents of ECX to EDX. This is a 32-bit data transfer. Indirect memory operations are performed by using [BX], as shown below:

```
MOV EAX,[BX].
```

This instruction loads 4 bytes from memory into EAX beginning with the address pointed to by the BX register.

The statements MOVSX and MOVZX permit data transfer from an 8- or a 16-bit register to a 32-bit register. The upper bits are either loaded with a sign bit (MOVSX) or 0s (MOVZX).

Use the .386 directive when compiling 80386 instructions.

Example 14.2

Write a program that first loads CL with 83h. Then load CL into AX and print the new value of AX in hex. Fill the upper bits in AX with 0s.

Solution   The MOVSX instruction can be used with just 16- and 8-bit registers. You do not have to use a 32-bit register. In the program below, CL is first loaded with 83h, then the MOVSX instruction is used to transfer CL to AX. Finally, AX is printed to the screen with the OUTHEX function. You will need to link with ASY.LIB to produce a working .EXE file.

```
.386
_stack segment para stack USE16 'stack'
        dw 100h dup(?)
_stack ends

_data segment word public USE16 'data'
_data ends

EXTRN outhex:near
_text segment word public USE16 'code'
main proc near
assume cs:_text
assume ds:_data
START:
        mov ax,_data
        mov ds,ax
        mov cl,83h          ;Load CL with 83h.
        movsx ax,cl         ;Transfer CL to AX.
        call outhex         ;Print AX.
        mov ah,4ch
        int 21h
main endp
_text ends
end START
```

BIT TEST INSTRUCTIONS

The 80386 introduced new instructions that can test bit positions in a register and set or reset the carry flag as a result. The instructions are given in Table 14.1.

For example, in the instruction **BTS AX,3,** the third bit in AX is tested. If it is equal to 1, the carry flag is set; otherwise, the carry flag is reset to 0. Note that these instructions count 0 as the LSB and 15 as the MSB.

Example 14.3

Write a program that tests and complements register AX. Have the user enter the bit position and display a message as to whether or not the carry flag is affected. Assume AX = 7.

Solution   The program below uses BTC to test and complement a selected bit in AX.

```
.386
_stack segment para stack USE16 'stack'
       dw 100h dup(?)
_stack ends

_data segment word public USE16 'data'
       InputMessage db 'Enter bit position to compare with number 7',0
       CarryMessage db 'Carry',0
       OutputMessage db 'Result = ',0
       NoCarryMessage db 'No Carry',0
_data ends

EXTRN outstring:near
EXTRN outdec:near
EXTRN getdec:near
EXTRN crlf:near

_text segment word public USE16 'code'
main proc near
assume cs:_text
assume ds:_data

START:
       mov ax,_data
       mov ds,ax
       mov bx,offset InputMessage      ;Enter message for bit position entry.
       call outstring
       call crlf
       call getdec                     ;Get bit position (0-15).
       mov bx,ax
```

```
        mov Ax,7h                            ;Load 7 into AX.
        btc ax,bx                            ;Complement AX with selected bit.
        jc next                              ;Jump over nocarry message if carry
                                              flag equals 1.
        mov bx,offset NoCarryMessage         ;Print nocarry message.
        call outstring
        call crlf
        jmp next1                            ;Jump to register output.
next:
        mov bx,offset CarryMessage           ;Print carry messsage.
        call outstring
        call crlf

next1:
        mov bx,offset OutputMessage          ;Print output message.
        call outstring
        call outdec                          ;Print new contents of register AX.
        call crlf
        mov ah,4ch
        int 21h
main endp
_text ends
end START
```

There are also two bit-scan instructions, BSF and BSR. The BSF instruction scans a register starting from the LSB and moves left toward the MSB. The first 1 that it encounters is recorded in the destination register. BSR scans the register in the same manner, but records the last 1 found in the register. For example, the instructions

```
MOV DX,0Ah
BSF AX,DX
```

will test DX until a 1 is found. The will be in position 1, as shown below:

```
Bit Position               3210
DX                 1010
```

A 1 is placed in AX as a result of the instruction.

TABLE 14.1   Instructions to test bit positions

Instruction	Operation
BTS	Sets selected bit.
BTR	Resets (clears) selected bit.
BTC	Complements (inverts) selected bit.

FLAG TEST INSTRUCTIONS

There are also flag test instructions in the 80386 and above processors. Three of the most common are SETB, SETZ, and SETS. These instructions set the destination register equal to 0 and copy the appropriate flag to bit 0. The flag registers associated with the instructions are shown in Table 14.2.

The program shown below forces a sign bit to 1 and displays the result in AL.

```
.386
_stack segment para stack USE16 'stack'
dw 100h dup(?)
_stack ends

_data segment word public USE16 'data'
_data ends

EXTRN outhex:near
EXTRN crlf:near
_text segment word public USE16 'code'
main proc near
assume cs:_text
assume ds:_data

START:
        mov ax,_data
        mov ds,ax
        mov dx,7h
        add dx,0fff3h      ;Force a sign bit in result.
        sets al            ;Clear AL and set bit 0 with sign bit.
        call outhex        ;Send to screen in hex.
        call crlf
        mov ah,4ch
        int 21h
main endp
_text ends
end START
```

TABLE 14.2   Flag Registers
Associated With the SET
Command

SETB	Carry flag
SETZ	Zero flag
SETS	Sign flag

CHAPTER 14 PROBLEMS

1. Describe the purpose of the LEAVE instruction. Why doesn't it need an operand, as ENTER does?
2. Write a procedure that multiplies two numbers. Use the ENTER stack for parameter passing.
3. The C language passes parameters through a temporary stack, much like the ENTER instruction. As stated in Chapter 11, you cannot alter the values on the stack. You can, however, pass addresses onto the stack and alter the values in the addresses, just as you can alter pointers in C. The routine shown below takes the addresses of DataA and DataB and pushes them onto an ENTER stack. Write the interchange procedure to exchange the values of DataA and DataB. The program should output:

```
DataA now equal to B
DataB now equal to A
```

Do not alter the program shown below when writing the interchange procedure.

```
.386
_stack segment para stack USE16 'stack'
        dw 100h dup(?)
_stack ends

;Data segment contains DataA = A and DataB = B
_data segment word public USE16 'data'
        DataAMessage db 'DataA now equal to ',0
        DataBMessage db 'DataB now equal to ',0
        DataA db 'A'
        DataB db 'B'
_data ends
EXTRN outchar:near
EXTRN outstring:near
EXTRN crlf:near

_text segment word public USE16 'code'
main proc near
assume cs:_text
assume ds:_data

START:
        mov ax,_data
        mov ds,ax

        ;Create stack.Need room for two offsets (4 bytes)
        ENTER 4,0

        ;Load address of DataA into upper offset
         mov [bp-3],offset DataA
```

```
                    ;Load address of DataB into lower offset
                    mov [bp-1],offset DataB

                    ;Call procedure to swap DataA and DataB
                    call Interchange

                    ;Destroy stack
                    Leave

                    ;Display new values of DataA and DataB
                    mov bx,offset DataAMessage
                    call outstring
                    mov al,DataA
                    call outchar
                    call crlf

                    mov bx,offset DataBMessage
                    call outstring
                    mov al,DataB
                    call outchar
                    call crlf

                    mov ah,4ch
                    int 21h
           main endp



           _text ends

           end START
```

4. Describe the difference between MOVSX and MOVZX.
5. Write a program to load 4 bytes of memory into EAX, starting at the current segment, offset 0. Display the results to the screen in hex.
6. Write program to print the first location of a 1 in AX to the screen. Assume AX = 724h.
7. Repeat problem 6, but display the last location of a 1 in AX.
8. Program an algorithm that sets the carry flag, sign flag, and zero flag. Use the SET instructions to obtain and display the flags.

APPENDIX A

BIOS Interrupts

INT 10H VIDEO FUNCTIONS

These functions control screen I/O on the PC. When Color is indicated, choose from:

Number	Color
0	Black
1	Blue
2	Green
3	Cyan
4	Red
5	Magenta
6	Brown
7	White
8	Gray
9	Light Blue
A	Light Green
B	Light Cyan
C	Light Red
D	Light Magenta
E	Yellow
F	Bright White

INT 10H FUNCTIONS

AH = 00h	Set display function
AL = 00h	BW text 40*25
AL = 01h	16-color text 40*25

AL = 02h	BW text 80*25
AL = 03h	16-color text 80*25
AL = 04h	320*200 CGA 4-color graphics
AL = 06h	640*200 CGA BW graphics
AL = 09h	320*200 16-color MCGA graphics
AL = 10h	640*350 16-color EGA graphics
AL = 12h	640*480 16-color VGA graphics
AL = 13h	320*200 256-color VGA graphics

AH = 02h	Set cursor position
BH	Page number (normally 0)
DH	Row number
DL	Column number

AH = 03h	Get cursor position
BH	Page number (normally 0)
On Exit:	
DH	Row number
DL	Column number

AH = 06h	Clear screen, scroll window
AL	Number of scroll lines
BH	Attribute for new lines (see text)
CH	Upper left row
CL	Upper left column
DH	Lower right row
DL	Lower right column

AH = 08h	Read character at cursor
BH	Page number (normally 0)
On Exit:	
AH	Attribute
AL	ASCII code for character

AH = 09h	Write attribute and character at cursor
BH	Page number (normally 0)
BL	Attribute
AL	ASCII code for character

AH = 0Ah	Write character at cursor
CX	Number of characters to write
BH	Page number (normally 0)
BL	Color (if in graphics mode)
AL	ASCII code for character

AH = 0Bh	Set background color
BH	00H
BL	Color

AH = 0Ch	Set pixel
AL	Color
BH	Page (normally 0)
CX	Column number
DX	Row number
AH = 0Dh	Read pixel
BH	Page (normally 0)
CX	Column number
DX	Row number
On Exit:	
AL	Color
AH = 0Fh	Get video mode
On Exit:	
AH	Number of character columns of screen
AL	Display mode
BH	Active page
AH = 12h	Configuration information
BL = 10H	
On Exit:	
BH	0 = Color; 1 = Monochrome
BL	Amount of memory on VGA board (0 = 64K, 1 = 128K, 2 = 192K, 3 = 256K
AH = 12h	Enable/Disable video
BL = 32h	
AL	0 = Enable; 1 = Disable
On Exit:	
AL	12H if successful

INT 14H RS232 FUNCTIONS

AH = 0H	Set parameters on serial port
DX = 0 COM1	
DX = 1 COM2	
AL:	
Bits 7–5	Baud rate

Baud rate	Bits 7–5 value
300	2
600	3
1200	4
2400	5
4800	6

9600	7
Bits 4–3	Parity

Parity	Bits 4–3 value
None	00
Odd	01
Even	11

Bit 2	Number of stop bits

Stop bits	Bit 2 value
1	0
2	1

Bits 1–0	Word length

Word Length	Bits 1–0 Value
7	10
8	11

AH = 1H	**Transmit character**
AL	Character to be sent
On Exit:	
AH	Bit 7 = 1 if unable to transmit
AH = 2H	Receive character
AL	Character received
On Exit:	
AH	Greater than 0 if error occurred
AH = 3H	Get line and modem control status
On Exit:	
AH	
Bit 7	time out
Bits 6–0	Same as Port 3FD in Appendix D
AL	
Bits 7–0	Same as Port 3FE in Appendix D

INT 16H KEYBOARD FUNCTIONS

AH = 00H	Read character from keyboard (pause until key is read)
On Exit:	
AH	Scancode
AL	ASCII character
AH = 01H	Keyboard status (no pause)
On Exit:	
AH	Keyboard scancode if ZF = 0
AL	Keyboard ASCII code if ZF = 0

AH = 02H   Keyboard flag status
On Exit:
AL   Keyboard flags, as shown below:

7	6	5	4	3	2	1	0
Insert	Caps	Num	Scroll	Alt	Ctrl	Left	Right
On	Lock	Lock	Lock	Key	Key	Shift	Shift
	On	On	On	Down	Down	Down	Down

AH = 03H   Set repeat rate
AL = 05H

BH:

BH value	Time delay before first repeat key
0	250 ms
1	500 ms
2	750 ms
3	1000 ms

BL:

BL value	Repeat rate
0	30.0
1	26.7
2	24.0
3	21.8
4	20.0
5	18.5
6	17.1
7	16.0
8	15.0
9	13.3
10	12.0
11	10.9
12	10.0
13	9.2
14	8.6
15	8.0
16	7.5
17	6.7
18	6.0
19	5.5
20	5.0
21	4.6
22	4.3
23	4.0
24	3.7
25	3.3
26	3.0

27	2.7
28	2.5
29	2.3
30	2.1
31	2.0

INT 19H REBOOT FUNCTIONS

This interrupt reboots the operating system.

INT33h

| AX=3 | Button Press (1 = Left Button, 2 = Right Button, 3 = Both Buttons) |
| AX=11 | Mouse Movement (CX negative = left, CX positive = right, DX negative = up, DX positive = down) |

APPENDIX B

DOS Interrupt Functions

AH = 01H   Input character with echo and pause
On Exit:
AL   If AL>0, AL = ASCII character
                    If AL = 0, second call gives AL = Extended ASCII character

AH = 02H   Output character to console
DL   ASCII character

AH = 05H   Output character to printer
DL   ASCII character to be sent to printer

AH = 06H   Input character with echo, without pause
DL = FFH
On Exit:
AL   If ZF = 0, AL = ASCII character (two calls needed for extended ASCII).
                    If ZF = 1, no character pressed.

AH = 08H   Input character without echo, with pause
On Exit:
AL   ASCII character (two calls needed for extended ASCII)

AH = 09H   Output string
DS:DX   Pointer to string

AH = 0AH   Input buffered string with echo
On Exit:
DS:DX   Byte 1 = number of bytes in buffer
                    Byte 2 = number of bytes returned
                    Remainder = String

AH = 0CH   Clear keyboard buffer and call function
                    AL = 01h, 06h, 08h, or 09h to substitute AH function call.
                    This call is identical to the keyboard functions listed above
                    except the keyboard buffer is emptied before the call is made.

AH = 2AH   Get current date
On Exit:
CX   Year
DH   Month
DL   Day of month
AL   Day of week (Sunday = 0)

AH = 2BH   Set current date
CX   Year
DH   Month
DL   Day of month
AL   Day of week (Sunday = 0)
On Exit:
AL   0 if date valid

AH = 2CH   Get current time
On Exit:
CH   Hour (0–23)
CL   Minutes (0–59)
DH   Seconds (0–59)
DL   Hundredths (0–99)

AH = 2DH   Set current time
CH   Hour (0–23)
CL   Minutes (0–59)
DH   Seconds (0–59)
DL   Hundredths (0–99)
On Exit:
AL   0 if time valid

AH = 30H   MS-DOS version number
On Exit:
AL   Major version number
AH   Minor version number

AH = 31H   Terminate and stay resident
AL   Return code
DX   Number of paragraphs to stay resident

AH = 35H   Get interrupt vector
AL   Vector number
On Exit:
ES:BX   Pointer to current interrupt handle

AH = 36H   Get disk free space
DL   Drive number (0 = current drive, 1 = A, 2 = B, etc.)
On Exit:
BX   Number of available clusters
DX   Number of clusters on drive

CX	Number of bytes/sector
AX	Number of sectors/cluster

AH = 39H   Create subdirectory
DS:DX   Pointer to ASCIIZ directory path
On Exit:
CF   0 if no error
AX   Error number (if CF = 1)

AH = 3AH   Remove subdirectory
DS:DX   Pointer to ASCIIZ directory path
On Exit:
CF   0 if no error
AX   Error number (If CF = 1)

AH = 3BH   Change directory
DS:DX   Pointer to ASCIIZ directory path
On Exit:
CF   0 if no error
AX   Error number (If CF = 1)

AH = 3CH   Create file
CX   File attributes (see text)
DS:DX   Pointer to ASCIIZ filename
On Exit:
CF   0 if no error
AX   Error number (if CF = 1), file handle (if CF = 0)

AH = 3DH   Open file
AL   Access mode (see text)
DS:DX   Pointer to ASCIIZ filename
On Exit:
CF   0 if no error
AX   Error number (if CF = 1), file handle (if CF = 0)

AH = 3EH   Close file
BX   File handle
On Exit:
CF   0 if no error

AH = 3FH   Read file
BX   File handle
CX   Number of bytes to read
DS:DX   Pointer to ASCIIZ buffer
On Exit:
CF   0 if no error
AX   Error number (if CF = 1), number of bytes read (if CF = 0)

AH = 40H   Write to file
BX   File handle

CX	Number of bytes to write
DS:DX	Pointer to ASCIIZ buffer
On Exit:	
CF	0 if no error
AX	Error number (if CF = 1), number of bytes written (if CF = 0)

AH = 41H	Remove file
DS:DX	Pointer to ASCIIZ filename
On Exit:	
CF	0 if no error
AX	Error number (if CF = 1)

AH = 42H	Move file read/write pointer
CX:DX	Offset
BX	File handle
AL = 0	Move beginning of file plus offset
AL = 1	Move current location plus offset
AL = 2	Move end of file plus offset
On Exit:	
CF	0 if no error, DX:AX = New pointer location
AX	Error number (if CF = 1)

AH = 47H	Get current directory
DS:SI	Pointer to a 64-byte buffer
DL	Drive number (0 = current drive, 1 = A, 2 = B, etc.)
On Exit:	
DS:SI	Pointer to path name
CF	0 if no error
AX	Error number (if CF = 1)

AH = 49H	Free allocated memory
ES	Segment of allocated block to free
On Exit:	
CF	0 if no error
AX	Error number (if CF = 1)

AH = 4CH	Terminate and exit
AL	Error level

APPENDIX C

Memory Map

The memory addresses defined in this map have been determined to be standard on all PCs. To maintain compatibility, however, it is better to use an interrupt or port address call wherever possible.

0–3FFh   **Interrupt Vector Area**

INT 0–7	80x86 vectors
INT 8–F	8259 vectors
INT 10–1F	BIOS vectors
INT 20–2F	DOS and network vectors
INT 30–4F	Device and assignable vectors (e.g., mouse, hard disk, etc.)

400–407h   **RS232 Asynchronous Adaptor Port Address**
Address of COM1, COM2, COM3, and COM4 (if available). For example, COM1, if at address 3F8, is represented as 400h-F8h and 401h-03h.

408–40Fh   **Parallel Printer Port Addresses**
Address of LPT1, LPT2, LPT3, and LPT4 (if available). For example, if LPT1 is at 378h, it is represented in little endian order as 408-78h and 409-03h.

413h   **Memory Size**
Size of system memory, not including video, given in multiples of 400h. For example, a reading of 280h is translated as A0000 hex, or 640K decimal.

417h   **Keyboard Flag Register**
The Num Lock, Caps Lock, and Scroll Lock indicator lights can be turned on (1) and off (0) here.

Bit 7	Insert key
Bit 6	Caps lock
Bit 5	Num lock
Bit 4	Scroll lock

	Bit 3	Alt key
	Bit 2	Ctrl key
	Bit 1	Left Shift key
	Bit 0	Right Shift key

41A **Head of Keyboard Buffer**
Next character to be obtained from the circular keyboard buffer.

41C **Tail of Keyboard Buffer**
Next unused position for entry when a key is pressed.

41E **Keyboard Buffer**
Circular buffer containing 15 usable entries. Each key is represented by ASCII/scancode in consecutive bytes.

43F **Drive Motor Status**
A 1 indicates a drive motor is running.

	Bit 0	Drive A
	Bit 1	Drive B
	Bit 2	Drive C
	Bit 3	Drive D

Bit 7   A 1 here indicates one or more of the drive motors are running.

46C **Timer**
A double word timer value that is incremented by IRQ0 (INT 8). The double word is in little endian order. The byte at 46C can be used as a pseudorandom number.

475 **Number of Hard Disks on System**

480 **Pointer to Start of Keyboard Buffer**
Offset from 400h.

482 **Pointer to End of Keyboard Buffer**
Offset from 400h.

700–9FFFFh **Program and Data Area**

4DB9 **Start of Device Drivers, Buffers, and File Control Entries, if in Low Memory**

53F0 **Start of Resident COMMAND.COM**

A0000–AFFFF **EGA/VGA Video Graphics Buffer Area**

B0000–B0FFF **Monochrome Video Buffer Area**

B8000–B0FA0 **Color Text Screen Area**

F0000–FFFFF **Rom Bios Information Area**
Differs greatly by machine.

FFFF0   **Power on Reset Vector**
                      This vector points to the address loaded into CS:IP when the PC is first
                      turned on. A call to this vector will reboot the system.

FFFFE   **Model Values**
                      FF = PC, FE = XT, and FC = AT.

APPENDIX D

Port Map

The ports indicated on this map have been determined to be standard on all PCs.

20H   **8259 Port Address**
Used to signal End Of Interrupt (EOI) when 20h is written to it.

21H   **8259 Interrupt Mask Register**
1 = disabled, 0 = enabled

BIT	7	6	5	4	3	2	1	0
IRQ	7	6	5	4	3	2	1	0

IRQ7 LPT1 Parallel printer port
IRQ6 Floppy disk controller
IRQ5 LPT2 Parallel printer port
IRQ4 COM1:COM3
IRQ3 COM2:COM4
IRQ2 Secondary I/O channel
IRQ1 Keyboard
IRQ0 System timer

40H   **8253 Programmable Interval Timer Channel 0**
A counter register that counts from 0 to 65535 approximately every 55 milliseconds. This port is routed through IRQ0 to INT 8.

41H   **8253 Programmable Interval Timer Channel 1**
Interrupts the direct memory access controller as part of the memory refresh cycle. Do not modify this register.

42H   **8253 Programmable Interval Timer Channel 2**
Used to specify the period for the speaker. Interfaced to the speaker through port 61h.

60H   **Keyboard Scancode**
Keyboard interfaced to this port.

61H   **8255 Interface Channel**
              Bit 7   Keyboard enable (0)
              Bit 6   Keyboard clicking on (1)
              Bit 4   RAM parity error enable (0)
              Bit 1   Speaker enabled (1)
              Bit 0   8253 Channel 2 (port 42h) clock (enable = 1)

201H   **Game Joystick Controller**
              0 = pressed, 1 = no contact
              Bit 7, joystick b, button #2
              Bit 6, joystick b, button #1
              Bit 5, joystick a, button #2
              Bit 4, joystick a, button #1
              Bit 3, joystick b, y value
              Bit 2, joystick b, x value
              Bit 1, joystick a, y value
              Bit 0, joystick a, x value

278H–27FH   **Possible Location of Parallel Printer Port (LPT1, LPT2, or LPT3)**

2F8H–2FFH   **Secondary Asynchronous Communications Adapter (Usually COM2)**

378H–37FH   **Possible Location of Parallel Printer Port (LPT1, LPT2, or LPT3)**

Base Port (i.e., 378)
Printer output data
Bit 0, pin 2 data bit 0
Bit 1, pin 3 data bit 1
Bit 2, pin 4 data bit 2
Bit 3, pin 5 data bit 3
Bit 4, pin 6 data bit 4
Bit 5, pin 7 data bit 5
Bit 6, pin 8 data bit 6
Bit 7, pin 9 data bit 7

Base Port + 1 (i.e., 379)
Printer status register
Bit 0, time out = 1
Bit 3, pin 15 error
Bit 4, pin 13 online
Bit 5, pin 12 out of paper
Bit 6, pin 10 acknowledge
Bit 7, pin 11 busy

Base Port + 2 (i.e., 37A)
Bit 0 Pin 1   Output data to printer (1)
Bit 1 Pin 14   Auto line feed (1)
Bit 2 Pin 16   Initialize printer (0)
Bit 3 Pin 17   Printer reads output (1)
Bit 4   IRQ7 enable for printer acknowledge (1)

3B8H–3BFH   **Possible Location of Parallel Printer Port (LPT1, LPT2, or LPT3)**

3F8H–3FFH   **Primary Asynchronous Communication Adapter (COM1)**

3F8H   **RS232 Transmit/Receive Buffer**
Store character to be transmitted here (if bit 7, port 3FB = 0).
Also receive character here (if bit 7, port 3FB = 0).
LSB of baud rate divisor (if bit 7, port 3FB = 1)

3F9H   **RS232 Interrupt Enable Register**
MSB of baud rate divisor (if bit 7, port 3FB = 1)

3FBH   **RS232 Line Control Register**
Bit 7   Divisor latch access bit (1)
Bit 6   Break enabled (1)
Bit 5   Parity enabled (1)
Bit 4   0 = odd parity, 1 = even parity
Bit 3   0 = no parity, 1 = parity
Bit 2   0 = 1 stop bit, 1 = 2 stop bits
Bits 1,0   00 = 5 bits per character, 01 = 6 bits per character,
            10 = 7 bits per character, 11 = 8 bits per character.

3FCH   **Modem Control Register**
Bit 1   Activate RTS (1)
Bit 0   Activate DTR (1)

3FDH   **Line Status Register**
Bit 6   Empty transmit shift register (1)
Bit 5   Empty transmit hold register (1)
Bit 4   Break error received (1)
Bit 3   Framing error received (1)
Bit 2   Parity error received (1)
Bit 1   Overrun error received (1)
Bit 0   Data received (1)

3FEH   **Modem Status Register**
Bit 7   Receive line signal detect (1)
Bit 6   Ring indicator (1)
Bit 5   Data set ready (1)
Bit 4   Clear to send (1)
Bit 3   Change in line signal detect (1)
Bit 2   Change in ring indicator (1)
Bit 1   Change in data set ready
Bit 0   Change in clear to send

Programming the RS232 Asynchronous Adaptor

Programming COM1 and COM2 using ports can be a tedious process, but it allows for faster communication with less overhead. Baud rates up to 115,200 are possible through the ports, while INT 16h in BIOS only allows up to 9600 baud.

To set up COM1 to send and receive, follow these steps:

1. Specify the baud rate. This can be done by first calculating the baud rate divisor from the formula below:

$$\text{baud rate divisor} = 1{,}843{,}200/(16*\text{baud rate})$$

For example, if a baud rate of 9600 is desired, the baud rate divisor equals 12 decimal, or C hex.
2. Set bit 7 of the line control register (3FB for COM1) to 1.
3. Store the number in LSB of the baud rate divisor into the transmit/receive buffer (3F8H for COM1). Store the MSB in the interrupt enable register (3F9H for COM1). For 9600 baud, store C in 3F8H and 0 in 3F9H.
4. Reset bit 7 of the line control register (3FBH for COM1) to 0.
5. Now set the parity and word length in the line control register. For example, suppose you want a 7-character word, even parity, and 1 stop bit. Set port 3FB equal to 1Ah. Note bits 7–5 are normally 0. Setting bit 5 to 1 allows for mark and space parity, and is not covered here.

To receive, follow these steps:

1. Read the line status register. If bit 0 = 1, data is in the input buffer.
2. If bit 0 = 1 in the line status register, read in port 3F8H, the transmit/receive buffer. This contains a character sent through COM1. If bit 0 = 0, repeat step 1.
3. Store the character, or print it to the screen.

To send a character, follow these steps:

1. Obtain a character from the keyboard, memory, or a file.
2. Check if the transmit hold bit (bit 5) is empty, in the line status register.
3. If bit 5 = 1 line status register, send the character to the transmit/receive buffer (port 3F8H).

APPENDIX E

8088 Instruction Set

AAA	ASCII adjust for addition.
AAD	ASCII adjust for division.
AAM	ASCII adjust for multiplication.
AAS	ASCII adjust for subtraction.
ADC destination,source	Add with carry destination and source.
ADD destination,source	Addition of destination and source.
AND destination,source	Boolean AND on destination and source.
CALL address	Call a procedure.
CBW	Convert AL to AX, sign bit is extended.
CLC	Clear carry flag.
CLD	Clear direction flag.
CLI	Clear interrupt flag.
CMC	Complement carry flag.
CMP destination,source	Compare destination to source. Set flags based on result. Destination not affected.
CMPS destination,source	Compare destination string to source string.
CWD	Convert AX to DX,AX. Sign bit is extended.
DAA	Decimal adjust for addition.
DAS	Decimal adjust for subtraction.
DEC destination	Decrement destination by 1.

DIV source	Divide AX by 8-bit source, or DX,AX by 16-bit source.
ESC opcode,source	Method for co-processors to receive instructions.
HLT	Places processor in halt mode until restored by a hardware RESET or interrupt.
IDIV source	Sign divide AX by 8-bit source, or DX,AX by 16-bit source.
IMUL source	Sign multiply AL by 8-bit source, or AX by 16-bit source.
IN accumulator,port	Input data from port to AL or AX.
INC destination	Increment destination by 1.
INT number	Execute interrupt number if interrupt flag = 1, pushing CS, IP, and the flag register.
IRET	Return from interrupt, popping the flag register, IP, and CS.
JA/JNBE short address	Jump if above/not below or equal.
JAE/JNB short address	Jump if above or equal/not below.
JB/JNAE short address	Jump if below/not above or equal.
JBE/JNA short address	Jump if below or equal/not above.
JC short address	Jump on carry (CF = 1).
JCXZ short address	Jump if CX = 0.
JE/JZ short address	Jump if equal/zero.
JG/JNLE short address	Jump if greater/not less or equal.
JLE/JNG short address	Jump if less or equal/not greater.
JMP address	Jump to address.
JNC short address	Jump on not carry (CF = 0).
JNE/JNZ short address	Jump if not equal/not zero.
JNO short address	Jump if not overflow.
JNP/JPO short address	Jump if not parity/parity odd.
JNS short address	Jump if not sign (SF = 0).
JO short address	Jump if overflow.
JP/JPE short address	Jump if parity/parity even.
JS short address	Jump if sign (SF = 1).
LAHF	AH = Flag register.
LDS destination,source	Load destination with source, and DS with source + 2.

LEA destination,source	Load offset of source to destination.
LES destination,source	Load destination with source, and ES with source + 2.
LOCK instruction	Lock bus while following instruction executes.
LODS source-string	Load AL or AX with byte or word from SI. Increment SI.
LOOP short address	Decrement CX. If CX = 0, jump to short address.
LOOPE short address	Decrement CX. If CX = 0 or ZF = 1, jump to short address.
LOOPNE	Decrement CX. If CX = 0 or ZF = 0, jump to short address.
MOV destination,source	Load source into destination.
MOVS destination string	Move byte or word from source string to destination string. Increment SI and DI.
MUL source	Multiply AL by 8-bit source, or AX by 16-bit source.
NEG destination	2's complement (invert + 1) destination.
NOP	No operation performed.
NOT destination	1's complement (invert) destination.
OR destination,source	Boolean OR on destination and source.
OUT port,accumulator	Output data from AL or AX to port.
POP destination	Pop a word off stack into destination.
POPF	Pop a word off stack into flag register.
PUSH source	Push source onto stack.
PUSHF	Push flag register onto stack.
RCL destination,CL	Rotate left through carry with wrap. Carry acts as a ninth bit in 8-bit register. Ninth (carry) bit wrapped to LSB.
RCR destination,CL	Rotate right through carry with wrap. Carry acts as a ninth bit in 8-bit register. LSB wrapped to ninth (carry) bit.
REP	Repeat string operation.
REPE	Repeat string operation while elements are equal.
REPNE	Repeat string operation while elements are not equal.
RET	Return from procedure.
ROL destination,CL	Rotate left with wrap. MSB wrapped to LSB.
ROR destination,CL	Rotate right with wrap. LSB wrapped to most MSB.
SAHF	Load AH into flag register.

SHL destination,CL	Shift left. Leading 0 introduced in first bit.
SAR destination,CL	Shift arithmetic right. Sign bit repeated in MSB.
SBB destination,source	Subtract with borrow (destination-source-carry flag).
SCAS destination string	Subtract destination string element pointed to by DI from AL or AX.
SHR destination,CL	Shift right. Leading 0 introduced in MSB.
STC	Set carry flag.
STD	Set direction flag.
STI	Set interrupt flag.
STOS destination string	Loads AL or AX into element in destination pointed to by DI.
SUB	Subtract destination-source.
TEST destination,source	Perform Boolean AND on destination and source. Flags are affected but destination not altered.
WAIT	Suspend operation of processor until TEST pin is high.
XCHG destination,source	Exchange destination and source.
XLAT AL	Replace AL with byte pointed to by BX+AL.
XOR destination,source	Boolean Exclusive OR on destination and source.

APPENDIX F

ASCII Table

ASCII NUMBER	HEX	CHARACTER
0	0	Null
1	1	☺
2	2	☺
3	3	♥
4	4	♦
5	5	♣
6	6	♠
7	7	BEEP
8	8	Back Space
9	9	Tab
10	A	Line Feed
11	B	Vertical Tab
12	C	Form Feed
13	D	Carriage Return
14	E	Shift Out
15	F	☼
16	10	▶
17	11	◀
18	12	↕
19	13	Device Control 3
20	14	¶
21	15	§
22	16	▬
23	17	↑
24	18	↑
25	19	↓
26	1A	End Of File

27	1B	Escape
28	1C	File Separator
29	1D	↔
30	1E	◣
31	1F	◥
32	20	Space
33	21	!
34	22	"
35	23	#
36	24	$
37	25	%
38	26	&
39	27	'
40	28	(
41	29	)
42	2A	*
43	2B	+
44	2C	,
45	2D	-
46	2E	.
47	2F	/
48	30	0
49	31	1
50	32	2
51	33	3
52	34	4
53	35	5
54	36	6
55	37	7
56	38	8
57	39	9
58	3A	:
59	3B	;
60	3C	<
61	3D	=
62	3E	>
63	3F	?
64	40	@
65	41	A
66	42	B
67	43	C
68	44	D
69	45	E
70	46	F
71	47	G
72	48	H

73	49	I
74	4A	J
75	4B	K
76	4C	L
77	4D	M
78	4E	N
79	4F	O
80	50	P
81	51	Q
82	52	R
83	53	S
84	54	T
85	55	U
86	56	V
87	57	W
88	58	X
89	59	Y
90	5A	Z
91	5B	[
92	5C	\
93	5D	]
94	5E	^
95	5F	_
96	60	`
97	61	a
98	62	b
99	63	c
100	64	d
101	65	e
102	66	f
103	67	g
104	68	h
105	69	i
106	6A	j
107	6B	k
108	6C	l
109	6D	m
110	6E	n
111	6F	o
112	70	p
113	71	q
114	72	r
115	73	s
116	74	t
117	75	u
118	76	v

119	77	w
120	78	x
121	79	y
122	7A	z
123	7B	{
124	7C		
125	7D	}
126	7E	~
127	7F	Delete
128	80	Ç
129	81	ü
130	82	é
131	83	â
132	84	ä
133	85	à
134	86	å
135	87	ç
136	88	ê
137	89	ë
138	8A	è
139	8B	ï
140	8C	î
141	8D	ì
142	8E	Ä
143	8F	Å
144	90	É
145	91	æ
146	92	Æ
147	93	ô
148	94	ö
149	95	ò
150	96	û
151	97	ù
152	98	ÿ
153	99	Ö
154	9A	Ü
155	9B	¢
156	9C	£
157	9D	¥
158	9E	P
159	9F	f
160	A0	á
161	A1	í
162	A2	ó
163	A3	ú
164	A4	ñ

165	A5	Ñ
166	A6	a
167	A7	o
168	A8	¿
169	A9	⌐
170	AA	¬
171	AB	½
172	AC	¼
173	AD	¡
174	AE	«
175	AF	»
176	B0	░
177	B1	▒
178	B2	▓
179	B3	│
180	B4	┤
181	B5	╡
182	B6	╢
183	B7	╖
184	B8	╕
185	B9	╣
186	BA	║
187	BB	╗
188	BC	╝
189	BD	╜
190	BE	╛
191	BF	┐
192	C0	└
193	C1	┴
194	C2	┬
195	C3	├
196	C4	─
197	C5	┼
198	C6	╞
199	C7	╟
200	C8	╚
201	C9	╔
202	CA	╩
203	CB	╦
204	CC	╠
205	CD	═
206	CE	╬
207	CF	╧
208	D0	╨
209	D1	╤
210	D2	╥

211	D3	⊫
212	D4	⊨
213	D5	⊧
214	D6	∏
215	D7	╫
216	D8	╪
217	D9	⌟
218	DA	⌈
219	DB	■
220	DC	▬
221	DD	▎
222	DE	▐
223	DF	▀
224	E0	α
225	E1	ß
226	E2	Γ
227	E3	π
228	E4	Σ
229	E5	σ
230	E6	μ
231	E7	τ
232	E8	Φ
233	E9	θ
234	EA	Ω
235	EB	δ
236	EC	∞
237	ED	ϕ
238	EE	ε
239	EF	$\cap$
240	F0	$\equiv$
241	F1	$\pm$
242	F2	$\geq$
243	F3	$\leq$
244	F4	$\int$
245	F5	$\int$
246	F6	$\div$
247	F7	$\approx$
248	F8	$\circ$
249	F9	$\cdot$
250	FA	$\cdot$
251	FB	$\sqrt{}$
252	FC	
253	FD	$\overline{}^2$
254	FE	■
255	FF	Blank

APPENDIX G

The Easy4 PC Software

The Easy4 is a system that simulates an early 4-bit microcomputer. It includes a hex keypad and single seven-segment LED as input/output devices. The appendix focuses on the setup and operation of the Easy4. Chapter 2 focuses on programming the Easy4.

Easy4 Setup

The Easy4 runs under Microsoft Windows 3.1 or Windows 95. It requires at least a 386 PC with a hard disk, 4 Mb of RAM, and an SVGA screen with at least 800x600 resolution. Easy4 is stored on a single floppy disk in a compressed format. To install Easy4, start Windows, then run

```
A:SETUP.EXE
```

from the Program Manager. Setup will prompt for the directory to load Easy4. After loading, an icon will be added to the EASY4 program group. To start the program, double-click on the icon. If the lower part of Easy4 does not appear on the screen, you will need to reconfigure Windows for a higher resolution.

Turning Easy4 On

Easy4 begins with a front panel display as shown in Figure 2.1. Before you can do anything with Easy4, you must first turn it on. Use the mouse to click the ON button. This button resets the stack pointer, instruction pointer, Register A, the carry and zero flags, and all memory data to 0. ON acts as a toggle switch, turning the Easy4 off and on. You can use this button later on to erase a program. Once the ON button is pressed, the screen appears as in Figure 2.2.

The RUN Button

The RUN button in Easy4 is designed for running a program previously stored in memory. Before running, it will set the instruction pointer, stack pointer, Register A, and the carry and zero flags to 0. A program will continue to run until a STOP instruction is encountered. In addition, an internal counter is incremented every time a loop sends the program address 0. If more than 100 iterations occur during a single run, the program terminates and an

```
Error...Infinite Loop. Press OK to Exit
```

message appears. Each time the program is stopped (whether through an infinite loop or STOP instruction), the internal counter is reset. This helps prevent Windows from crashing due to an infinite loop.

Step Button

The Step button steps through a program, one instruction at a time. It does not reset any registers or flags. Step is good for tracing through a program, often to debug it. It is also good for stopping a program to read input from the keyboard buffer.

RESET Button

The RESET button resets the instruction pointer, stack pointer, Register A, and the carry and zero flags to 0. In addition to this button, the instruction pointer can also be preset by clicking on a memory address.

Menu Commands

When File is selected on the upper left of the screen, a menu appears as shown below:

```
Load
Save
Disassemble
Show Easy4 Bus
Hide Easy4 Bus
Exit
```

Load is used to load a previously saved Easy4 program into memory. The file must end with the EZ4 extension.

Save is used to save a program to disk. All registers and flag values are not saved. The file must be saved with an EZ4 extension.

Disassemble takes the op-codes in memory and interprets them as instructions. All of memory is included, so even information that was stored as data is interpreted as instructions. The program can be printed with the PRINT button.

Show Easy4 Bus displays the address, data, and control buses. You cannot program in this mode. It is simply for observing how the LED, keypad, and memory are interfaced to the CPU.

Hide Easy4 Bus returns the screen to programming mode after Show Easy4 Bus was selected.

Exit terminates Easy4 and returns to Windows.

APPENDIX H

PC Interfacing Experiments

The ISA bus, described in Chapter 5, provides an ideal way of interfacing the PC to the outside world. This appendix contains a series of experiments designed to I/O on the ISA bus. This appendix assumes the student has had a course in circuit analysis and has concurrent courses in digital and analog electronics.

Equipment List

This appendix uses the following TTL chips:

7404 hex inverter
7430 eight input NAND gate
7432 two input OR gate
74LS244 buffer chip
74LS373 latch

It also uses the following linear devices:

ADC0801 analog-digital converter
LM2601 frequency to voltage converter
2N2222A small signal transistor

The following equipment is needed to operate the chips:

1 PC breadboard. (A low-cost, effective version is available from Global Industries.)
1 digital breadboard trainer
1 data analyzer
1 frequency counter
1 oscilloscope
1 signal generator
2 1K resistors
1 47K resistor
1 10K resistor

1 150pf capacitor
2 .01uf capacitors
1 5V Zener diode

EXPERIMENT 1: GETTING ACQUAINTED WITH THE ISA BUS

Objective:
To observe the operation of the ISA bus, including the clock pins and the data bus.

Procedure:
1. Install the PC breadboard into the PC chassis. Note that the ISA bus contains an OSC and a CLOCK pin. The OSC pin is the system clock for the PC. The CLOCK pin is one-third the OSC frequency. Turn on the PC, insert the frequency counter probe into OSC, then CLOCK and record the frequencies.

OSC = _____Mhz

CLOCK = _____Mhz

2. The CLOCK pin has a 33% duty cycle. Duty cycle is defined by the following formula:

Duty Cycle (%) = 100 * Length of Time Signal is High/Period

Using this formula, a 33% duty cycle occurs when the signal is low twice as long as it is high. Insert the oscilloscope probe into the CLOCK pin and fill in the data below:

Length of time signal is high = _____

Period = _____

Duty Cycle = _____

3. In order to see what information is on the data bus when an I/O operation occurs, it is necessary to decode the data bus. This ensures that the data analyzer only receives information about the bus when an I/O operation occurs. Wire a 74LS244 bus transceiver to the data bus as shown in Figure H.1. Wire the 74LS244 outputs to the data analyzer and the inputs to the data bus. Connect the two enables together and wire the IOW signal to one of them.
4. If you are in Windows, exit to DOS. Enter the following program into DEBUG.

```
100   MOV DX,FB00
103   MOV AL,9
105   OUT DX,AL
106   JMP 105
```

5. Place the data analyzer in parallel state mode and run the program (see Chapter 3 for information about DEBUG).
6. The 74LS244 passes data from the inputs to the outputs when the enables are low. Thus the data analyzer receives information from the data bus when IOW is low. The program sends a "9" on the data bus when IOW is low, so this is what the data analyzer should read. The 74LS244 should be wired as shown in Figure H.1.

FIGURE H.1   74LS244

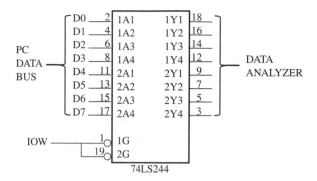

74LS244

EXPERIMENT 2: DECODING THE ADDRESS BUS

Objective:

The procedure used in Experiment 1 would work for any address on an OUT instruction. This experiment describes how to decode the address bus for an output port at FB00.

Procedure:

1. Wire the schematic shown in Figure H.2. Note that VCC and ground for each chip is not shown in the drawing. Consult a logic data book or the TTL pinout section of this appendix for information on connecting ground and power (see Figure H.2).

   When the address bus has FB00 on it, the bit combinations appear as shown below:

A15	A14	A13	A12	A11	A10	A9	A8	A7	A6	A5	A4	A3	A2	A1	A0
1	1	1	1	1	0	1	1	0	0	0	0	0	0	0	0

   All of the address pins are wired to two 74LS30 eight input NAND gates. This gate outputs a 0 only when all inputs are high. Note that pins A10 and A7-A0 contain 0. Each of these pins is inverted through a 7404 so that a 1 is sent to 74LS30 when FB00 appears on the address bus. The two 74LS30 outputs are sent to a two-input 74LS32 OR gate. The output of this gate is 0 only when both inputs are 0.

   The output of the 74LS32 is sent to another 74LS32 gate. The other input to this gate is IOW. The output of this gate only goes low when FB00 appears on the address bus and IOW goes low.

2. Set the oscilloscope on 5 volts/div and ground. Adjust the trace to the center of the screen. Now set the scope on DC.

3. Connect the oscilloscope to the output of the second 74LS32. Turn on the PC, and run the following program in DEBUG (note that this same program also appeared in Experiment 1).

```
100   MOV DX,FB00
103   MOV AL,9
105   OUT DX,AL
106   JMP 105
```

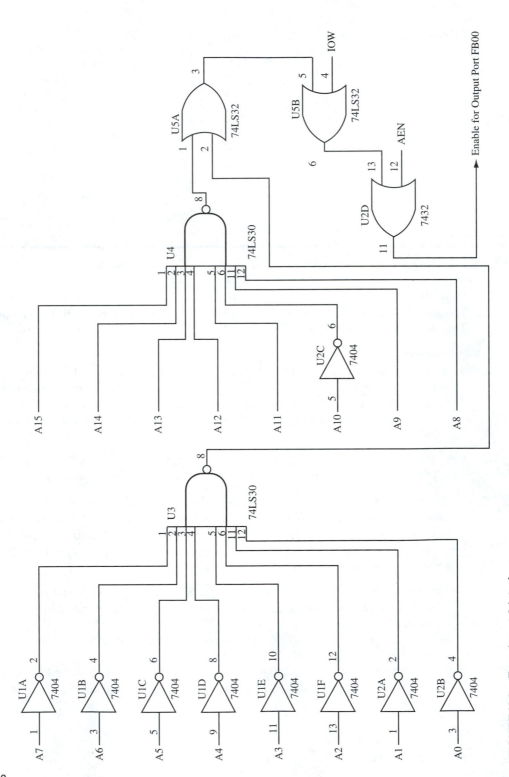

FIGURE H.2 Experiment 2 Interface

If working properly, the output of the scope should now be high with short spikes going low. These spikes occur when the program issues the OUT instruction. If not working, use the scope probe to find the problem. Start with the final output and go back to the address bus to locate a changing signal. This will help locate the problem.

EXPERIMENT 3: DESIGNING AN OUTPUT PORT

Objective:
To use the knowledge gained in Experiments 1 and 2 to build an output port using a 74LS373 latch. A set of LEDs are connected to the port to demonstrate its operation. 80x86 Assembly language is used to control the port.

Procedure:
Normally, output ports are latched. As was seen in Experiment 2, the enable output goes low only for a short period of time. If the data was not latched, it would be lost when the enable goes high. A 74LS373 is a set of 8 D latches. When the enable is high, data is sent from the input to the output. When the enable is low, previous data is latched and held at the output.

1. Add a 74LS373 D latch to the output of the schematic in Experiment 2, as shown in Figure H.3.
2. Enter the program below in DEBUG. It first turns all the LEDs on, then, after a key-press, turns them all off. Run the program and observe the LEDs before and after a key-press.

```
100 MOV DX,FB00
103 MOV AL,FF
105 OUT DX,AL
106 MOV AH,8
108 INT 21
10A MOV AX,0
10D OUT DX,AL
10E INT 20
```

3. Write a program in MASM that operates the LEDs as a ring counter. The bit pattern should appear as shown below:

LED	0	1	2	3	4	5	6	7
	0	0	0	0	0	0	0	1
	0	0	0	0	0	0	1	0
	0	0	0	0	0	1	0	0
	0	0	0	0	1	0	0	0
	0	0	0	1	0	0	0	0
	0	0	1	0	0	0	0	0
	0	1	0	0	0	0	0	0
	1	0	0	0	0	0	0	0

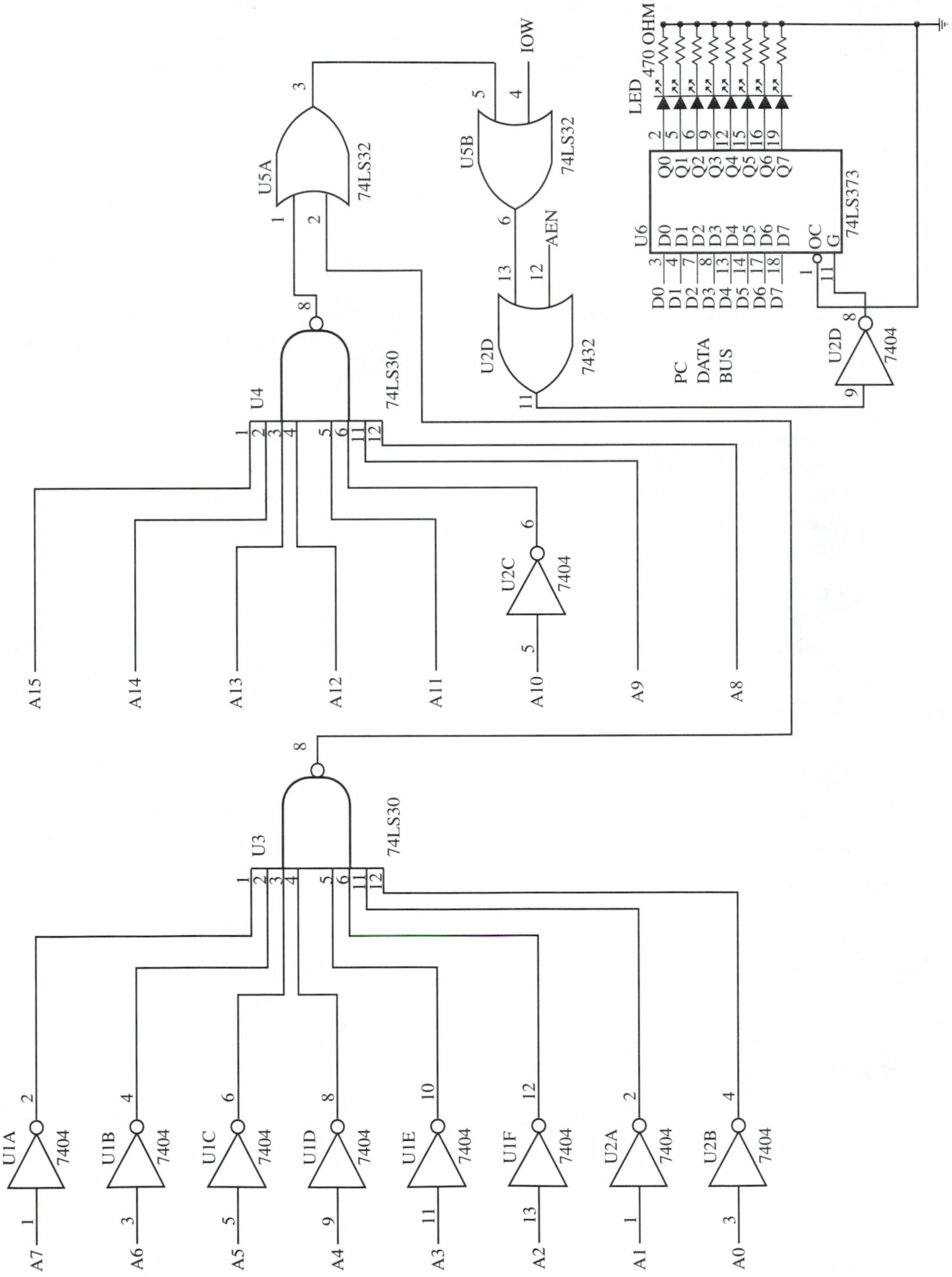

FIGURE H.3 Experiment 3 Interface

EXPERIMENT 4: ANALOG-DIGITAL CONVERSION

Objective:

To design an analog interface to the PC. A digital oscilloscope capable of displaying and calculating the DC and RMS values of waveforms is used as an example. Microsoft C is used to read and display the voltages.

Procedure:

1. Revise the schematic in Figure H.2 as shown in Figure H.4. The ADC0801 has the CS (pin 1) connected to the enable output from Experiment 2.

   The ADC0801 has an INTR pin that goes low after a conversion has been made. There is also a WR pin that is set low at the start of a conversion. By tying these two pins together, a continuous read is obtained. When the data is read, it is placed in a temporary storage buffer inside the chip. The RD pin is tied low to release the data from the buffer to the data bus. The data does not actually appear until the CS pin is set low by the enable from the 7432. An RC circuit is used to control a clock. The frequency of the clock is calculated by:

$$f = 1/(1.1*R*C)$$

For R = 10K and C = 150pf, the clock frequency is 606Khz.

   The ADC0801 also has a reference voltage input (VREF) that allows an input to be scaled. The range is determined by the voltage on VREF. The Zener diode protects the ADC from voltages greater than 5 or less than −.7v.

2. After wiring Figure H.4, enter the program below in QuickC or Microsoft C.

```
#include <stdio.h>
#include <graph.h>
#include <math.h>
#include <conio.h>
float v[640];
main()
{
/*Define Variables*/
int  x,xmax,xmin,xm,xn;
float  vmax,vmin,vm,vn,vdc,vs,a;
/*Set Screen for VGA, 16 color*/
_setvideomode(_VRES16COLOR);
/*Clear the Screen*/
_clearscreen(_GCLEARSCREEN);

/*Read inputs into array and draw on screen*/
for (x=0;x<=640;x++){
v[x]=inp(0xfb00);
if (x==0)
_moveto(x,480-(int)(v[x]));
_lineto(x,480-(int)(v[x]));
}
```

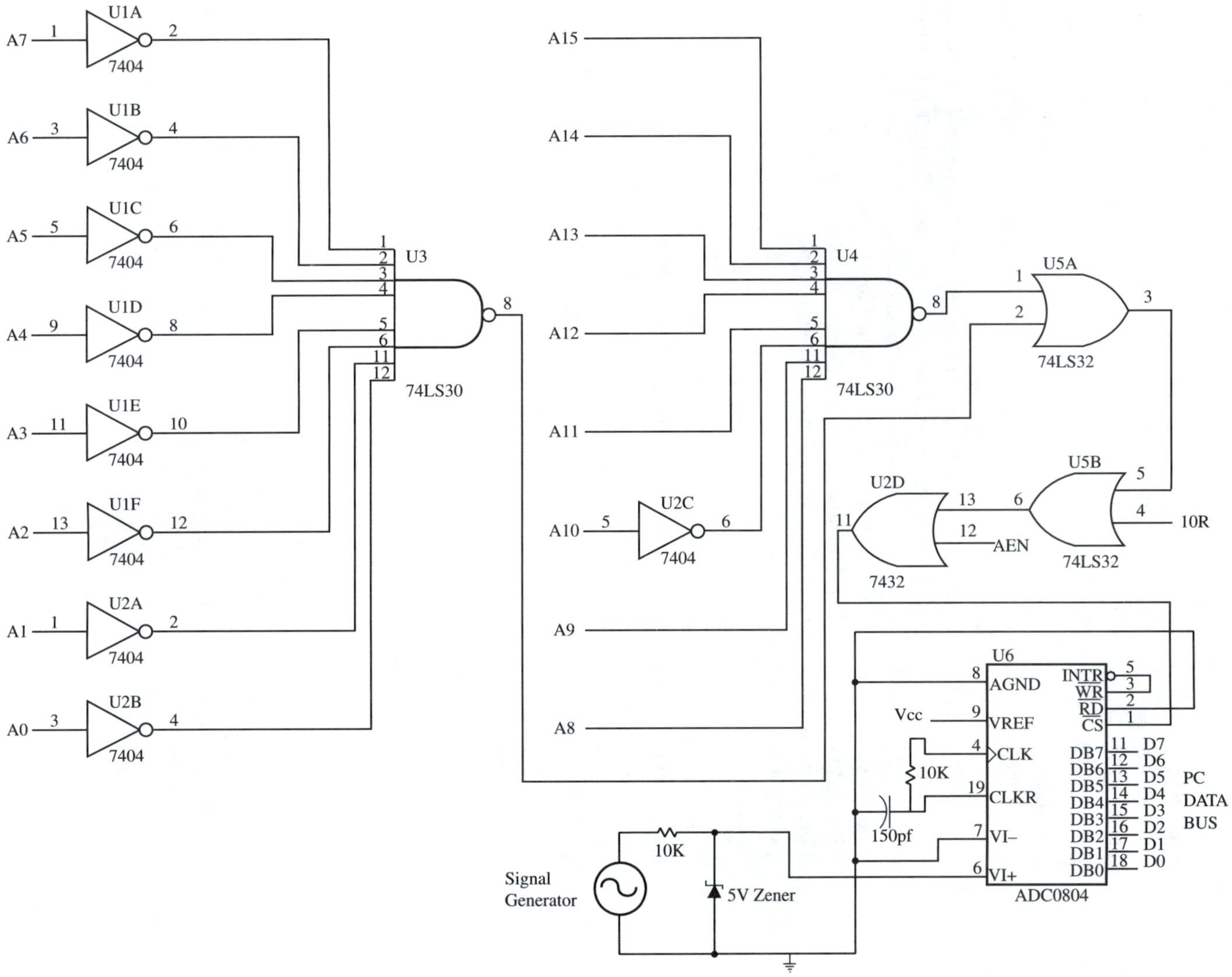

FIGURE H.4 Experiment 4 Interface

```
/*Wait for keypress*/
getch();
/*Restore screen*/
_setvideomode(_DEFAULTMODE);
}
```

3. Adjust a signal generator such that the higher peak is about 5 volts, and the lower peak is about 0 volts. Connect the signal generator to the input of the circuit and ground. Compile and run the C program. A waveform should now appear on the screen. Adjust the frequency, amplitude, and type of waveform to observe that the interface is working correctly.

4. An approximate reading of the DC and RMS value of the waveform can be calculated. The DC content is found by subtracting the lower from the higher peak and dividing by 2, then adding the lower value to the result. The RMS value can be calculated by reading the term backwards; in other words, first square the waveform, find its mean, then take the square root of the mean. The mean can be found by first integrating to find the area under the waveform, then dividing by the period. To find the period, the distance (in pixels) between the two upper peaks is first determined. All of the samples between these peaks are then squared and added. In this way, an approximation of the integral of the square of the waveform is obtained. The sum is then divided by the period to find the mean. Finally the square root of the mean is taken to find the RMS value. The advantage to doing this (as opposed to simply multiplying the peak by 0.707) is that the RMS value for any waveform can be found, not just a sine wave.

5. The program below finds the approximate DC and RMS values of a sampled waveform. The accuracy of the readings is determined by the influence of quantization error, other types of noise, and an assumption that the bus voltage is exactly 5 volts. Revise the program to add the lines of code shown below:

```
#include <stdio.h>
#include <graph.h>
#include <math.h>
#include <conio.h>
float v[640];
main()
{
/*Define Variables*/
int x,xmax,xmin,xm,xn,xtemp;
float vmax,vmin,vm,vn,vdc,vs,a;
/*Set Screen for VGA, 16 color*/
_setvideomode(_VRES16COLOR);
/*Clear the Screen*/
_clearscreen(_GCLEARSCREEN);

/*Read inputs in to array and draw on screen*/
for (x=0;x<=640;x++){
v[x]=inp(0xfb00);
if (x==0)
_moveto(x,480-(int)(v[x]));
_lineto(x,480-(int)(v[x]));
}
```

```
xmax = 0.0;
vmax = 0.0;

/*Find First Upper Peak*/
for (x=0;x<=640;x++){
if(v[x] > vmax){
vmax = v[x];
xmax = x;
}
}
vm = vmax;
xm = xmax;

xmax = 0.0;
vmax = 0.0;

/*Find Second Upper Peak*/
for (x=0;x<=640;x++){
if (v[x] > vmax && ((x < (xm - 3)) || (x > (xm + 3)))){
vmax = v[x];
xmax = x;
}
}

xmin = 0;
vmin = 5000.0;

/*Find First Lower Peak*/
for (x=0;x<=640;x++){
if(v[x] < vmin){
vmin = v[x];
xmin = x;
}
}

vn = vmin;
xn = xmin;
xmin = 0.0;
vmin = 5000.0;

/*Find Second Lower Peak*/
for (x=0;x<=640;x++){
if (v[x] < vmin && ((x < (xn - 3.0)) || (x > (xn + 3.0)))){
vmin = v[x];
xmin = x;
}
}

/*Print Vmax and Vmin*/
printf("Vmax = %f\n",vmax*5.0/256.0);
printf("Vmin = %f\n",vmin*5.0/256.0);

/*Find DC Value*/
```

```
vdc = ((vmax - vmin) / 2.0)+vmin;
printf("Vdc = %f\n", vdc * 5.0 / 256.0);

/*Find start of period*/
if(xmax>xm){
xtemp=xm;
xm=xmax;
xmax=xtemp;
}
/*Find RMS Value*/
a = 0;
for (x=xmax;x<=xm;x++){
/*Reference waveform to 0*/
vs = v[x] - vdc;
/*Square waveform and add to previous value*/
a = a + vs * vs;
}

/*Take square root of waveform*/
a = sqrt(a / (float)((xm - xmax)));
/*Print RMS value*/
printf( "Vrms = %f\n", a * 5.0 / 256.0);
/*Wait for keypress*/
getch();
/*Restore screen*/
_setvideomode(_DEFAULTMODE);
}
```

6. Run the program. It should display the DC and RMS values in addition to drawing the waveform.
7. Quantization error is caused by an LSB error in the ADC. Each LSB change in the output of the ADC corresponds to a discrete change in the input voltage. The quantization error for a 2-bit ADC is shown below. Note that a 2-bit ADC has 2^2, or 4 binary output states.

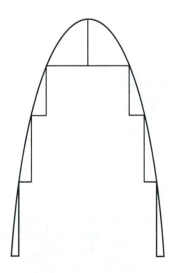

TABLE H.1

Analog Input Voltage	Digital Output Byte
0	00000000
.01953125	00000001
.03906250	00000010
.07812500	00000011
.15625000	00000100
.....	......
4.9804688	11111111

As the input waveform changes from 0 to 5 volts, the step change does not approximate the waveform very well. For a 5-volt 8-bit ADC, the change is $5*2^{-8}$, or .01953 volt. A table of input and output voltages for an 8-bit ADC is shown in Table H.1.

Quantization error occurs when an input voltage is between the steps in Table H.1. For instance, an input voltage of 0.07 volt would be read as the next lowest step input, or 0.0390625. A 12- or 16-bit ADC significantly reduces the quantization error. A close observation of the waveform on the screen shows discrete step changes for small changes in the input voltage. This is especially noticeable at lower frequencies.

8. Sampling error is caused by sampling at a rate that is too slow. Sampling error is demonstrated by increasing the frequency until a valid reading and/or visible waveform can no longer be obtained. This is the maximum frequency that the computer can read. Write the result below.

Maximum frequency = _____hz

9. Now decrease the frequency until exactly one cycle appears across the screen. Measure the period of the waveform with an oscilloscope or frequency counter. Since there are 640 pixels across the screen, divide the period by this number. This will give the sample rate. The sample rate is defined as the time between samples.

Sample rate = _____

Nyquist's sampling criteria states that the sample frequency must be at least two times the maximum frequency.

EXPERIMENT 5: FREQUENCY MEASUREMENTS

Objective:
To measure frequency using an LM 2907 chip. Microsoft C is used to read, calculate, and display the frequency.

Procedure:
1. Besides reading the DC, peak, and RMS voltage, it is also useful to read in the frequency of the incoming signal. The LM2907 is a frequency-to-voltage converter. It

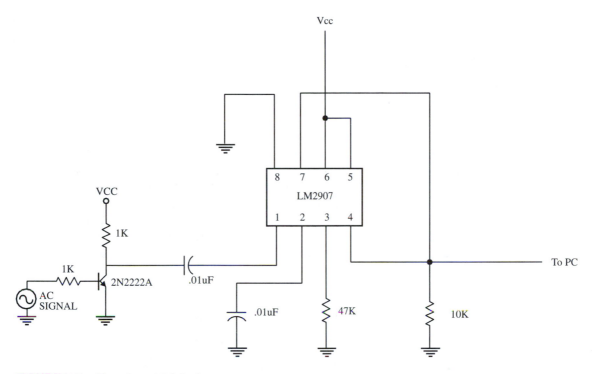

FIGURE H.5   Experiment 5 Interface

outputs a voltage proportional to the input frequency. This experiment uses the LM2907 to send a 0–5V DC voltage to the PC that is proportional to the frequency of the signal generator. Wire the schematic shown in Figure H.5 on a breadboard.

2. Disconnect the signal generator in Experiment 4 and move it to the input of Figure H.5. Set the generator of a 0–5-volt square wave. Place a voltmeter on the "To PC" connection. Turn the frequency on the generator to 1000 hz. The output voltage of the LM 2907 is defined by the formula:

$$Vo = V*R*C*fin$$

in this case, the output equals:

$$Vo = 5*47K*.01uf*fin = .00235fin$$

If fin = 1000 hz, Vo = 2.35 volts.
   With the frequency generator at 1000 hz, record Vout:

$$Vout = \underline{\hspace{2cm}}$$

Your actual reading may be slightly off due to resistor and capacitor tolerance and a opamp gain other than 1. The input 2N2222A transistor act as an AC coupler for the signal generator.

3. Place the plug-in breadboard into the PC. Connect the "To PC" output to the PC breadboard signal generator input in Figure H4. Turn on the PC.

4. Enter and run the short C program shown below.

```
#include <stdio.h>
#include <conio.h>
main()
{
int f;
f=inp(0xfb00);
printf("Frequency = %d",f);
}
```

5. This program will read in the input voltage from the LM2907 and print it to the screen. It must be calibrated to the proper frequency. This can be done with linear interpolation. This process starts with taking a set of maximum and minimum readings for the PC program display and the corresponding frequencies. The frequency should be read at the output of the signal generator with a frequency meter. The PC display is simply the value shown on the screen from the printf statement. Fill in the table below for a 400 hz and 1600 hz reading:

$$F(400 \text{ hz}) \quad \text{PC display minimum} = \underline{\hspace{2cm}}$$

$$F(1600 \text{ hz}) \quad \text{PC display maximum} = \underline{\hspace{2cm}}$$

6. The linear interpolation equation is shown below:

$$f = 400 + (f - PC \text{ min})*/(1600 - 400)/(PC \text{ max} - PC \text{ min})$$

Insert the PC minimum and PC maximum readings obtained from step 5 into the equation above. For example, if PC minimum = 1 volt and PC maximum = 5 volts, the equation would appear as shown below:

$$f = 400 + (f - 1)*(1200)/(4)$$

7. Insert this equation into the program in step 4. Run the program and vary the input frequency over a range between 400 and 1600 hz.

In the example shown below, IRQ4 is used along with a data acquisition board to read port FB00h. A laboratory experiment using ISR.ASM is described in Appendix H.

EXPERIMENT 6: IMPLEMENTATION OF AN ISR SERVICE ROUTINE

Note: This experiment uses the IRQ4 line on the ISA bus to generate an interrupt. Most modern computers use this line for .COM1. If the line is also used in this experiment, it could cause bus conflicts and lock up the computer. Because of this, it is best to perform this experiment on an older XT model computer, where there is a high probability the IRQ line is not used.

Objective:

To observe how an interrupt request on an IRQ line generates a hardware interrupt. This experiment uses the analog-digital converter from Experiment 3. 80x86 assembly language is used to generate the IRQ.

Procedure:

1. Use MASM to enter and compile the program shown below:

ISR.ASM

```asm
;MASM Assembly language interrupt program to read and print an
;analog signals to the screen.

_stack segment para stack 'stack'
   dw 100h dup(?)
_stack ends

screen segment at 0b800h
   corner db 10 dup (?)
screen ends

_data segment word public 'data'
   intro db 100 dup (?)
_data ends

_text segment word public 'code'
main proc
     START:
             assume cs:_text
             assume ds:_data
             assume es:screen
             mov ax,_data
             mov ds,ax
             mov ax,screen
             mov es,ax

             ;Enable IRQ4
             in al,21h
             and al,0efh
             out 21h,al

             ;Set IRQ4 vector to the inter procedure
             mov ax,_text
             mov ds,ax
             mov dx, offset inter
             mov ax,250ch
             int 21h
             mov ax,_data
             mov ds,ax

             ;Wait for keypress
             mov ah,1
             int 21h

             ;Reset IRQ4 8259 interrupt mask
             in al,21h
             or al,10h
```

```
                      out 21h,al

                      ;Exit to DOS
                      mov ah,4ch
                      mov al,0
                  int 21h

      main endp

      inter proc
                      push ds
                      push ax
                      push bx
                      push cx
                      push dx

                      ;Notify 8259 that interrupt is being serviced
                      mov al,20h
                      out 20h,al

                      ;Read in port value
                      mov dx,0fb00h
                      in al,dx

                      ;Place a "1" or "0" on upper left corner of screen,
                      depending on switch state.
                      cmp al,250
                       jl zero
                      mov corner,'1'
                      jmp one
      zero:
                      mov corner '0'
      one:
                      mov bx,ax
                      pop dx
                      pop cx
                      pop bx
                      pop ax
                      pop ds
                      sti
                      iret

      inter endp
      _text ends
      end START
```

2. Remove the signal generator shown in Figure H4. Replace it with a switch, as shown in Figure H.6.
3. Connect a wire to IRQ4 in the PC breadboard. Tie the other end of the wire to a switch as shown in Figure H6. Run the compiled ISR.EXE program. Turn the IRQ4 off and on

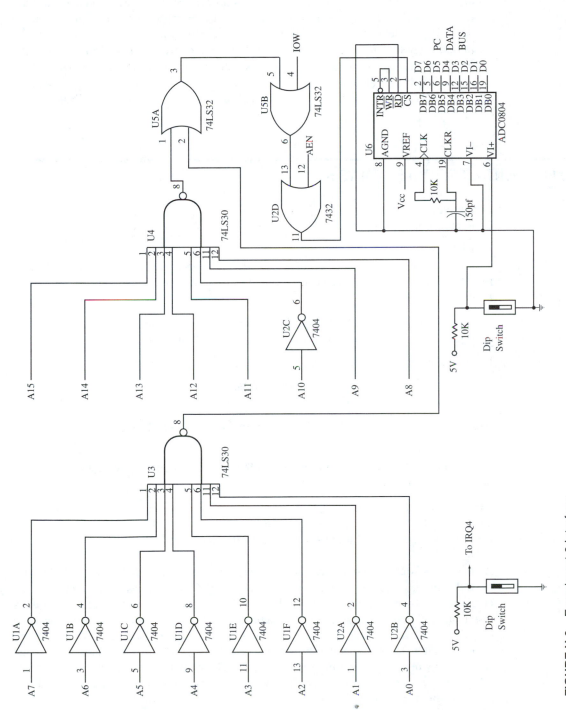

FIGURE H.6 Experiment 6 Interface

again (do not leave the switch off). If there is no voltage at the ADC input, a 0 will appear on the upper left corner of the screen. If the switch is open, a 1 appears on the upper left corner of the screen. The program terminates when a key is pressed. It is important to note that there is a significant difference between ISR.ASM and other programs in this appendix. This program continually monitors the keyboard for a keypress. It does *not* monitor an input port. Only when IRQ4 is set low is a port reading taken. When a key is pressed, IRQ4 is disabled, and the program exits to DOS.

EXPERIMENT 7: SPECTRAL ANALYSIS

Objective:
To demonstrate how signals can be analyzed using the discrete Fourier transform.

Procedure:
Fourier's great contribution to mathematics was his concept that any function can be represented by a series of sine and cosine terms. The general form of the Fourier series for any function $y = f(x)$ is:

$$y = (1/2)a0 + a1\cos(x) + a2\cos(2x) + \ldots a_n\cos(nx)$$
$$+\ldots b1\sin(x) + b2\sin(2x) +\ldots b_n\sin(nx)$$

It can be shown that the Fourier series of a square wave is made up of odd sine terms, or

$$f(t) = (4/\pi) \sum (1/n) \sin[(n*2\pi t)/T]$$
$$n = 1,3,5,\ldots$$

where
T = the period of the square wave
t = time

A Fourier series expansion for the first few terms of a square wave are shown in Figures H.7, H.8, and H.9.

$n = 1$, $f(t) = (4/\pi)*\sin((2\pi t)/T)$
$n = 3$, $f(t) = (4/\pi) * [\sin(2\pi t)/T] + 1/3*[\sin(3*2\pi t)/T]$
$n = 5$, $f(t) = (4/\pi) * [\sin(2\pi t)/T] + 1/3*[\sin(3*2\pi t)/T] + 1/5*[\sin(5*2\pi t)/T]$

As is shown from the above example, the more terms that are added to the series expansion, the closer a square wave is approximated. If the Fourier series is implemented on a computer, a complex waveform could be stored as a series of sine waves. This requires less data storage than recording every sample. The Fourier series is a continuous time equation. Unfortunately, an analog/digital converter reads discrete samples of a waveform. In other words, the computer doesn't know whether the waveform is a square wave, a sine wave, or any other type. This must be known in order to apply a continuous Fourier series.

The discrete Fourier transform allows data samples to be read in and analyzed as a series of sine waves. The equation can be written as shown below:

$$F(m) = \sum x(n) * [\sin (2\pi mn/N) - j \cos (2\pi mn/N)]$$

FIGURE H.7

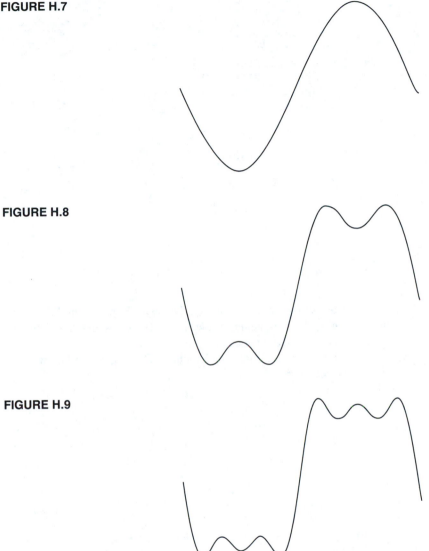

FIGURE H.8

FIGURE H.9

1. Before writing a program that implements the DFT, a set of samples for a waveform is sampled and saved to disk. Enter, compile, and run the program shown below:

```
#include <stdio.h>
#include <graph.h>
#include <math.h>
#include <conio.h>
float v[640];
char s[50];
FILE *fh;
```

```
main()
{
int x,xmax,xmin,xm,xn;
float vmax,vmin,vm,vn,vdc,vs,a;
_setvideomode(_VRES16COLOR);
_clearscreen(_GCLEARSCREEN);
for (x=0;x<=640;x++){
v[x]=inp(0xfb00);
if (x==0)
_moveto(x,(int)(v[x]));
_lineto(x,(int)(v[x]));
}
puts("Enter filename");
gets(s);
fh=fopen(s,"w");
for (x=0;x<640;x++)
fprintf(fh,"%f\n",v[x]);
fclose(fh);
_setvideomode(_DEFAULTMODE);
}
```

2. Connect the signal generator to the ADC as in Experiment 4. Run the program. Continue running the program until at least 1 to 10 cycles appear on the screen. Enter a filename to save the data to disk.

3. A Microsoft C program that implements a DFT is shown below. Enter, compile, and run the program.

```
#include <stdio.h>
#include <graph.h>
#include <math.h>
float a,b,value,x[1000],v;
char s[50];
FILE *fh;
main()
{
int pos=0;
int m,n,p,total=64;
float PI=3.1415927;
p=0;
/*Configure monitor for VGA 16 color*/
_setvideomode(_VRES16COLOR);
_clearscreen(_GCLEARSCREEN);
/*Set color to cyan*/
_setcolor(3);
/*Get filename*/
puts("Enter filename\n");
gets(s);
_clearscreen(_GCLEARSCREEN);
fh=fopen(s,"r");
while(!feof(fh))
```

```
{
/*Read saved sample from disk*/
fscanf(fh,"%f",&x[p]);
x[p]/=255.0;
p++;
}
total=p;
fclose(fh);
_moveto(0,100);
for(p=0;p<=total-1;p++){
/*Plot samples to screen*/
_lineto(p*(10/(total/64)),480-(340+(int)(x[p]*100.0)));
}
_setcolor(7);
for(m=0;m<=total/2;m++)
{
a=0.0;
b=0.0;
for(n=0;n<=total-1;n++)
{
/*DFT algorithm*/
a = x[n] * cos(2.0 * PI * (float)(m) * (float)(n) / (float)(total)) + a;
b = x[n] * -sin(2.0 * PI * (float)(m) * (float)(n) / (float)(total)) + b;
}
/*Combine read and imaginary results for DFT value*/
value=sqrt(a*a+b*b);

/*Scale to first reading*/
if (m==0)
v=value;

else{
value*=480/v;
/*Plot DFT values to screen*/
_moveto(pos,480);
_lineto(pos,480-(int)(value));

pos++;
}
}
getch();
_setvideomode(_DEFAULTMODE);
}
```

4. The results for a square wave are shown in Figure H.10. The type of graph is called a spectral graph. Amplitude is on the y-axis, and frequency on the x-axis. Note that the second peak is one-third of the first, and the third peak is one-fifth of the first. This follows the Fourier series formula for a sine wave.
5. As a challenge, rewrite portions of the DFT C code in 80x87 floating point assembly.

FIGURE H.10

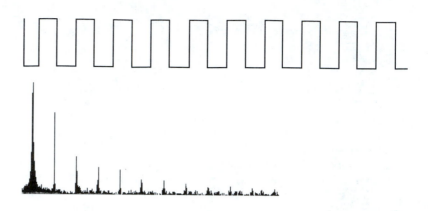

TTL Chip Pinouts

Figure H.11 shows the pinouts for the TTL chips used in this appendix.

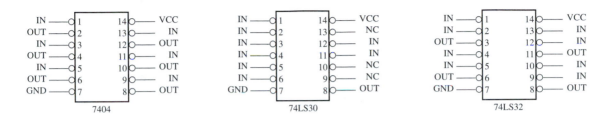

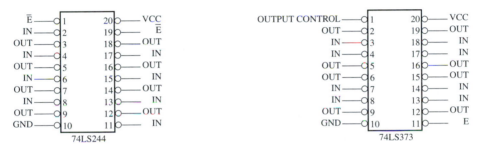

FIGURE H.11 TTL Chip Pinouts

INDEX